Bipolar Disorder

Danny Walsh and Roger Smith

A guide for mental health
professionals, carers and
those who live with it

Pavilion

Bipolar Disorder: A guide for mental health professionals, carers and those who live with it

Published by:
Pavilion Publishing (Brighton) Ltd
Richmond House
Richmond Road
Brighton
BN2 3RL
Tel: 01273 623222
Fax: 01273 625526
Email: info@pavpub.com

Published 2012

A catalogue record for this book is available from the British Library.

ISBN: 978-1-908066-15-2

Pavilion is the leading training and development provider and publisher in the health, social care and allied fields, providing a range of innovative training solutions underpinned by sound research and professional values. We aim to put our customers first, through excellent customer service and value.

Authors: Danny Walsh and Roger Smith
Production editor: Catherine Ansell-Jones, Pavilion
Cover design: Emma Garbutt, Pavilion
Page layout and typesetting: Emma Garbutt, Pavilion
Printing: Ashford Press

Contents

Introduction

This handbook is written by a mental health nurse with experience of working with people with bipolar disorder during acute episodes and through recovery, and by a researcher with experience of bipolar disorder and recovering from it. It also draws upon the experiences of other people whose lives have been disrupted by the disorder. The disorder itself can be both a cruel friend and a worst enemy. It can drop you into the depths of despair and threaten your very existence. At the other extreme it can fill you with such vigour that nothing seems beyond your capability, but the knowledge that such energy can damage everything and everyone you care about is always present.

There has been an awareness of mood disorders for centuries. The ancient Greeks noted states of high elation and euphoria and the depression that they called 'melancholia'. However, it was not until the 19th century that Emil Kraepelin asserted that there were differences between mood disorders like mania and depression in order to distinguish them from other forms of psychosis such as schizophrenia and dementia. In the 1940s and 1950s, experiments with chemicals that could change moods led many medical professionals and pharmaceutical companies to say that mood disorders were caused either by faulty electrical activity in the brain or a chemical imbalance. The isolation of chemical messenger compounds, such as serotonin and dopamine, in animal brains meant that by the mid-1950s the 'chemical model' dominated thinking, leading to many patients being told that their disorders were due to chemical imbalances, despite there being no tests to prove this theory.

Following on from the idea of chemical imbalances, in 1959 the newly developed chemical imipramine was the first medication to be called an antidepressant. In the 1960s, chlorprozamine, a chemical that had been found to calm patients, was one of the first medications to be described as an antipsychotic. Lithium was chosen as it seemed to make extremes of depression and mania less likely and eventually became the first chemical to be described as a mood stabiliser. With the availability of these drugs, the medication of anyone who was seen to experience extreme highs and lows became possible. For many this seemed to prove the existence of the 'chemical imbalance' and supported the idea that bipolar disorder was a physical illness that could primarily be treated with medication.

The partnership approach to modern nursing underpins the reason for this handbook, which is to arrive at a shared view of bipolar disorder between health professionals and those who experience it. There is much that is still not known about the disorder and if, indeed, it is a specific disorder. Thus there is often little consensus and much theorising. However, what is known can help us to bring the disorder under a significant degree of control. Those with bipolar have tried and tested many ways of coping, improving control over their moods and finding their feet again in recovery. This handbook aims to aid this process by providing professional and expert experience. It avoids exploring aspects in any great theoretical depth in order to provide a more practical guide to bipolar disorder. This book is not about providing all the answers; it is as much about raising the relevant questions.

The information in this handbook is divided into four sections. **Section 1: Theories and approaches** gives background information on bipolar disorder. **Section 2: Inpatient/acute care** focuses on inpatient areas. This section will also be of interest to relatives to help them understand treatments and to interact with staff as necessary. People with a bipolar diagnosis or suspected bipolar diagnosis may also find useful information here whether they are an inpatient or reading up in case of re-admission. **Section 3: Bipolar in the community** is both for the professional and non-professional supporters of people with the disorder. It explores issues in relation to recovery and survival and even flourishing in the community. **Section 4: Related conditions and conclusions** looks at diagnosis overlap and conditions similar to bipolar. It also explores the importance of maintaining balance as well as future possibilities. Many of the chapters contain reflection exercises, questions and consideration points that can be completed to help learners further develop their knowledge. **Answers to the questions can be found at the end of each chapter.**

We have chosen to use both the words 'patient' and 'client' in this book. We tend to use 'patient' when the person is on the ward and 'client' when the person is in the community. It is important to be aware that the words we use may need to be flexible according to the culture we find ourselves in. Some people may not like to be called a patient, while others may not want to be called 'client'. Many people find the phrase 'service user' very acceptable while others will fervently reject this term, saying it suggests they are merely using services when they do far more than that.

Further reading
Whitaker R (2010) *Anatomy of an Epidemic*. New York: Random House Publishing.

Section 1
Theories and approaches

Chapter 1

What is bipolar disorder?

Key issues

■ It is important to ensure there is a shared understanding of bipolar disorder.

■ It is important to clarify definitions and terms.

Consideration points

Before reading the chapter, consider your own preconceptions of bipolar disorder/manic depression.

■ What do you think the characteristics are?
■ How do you think it affects a person?

Manic depression and bipolar disorder

It could be said that the bipolar diagnosis did not exist prior to 1980 when it was first included in the *Diagnostic and Statistical Manual of Mental Disorders* (DSM-III). Prior to this the term 'manic depression' was used to describe patients who were seen to swing between manic and depressive states. It is important to be aware that significant numbers of people continue to prefer (and perhaps will only ever use) the term 'manic depression' as it accurately describes the main aspects of the disorder.

For many people diagnosed with bipolar disorder, the first step towards recovery is to try and understand it. Considering this statement, it is essential that you and the person you are supporting use the same language. Many health professionals make the mistake of expecting a client to use their personal mix of medical and technical terms. This mistake is further compounded as every health professional has their own preferences regarding terms.

The following pages cover the definitions of medical terms and classifications for bipolar disorder. In supporting people with bipolar disorder it is important that health professionals understand all the medical terms so that they can explain them to their clients. Each individual with bipolar will also have their own preference regarding the use of medical terms. To be most effective, health professionals will need to be able to discuss everything to do with mood swings without recourse to medical terms or jargon. It is important to be aware that language always affects feelings and can influence mood.

Question 1

Explain the following medical terms in plain English.

- Acute
- Anxiety
- Delusion
- Depression
- Differential diagnosis
- Hallucination
- Hypomania
- Insight
- Libido
- Prodome
- Prognosis
- Psychiatry
- Psychosis
- Stigma

Question 2

What is meant by 'positive language'?

> ## Consideration points
>
> - Why is positive language important in mental health care?
> - Can you ever be too positive?

Definitions and terminology

Bipolar disorder and manic depression both describe a brain disorder that renders a person liable to profound or extreme mood swings that frequently range from severe depression to unbridled mania. Between these episodes there are usually stable periods of normal mood variation. There are many variations and combinations of mood. Generally, the moods of those with bipolar tend to be much more variable than the mood swings experienced by the rest of the population.

The effects, like the moods, can be extreme. Careers can be ruined and families split up. Suicide rates are higher among this population and people have died during manic episodes. At the other extreme, there can be energetic, productive periods and great creativity. Whatever the picture, the disorder can be mastered and those with it can lead fulfilling lives.

The *Diagnostic and Statistical Manual of Mental Disorders* (DSM-IV) and the *International Classification of Mental and Behavioural Diseases* (ICD-10) both subdivide the disorder into numerous categories. The IDC-10 has separate categories for mania and different types of depression and breaks bipolar affective disorder (BAD) into the following sub-categories:

F31.0 BAD, current episode hypomania
F31.1 BAD, current episode manic without psychotic symptoms
F31.2 BAD, current episode manic with psychotic symptoms
F31.3 BAD, current episode mild or moderate depression
F31.4 BAD, current episode severe depression without psychotic symptoms
F31.5 BAD, current episode severe depression with psychotic symptoms
F31.6 BAD, current episode mixed
F31.7 BAD, current episode in remission
F31.8 Other bipolar affective disorder
F31.9 Bipolar affective disorder, unspecified

The DSM-IV has the following major bipolar categories:

296.0x Bipolar I disorder single manic episode
296.40 Bipolar I disorder most recent episode........hypomanic
296.4x Bipolar I disorder most recent episode........manic
296.5x Bipolar I disorder most recent episode........depressed
296.6x Bipolar I disorder most recent episode........mixed
296.7   Bipolar I disorder most recent episode........unspecified
296.80 Bipolar disorder NOS (not otherwise specified)
296.89 Bipolar II disorder

In the DSM-IV the single manic episode and the manic, depressed and mixed categories are further broken down according to severity, degrees of remission and presence or otherwise of psychotic symptoms.

Glossary

Having outlined the importance of language, it is pertinent to examine the key terms in detail to clarify their meaning. Many are explained in greater detail in Chapter 3: Symptomatology.

Affect
The observable expression of emotions/feelings.

Affective disorder
A group of disorders characterised by changes to mood.

Bipolar
Having two extremes (or 'poles', hence bipolar).

Bipolar affective disorder/bipolar disorder
Having both manic and depressive episodes severe enough to cause significant personal distress, impairment to daily living, social functioning, and loss of the ability to think clearly and reason.

Bipolar I (BPI)
Defined by the DSM-IV as a severe form of bipolar disorder where episodes of depression are interspersed with at least one episode of full blown mania, which has lasted more than a week and often requires hospitalisation.

Mood is 'normal' between such episodes. There are six major variants of bipolar I in the DSM-IV, differentiated according to the nature of the last episode, being either manic, depressive or of mixed presentation.

Bipolar II (BPII)

This is a form of bipolar disorder with more than one episode of major depression and one or more period of hypomania. The manic episodes are much less intense than in bipolar I but can still cause disruption to normal functioning. Hypomanic episodes can often go unrecognised, thus it is often wrongly diagnosed as unipolar depression.

Cycling

This refers to the cyclical nature of episodes. Every bipolar person who is able to plot their moods will create a unique pattern. Cycles with symptom-free periods between mood swings may be seen within the pattern. These cycles may occur over months and even show many years between episodes. Where four or more episodes of depression or mania are seen per year, the medical term 'rapid cycling' can be used.

Cyclothymia

Having multiple periods of elevated mood (hypomania) interspersed with periods of low mood, but in which neither is severe enough to merit being called bipolar. The term is also used to refer to a personality type that is prone to changes in mood. This diagnosis can also represent chronic bipolar affective disorder without acute phases, yet still causing problems in functioning.

Depression

A state of sustained (two or more weeks) deep, lowered mood beyond that regarded as normal, to the degree that it interferes with the person's ability to carry out everyday tasks. It affects sleep, diet and social interaction. There is a loss of energy, interest and motivation. At its worst it makes the person with bipolar believe that they are worthless. The resulting low self-esteem renders many liable to suicidal thoughts and thus the incidence of suicide is high. For a major depressive illness to be diagnosed, five key symptoms must have been present for at least two weeks and must include either depressed mood for most of the day, nearly every day, or diminished interest or loss of pleasure in activities.

Differential diagnosis

A state of uncertainty with respect to diagnosis. In North America this term is sometimes used for bipolar-type disorders, which are caused by medication or physical illnesses, and is often referred to as bipolar IV. (This does not include mood swings caused by illegal drugs.) This can include mania caused by antidepressant use or depression caused by an antipsychotic.

Dysphoria
An unpleasant condition of general unhappiness, discontent and anxiety.

Dysthymia
This describes mild but persistent symptoms of depression over a number of years. Symptoms are usually present throughout most of the day and often on a daily basis.

Episode
A period when the bipolar person's mood is so high or so low that they are unable to cope as well as they would normally.

Euphoria
An exaggerated feeling of well-being.

Hypo
Below or less than.

Hypomania
Elated mood typified by great energy, quick speech and more activity than usual. Anyone can experience short periods of hypomania. It is only usually considered symptomatic of bipolar disorder when it starts to impair social/daily functioning and/or continues for periods long enough to concern observers. Hypomania (being less extreme than mania) is usually seen as less damaging, having a reduced impact upon personal life or work.

Mania
This is characterised by personally and/or socially harmful behaviours, arising out of a feeling of high energy and abnormal thinking such as feelings of infallibility. This persistently elevated, expansive or irritable mood, lasting at least one week, often includes: inflated self-esteem, decreased need for sleep, flight of ideas, racing thoughts, overtalkativeness, restlessness, distractibility, inability to concentrate, increased libido, creativity, overexaggerated belief in own powers, poor judgement, loss of financial inhibitions and risky sexual behaviour. Mania is often described as the opposite to depression and as an intense high. It is likely to ruin aspects of one's life impacting on relationships, work life and personal finances.

Manic depression/manic depressive psychosis

This is the older terminology for bipolar disorder, which is gradually being used less in English speaking countries such as the UK, Canada and Australia. It is classed as a psychotic disorder due to the severity of its symptoms, especially the extreme changes in mood and potential loss of touch with reality.

Mixed state

Signs of depression and mania are simultaneously present, fluctuating within the day and present every day for at least a week. Typically a person will show signs of agitation, anxiety, fatigue, guilt, impulsiveness, irritability and suicidal ideation. They may, for example, become tearful during manic phases or be overactive during a depressive period.

Mood scale

These allow people to express their feelings or moods as numbers. This can help a person to understand their mood and help with sharing experiences with supporters.

Mood chart

Numbers from a mood scale can be charted over any period from hours and weeks to years and even decades. Mood charts allow us to see 'cycles'. More importantly they can help with the understanding of stressors and triggers that may need to be avoided and the development of plans to avoid future episodes.

Psychosis

Psychosis is characterised by lack of insight, loss of contact with reality and often a change in personality. Severe symptoms such as hallucinations and delusions are often present alongside a range of thought disorders such as feeling that others are listening to your thoughts or that your thoughts are being interfered with.

Rapid cycling (see cycling)

This term refers to four or more episodes of depression or mania per year. However, people whose moods frequently fluctuate between extremes several times in a day will struggle to understand why their more stable peers should be termed 'rapid cyclers'.

Trigger

Triggers are stressors that appear to cause an episode to start or to become more intense. These may range from obvious events to what an outsider may perceive as trivial irritations.

Unipolar affective disorder
This describes recurrent depressive or manic episodes. These are usually unipolar depression as repeated mania without depression (unipolar mania) is rare.

Question 3
Are cyclothymia and bipolar II identical?

Consideration point
■ In what ways could hypomania be more damaging than mania?

Question 4
When will a person exhibiting hypomania realise that they are in a state of hypomania?

Mood charts

The following charts illustrate the use of a mood scale to show mood variations.

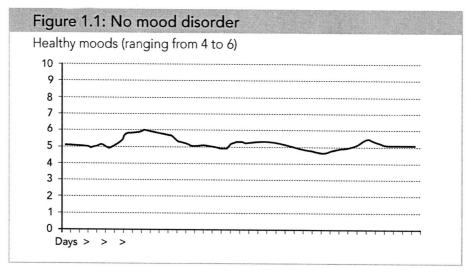

Figure 1.1: No mood disorder
Healthy moods (ranging from 4 to 6)

This chart shows a 'normal' range of ups and downs in mood within a day and over a few days.

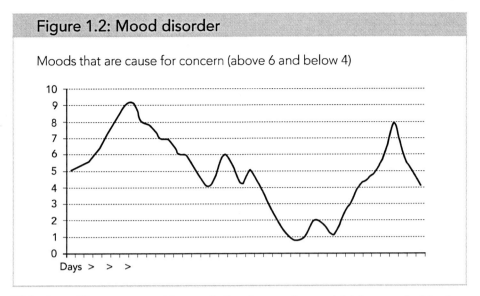

This chart illustrates a wider variation in mood, as might be seen in bipolar disorder.

What bipolar is not

Some people think that manic depression is an extreme form of long lasting depression, while others think it is a state in which the person is constantly high and manic. Explaining that the disorder is also known as bipolar disorder can help with understanding that people who have it are not necessarily always very depressed or elated, but are simply prone to variations in mood that can occasionally be extreme.

There can be an assumption that because people with bipolar have periods of stability and periods of being high, that their depressions are not as severe as for those with unipolar depression. This is not true as clearly indicated by the high level of suicide in those diagnosed with bipolar disorder.

Bipolar disorder can conjure up images of creative, successful or famous people who are known to or believed to be bipolar by nature. This can give exaggerated ideas about the benefits of the disorder. There can be benefits to mood swings, but these are only possible for those who are able to take some control of their moods. (See Chapter 35: Creativity)

Is bipolar disorder a gift or a curse? For most it is a bit of both, but only those in recovery are likely to appreciate it as a gift. When it is out of control the disorder is always a 'curse'.

Answers to questions

1. **Explain the following medical terms in plain English.**

- *Acute: happening over a short period and needing an immediate response.*

- *Anxiety: can be a feeling, an emotion or a mood accompanied by uncomfortable and sometimes frightening physical symptoms. Anxious moods tend have high energy with negative feelings. Although it is not the same as stress, the words anxiety and stress are often used interchangeably.*

- *Delusion: a belief that is not shared by the majority. It is usually a belief with little evidence/not supported by facts.*

- *Depression: may be used to describe any low mood, with it frequently being used by people who are only a little saddened for a short period. When depression is used to describe an illness this is a far lower energy state with ongoing negative feelings. Extremes of depression are always accompanied by much negative thinking.*

- *Hallucination: sensing things that are not there eg. hearing voices or seeing things. All the senses can be affected by hallucinations.*

- *Hypomania: an exceptionally energetic mood, likely to be accompanied by positive feelings and positive thinking.*

- *Insight: describes the ability to recognise one's wellness/illness. It is a vital component of bipolar recovery. People who gain better insight can communicate their feelings and thoughts more clearly, as well as take actions necessary to change their mood using strategies they have practised.*

- *Libido: feelings/urge associated with sexual desire.*

- *Prodome: a warning sign. A symptom which is predictive of oncoming illness or relapse.*

- *Prognosis: an outlook; it describes the likelihood of recovery.*

- *Psychiatry: the medical speciality relating to mental illness.*

- *Psychosis: involves a loss of touch with reality. There can be extremes of distorted thinking during psychosis. Delusional thoughts are often present. It is usually accompanied by a loss of insight, although importantly this does not mean necessarily a loss of awareness or any loss of memory of what happens during a psychotic episode.*
- *Stigma: being marked as different and the feelings associated with this.*

2. What is meant by 'positive language'?

A simple answer to this question is that everything that is not negative language might be positive. With a little training negative language is easy to recognise, and is characterised by the excessive use of expressions such as 'cannot', 'got to', 'but', 'impossible', 'incurable', 'hopeless'.

Positive alternatives include: 'I can', 'I like to', 'that's possible', 'I can recover', 'I hope that'. Positive language reflects hope rather than doubt.

3. Are cyclothymia and bipolar II identical?

Distinguishing between cyclothymia and bipolar II is never easy. When we consider that no one in the world ever perfectly fits a diagnosis, there are certain to be many patients who believe they have cyclothymia where undesirable moods (especially lows) last far too long without reaching disabling extremes. Other patients with very similar symptoms may prefer to consider that they have bipolar II if they feel their highs are a little higher and their lows are a lot lower.

4. When will a person exhibiting hypomania realise that they are in a state of hypomania?

The first time a person experiences a period of unusually high energy they are unlikely to be thinking 'Am I hypomanic?'. This means that during a first period of hypomania it is extremely unlikely that the person will be aware that what they are experiencing could be hypomania. However, hypomania is such an altered state that people talk about 'feeling odd' or 'feeling different' – there is certainly an awareness that something has changed.

> For later episodes the term 'insight' is used to describe people who are able recognise their moods and understand when others see them as just a little bit high, or even as hypomanic. Having this insight allows the individual to take action to control their mood and most often keeps them well. However, simply because someone knows they are hypomanic does not mean they will do whatever it takes to lower their mood. Some people who know they are hypomanic go on to become manic as insight is lost as the mood moves towards an extreme.

Further reading

Antai-Otong D (2003) The client with a bipolar disorder. In: D Antai-Otong *Psychiatric Nursing: Biological and behavioural concepts*. New York: Thomson/Delmar Learning.

Craig T (2000) Severe mental illness: symptoms, signs and diagnosis. In: C Gamble & G Brennan (Eds) *Working with Serious Mental Illness: A manual for clinical practice*. Edinburgh: Bailliere Tindall.

Goodwin G & Sachs G (2004) *Fast Facts: Bipolar disorder*. Abingdon: Health Press.

Fink C & Kraynak J (2005) *Bipolar Disorder for Dummies*. Hoboken, New Jersey: Wiley. (See Chapter 2: Demystifying bipolar disorder.)

Johnstone L (2008) Psychiatric diagnosis. In: R Tummey & T Turner (Eds) *Critical Issues in Mental Health*. Basingstoke: Palgrave MacMillan.

MDF The Bipolar Organisation (2008) *Manic Depression / Bipolar Affective Disorder* [online]. London: MDF/The Bipolar Organisation. Available at: www.mdf.org.uk (accessed August 2011).

Parsons S (2004) The person with a mood disorder. In: I Norman & I Ryrie (Eds) *The Art and Science of Mental Health Nursing: A textbook of principles and practice*. Maidenhead: Open University Press.

Perkins R (1999) My three psychiatric careers. In: P Barker, P Campbell & B Davidson (1999) *From the Ashes of Experience: Reflections on madness, survival and growth*. London: Whurr Publishers.

Chapter 2

Causes and prevalence

Key points

- There is a wide range of causal factors for bipolar disorder cited in the literature.

- Statistics relating to prevalence are affected by cultural variations and differing definitions.

- It is essential not to lose sight of the fact that each individual is unique and has a unique set of causal and contributory factors.

Consideration point

- What do you think might be the possible causes or reasons that a person has bipolar disorder?

High and low moods are universal experiences and moods can have a positive or negative effect on a person's ability to function. For most people changes in mood reflect everyday activities and so are considered to be normal. It is this normality that makes determining the causes and prevalence of bipolar disorder so challenging. There is an indistinct blurring of boundaries or parameters. When is a mood beyond the norm? Many people experience bad mood swings, yet they do not seek medical help and never see a psychiatrist. Even when people do seek help, professional health carers often only ever see the more common depressive side of the disorder.

Statistics are difficult to interpret as many studies do not differentiate between bipolar affective disorder and the unipolar affective disorders of depression and mania. The picture is further complicated because some bipolar symptoms can also lead to misdiagnosis.

> ## Consideration points
>
> - What other disorders might be mistaken for bipolar disorder?
> - Can you think of ways in which jargon might cause exclusion?

> ## Jargon
>
> **Aetiology** is the medical term for the examination of causes.
>
> **Epidemiology** relates to the study of prevalence or how often the disorder occurs in different groups.
>
> It is important to understand medical terms in order to demystify them and promote inclusion.

Prevalence (epidemiology)

Numbers

Research suggests that one in 100 people will be diagnosed with bipolar I at some point during their life, while a far greater number may have bipolar II and cyclothymia. However, the statistics are likely to be underestimated as diagnosis will vary and there is anecdotal evidence that many will be misdiagnosed as being depressed when they may have bipolar disorder. In the UK the annual incidence of diagnosis with bipolar has been seven per 100,000, equivalent to roughly 4,200 new diagnoses a year (NICE, 2006a).

The exact number of people who have a bipolar diagnosis continues to be unknown, not least because the age of diagnosis has lowered and the rate of diagnosis has been continuing to increase. Adding to this uncertainty are the increasing numbers of people who, after years of stability, claim they were incorrectly diagnosed.

Bipolar Disorder: A guide for mental health professionals, carers and those who live with it
© Pavilion Publishing (Brighton) Ltd 2012

Sex

Evidence suggests that bipolar disorder tends to occur equally in men and women. However, the National Institute for Health and Clinical Excellence (NICE) cites several recent studies that suggest that bipolar II is more prevalent in women (Baldassano *et al*, 2005; Arnold, 2000, Hendrick *et al*, 2000). Also, there is some evidence that shows the presence of rapid cycling is greater in women (Arnold, 2003).

Moods related to gender are often the butt of jokes but the question remains as to whether there are significant differences between the sexes.

Consideration points

- Are mood swings different between the sexes?
- Is the capacity to deal with mood swings different between the sexes?
- Do men and women cope differently?
- What are the effects of different coping mechanisms chosen by men and women?

Age of onset

It is often difficult to know the age of onset for an individual. After diagnosis many people will look back at their lives and say they have *always* had greater mood swings than their peers, while others will identify a time or age when the mood swings started. In the USA children as young as four have been diagnosed, but this is rare. In the UK it is generally accepted that bipolar disorder can occur any time from adolescence onwards. Although the average age of onset is around 15–21 years, some people will live without significant mood swings well into adult life when the disorder is suddenly triggered by a life event. In older adults too, symptoms can easily be misinterpreted leading to an incorrect diagnosis.

Class

There is a very strong link between poverty or low socio-economic status and higher rates of physical and mental illnesses (Pilgrim, 2009; Whitehead *et al*, 1992; Wilkinson, 1996; Murali & Oyebode, 2004). There is research which suggests bipolar is more prevalent in higher socio-economic groups and in those deemed to be creative or artistic (see Chapter 35: Creativity), but the evidence for this is not particularly strong.

Consideration points

- How does socio-economic status affect physical health?
- How does low socio-economic status impact on mental health?
- What are the implications of this for health promotion?
- Can you think of illnesses which might be more prevalent in the wealthy?

Culture

This is an area lacking in research but most studies show a similar prevalence of bipolar disorder across the cultures and races. What is seen when comparing statistics for different countries is the different ways in which they are presented. For example: '*Almost five per cent of Australians have the less severe bipolar II disorder, experiencing dramatic swings from highs to depression but not psychotic episodes.*' (Parker *et al*, 2006). This appears to be far higher than the '*1 in 100 will have bipolar at some time during their lives*' often quoted for the UK (Royal College of Psychiatrists, 2011). However, this is likely to be a matter of not comparing like with like and the differences between diagnostic practices in different countries. Figures in the UK generally relate to severe forms and the Australian research by Parker *et al* (2006) includes less severe forms, hence the apparent higher prevalence.

Having said this, recent research from the UK and US suggests that there are higher rates of the disorder within black and ethnic minority groups. The evidence suggests that as well as higher prevalence, these groups have more psychotic episodes, more hospitalisations, higher attempted suicide rates and a later presentation. This evidence (cited by NICE, 2006b) is tentatively explained in terms of social exclusion. The later presentation reflects the difficulties this group has in accessing services, thus the disorder is more severe when finally diagnosed. This also mirrors other evidence from both the UK and the US which suggests that ethnic minorities fare much worse in the psychiatric system, regardless of diagnosis.

Consideration point

■ What are the possible reasons for the comparatively poor experiences of ethnic minorities within the psychiatric system?

Case study: Culture

I was born to Indian parents in Africa. I have experienced extremely high moods while in the UK and in India. My treatment has been very different according to where I was and who I was with.

When I first flew to India to spend time with relatives the change of time zone was probably the cause of an extreme high, and I completely lost touch with reality. My relatives believed I was having a religious experience and stayed with me listening to my ramblings day and night. There was no panic. They calmly listened while encouraging me to eat well and drink plenty of water. I recovered well.

A subsequent extreme high occurred in London when I was over the moon about completing my studies. This time the trigger was probably staying out all night celebrating and drinking alcohol, which I do not tolerate at all well. My British relatives called the crisis team and I spent a long time in hospital on antipsychotics. The hospital experience was awful and it took years to make any sort of recovery.

I appreciate that the two episodes were different, but both would have been described as 'manic' in the UK, and as a religious experience by my Indian relatives.

Causes (aetiology)

There are many causes for bipolar disorder cited within the literature and great caution is necessary before drawing any firm conclusions. It is wise to keep an open mind. The only certainties are that there is no single cause and that in every case there is likely to be a combination of several causal factors.

Genetics

A number of studies have shown that a predisposition to bipolar disorder can be inherited. One theory suggests that the disorder is related to a combination of genes, giving rise to a predisposition to being an 'anxious worrier'. Blows (2003) suggests that first-degree relatives of a person with bipolar have a 19% chance of developing it, while the concordance rate for monozygotic twins is around 65%. (Monozygotic twins are derived from a single egg, which splits into two embryos, so twins share the same DNA). Others suggest that offspring have a one in 10 chance of developing the disorder if one parent has a bipolar diagnosis. Stimmel (1996) suggests that as many as 60% of those diagnosed will have a family member with bipolar. There can be little doubt that a combination of genetic factors are involved (Hyman, 1999).

Major research projects including St Clair *et al* (1990), Blackwood *et al* (2007), Millar *et al* (2001), Klar (2002) and Millar *et al* (2005) have led to the identification of a specific 'disrupted' gene, known as DISC1, which increases the likelihood of diagnosis with psychotic disorders. Roberts (2007) said: '*Converging evidence from cell culture, mice mutants, brain post-mortem and genetics implicates mutant DISC1 in the pathophysiology of schizophrenia and other mental illnesses. The mechanisms by which genetics influence susceptibility to bipolar are becoming more apparent, while genetics alone cannot explain the cause of bipolar disorder*'. However, Hodgkinson *et al* (2004) suggest that the evidence is strong that genes may predispose people to developing mood disorders. However, it is suggested that many people avoid the disorder by developing and maintaining good physical and mental health.

Brain pathology

Brain chemistry disturbance is a medical explanation of bipolar disorder as a disturbance in the levels of neurotransmitters, which affects how a person feels. The neurotransmitters noradrenaline, serotonin and dopamine are said to become depleted in depression and it is thought that high levels of these neurotransmitters may cause manic episodes. Brain pathology research is insufficient to point to any one brain abnormality being the causal factor.

Body clock theory (biological clock)

Significant changes in sleep patterns during depression are extremely common. According to participants on bipolar recovery courses, the most commonly reported warning sign for mania is a reduction in the amount of hours slept. Information like this, together with cases of mania coinciding with jet lag, led some researchers (eg. Roybal *et al*, 2007; McClung, 2007) to consider whether many, or even most, manic episodes (and many depressive episodes) may be related to the disruption of the biological clock. Susceptible individuals need to consider how they will cope with long distance travel or even the occasional very late night that could confuse their body clock.

Case study: Interpretation

I remember saying to my psychiatrist that I felt the manic episode I was recovering from had been brought on by a lack of sleep. Five nights without sleep with no significant symptoms and then suddenly I lost touch with reality. He said: 'No. The lack of sleep is simply a symptom of mania.' It made me wonder if he was talking about some other disorder, as that certainly was not how it felt to me.

Consider

- Where do the differences in interpretation come from?
- Which is the cause and which is the effect here? Which came first?
- Do you have personal experience of changes in mood due to insufficient sleep?

Life events

Life events rather than biological events are a common cause of most depression. Similarly, life events may trigger the initial onset of bipolar disorder and be the cause of recurring episodes. While particular stressful events may trigger the disorder in some people, others will cope well. This variation may be explained by the Stress Vulnerability Model. This suggests that it is a *combination* of the nature and intensity of the stress, levels of support at the time, personality, coping skills, physical health and many other factors which determine whether someone will cope or become ill.

Put simply, there is no one single causal factor, but life stresses are a major trigger. One increasingly recognised causal stress is abuse during childhood when the mood swings may start immediately or occur long after the events (Alston, 2000). Other anecdotal evidence arises from recovery courses where people choose to share their life story in a safe environment. Here, extreme events such as rape, abuse, witnessing traumatic events etc. are often talked about for the first time.

Ongoing/everyday stress

It is sometimes said that those with bipolar disorder may be more vulnerable to general stresses and thus prone to relapse in the face of stressful events. However, relapse can also happen without any obvious major life events, and long periods of stability can be achieved if the person can learn to manage and overcome the stresses that have made them ill in the past.

Reflection exercise: Stressors

- List some stressors that cause you anxiety or changes in mood. Try and rank these in order of their impact on your life.
- With colleagues, compare your lists and note the individual variation of the different impacts of similar stresses.
- Consider how you usually manage such stresses. Note how few of your coping mechanisms rely on medication.

Lack of support

The absence of a supportive relationship or other forms of support can be a major factor in the development of bipolar disorder and mood swings. Going to university, moving to a new town or changing jobs are all potential triggers, as are family arguments and separation from a supportive partner. All these factors make the individual more vulnerable due to the absence of previously available support systems, and especially the lack of a close, confiding relationship.

Drugs

There is much debate about the role of cannabis and other illegal drugs and the experience of psychosis later in life (Moore *et al*, 2007). The debate is controversial as many people who use cannabis and other drugs recreationally do not have any significant mental health issues. However, there are large numbers of people who say that their first experience of psychosis was directly related to the use of cannabis.

Case study: Drug use

I had tried dope a few times with no problems. My first experience of psychosis was the result of a couple of drags on a joint that had been made with opiated dope. This experience, I feel, opened me up to a new level of experiencing terror and torment while awake. I think that being 16, a long way from home for the first time and being bullied by local kids must also have been a factor in this bad experience. Strangely, I kept trying dope when offered to see if I could 'get over it'. Occasionally, I felt relaxed in the way I suspect most people who smoke dope feel – it was pleasant. One time, however, I was in a hotel and having taken one drag on someone else's joint, I needed to lock myself in the closet to stop me throwing myself out of the window. I had not been diagnosed by this stage as having bipolar. It took a few more years and another bad trip to appreciate that I had bipolar disorder and that dope did not suit me!

Case study: Clare

A woman in her 20s is brought from the general hospital to the psychiatric unit. She tells staff that she is being followed by the CIA who will kill her if they get a chance but it is OK because she is protected by hundreds of allies. She then answers all questions by signing rather than talking. She refuses to drink because she believes all drinks, including tap water, have been poisoned. Her parents arrive and say the woman has no history of mania or depression and four hours earlier she had none of these strange beliefs.

■ Consider some of the possible causes for Clare's behaviour.

An adverse reaction to a prescribed medication can trigger psychotic episodes, just as infections can be the cause of confusional states. A thorough screening and physical assessment are crucial in order to rule out such treatable causes.

Case study: Clare – what happened next, and why?

Clare stayed on the psychiatric ward overnight, talking to staff through most of the night before calming down and sleeping a few hours until breakfast time. At breakfast she was delightful and calm but remembered little of what had happened the day before. She had experienced an adverse reaction to an antibiotic that had caused a manic state. Once the antibiotic was out of her system her mood returned to normal. She was discharged when her parents arrived mid-morning. There was no question of her having bipolar disorder although the symptoms at the time were typical of mania.

Physical illness

Being physically unwell or 'run down' can greatly increase a person's vulnerability to stress and relapse. Things we normally cope with can easily get the better of us when we are physically weak through illness or simply not looking after ourselves.

Personality type

Some people can be mildly depressed for years and then have short periods of hypomania. Friends and relatives may not have noticed the episodes of hypomania. Whether they do or not they are likely to dismiss the person's moods simply as a personality trait unless severe episodes are noticed. This condition is described as cyclothymia and may also be diagnosed as bipolar II (see Chapter 1: What is bipolar disorder? for information on the different types of the disorder).

Consideration points

- Do you know people who seem to be down or in a low mood almost all the time?
- Would you know if they had cyclothymia?
- How else might their behaviour be explained?

Season of birth

As is the case for schizophrenia there is some research which suggests that people born in the winter and spring months are more likely to develop bipolar disorder (Walshe & Murray, 2011). Several reasons are cited, such as:

- viral infections during pregnancy or around the time of birth

- lack of nutrients such as vitamin D during pregnancy and/or the same for the baby in the months following birth (McGrath, 1999).

Seasonal triggers

In countries close to the equator there is little variation in the numbers of high and low episodes for the population as a whole during the year, other than at times of major festivals, such as Christmas, which may be possible triggers. Away from the equator where there is much more variation in weather between the seasons, pronounced seasonal trends variations in mood are also seen. For example, there is more hypomania and mania in the spring and early summer, and more depression in the late autumn and winter (Baldwin & Hirschfeld, 2001).

Regular patterns may be reported, such as 'I always go high this time of year' or 'I always get depressed as soon as the clocks go back'. The research base for this is slim but it does seem that, in some cases, seasonal weather has a real effect on mood. In the UK, when it rains for days on end it can make us feel gloomy despite the fact that we should be accustomed to this. Persaud (1997) suggests that a significant minority of the population are extra sensitive to sunlight or a lack of sunlight.

Hormonal/postpartum depression

Pregnancy can be a trigger for mood swings. For women with a diagnosis of bipolar disorder, pregnancy can present an additional risk as decisions need to be taken regarding any changes to medication. The period following childbirth brings with it a very significant increase in the risk of experiencing severe mood swings. Post-natal depression is well reported. Less well known is that women with no history of mania can become manic shortly after giving birth as happens in puerperal psychosis, which affects approximately one in 1,000 women.

Case study: Pregnancy

'The rest of my pregnancy proceeded well but I was warned that I was at high risk (25–50%) of another episode of postpartum depression. Naïvely, I believed that because everyone was prepared for it, it would be averted. A week after my son was born I was hospitalised for another month with puerperal psychosis.'

Source: *Pendulum: The Journal of MDF The Bipolar Organisation* **23** (2).

Caution

We must never lose sight of the fact that each person with bipolar disorder is an individual and will have a unique set of causal factors at play in their lives, and thus require a unique approach to helping them. While there may be treatments which work well for some people, every person's experience of the disorder is different so treatment plans must vary to reflect this. This book is essentially an introduction to what we know about bipolar disorder and what might help. Having said this, an enlightened client will not touch a treatment plan – only a recovery plan. Bipolar people start to get well when they become determined to start recovering and have a plan that they believe in – it is more hopeful to believe in a recovery plan than a treatment plan.

References

Alston J (2000) Correlation between childhood bipolar I disorder and reactive attachment disorder: disinhibited type. In: T Levy (Ed) *Attachment Interventions*. San Diego: Academic Press.

Arnold LM (2003) Gender differences in bipolar disorder. *Psychiatric Clinics of North America* **26** (3) 595–620.

Baldwin D & Hirschfeld R (2001) *Fast Facts: Depression*. Oxford: Health Press Limited.

Baldassano CF, Marangell LB, Gyulani L, Nassir Ghaemi S, Joffe H, Kim DR, Sagduyu K, Truman CJ, Wisniewski SR, Sachs GS & Cohen LS (2005) Gender differences in bipolar disorder: retrospective data from the first 500 STEP-BD participants. *Bipolar Disorders* **7** (5) 465–470.

Blackwood DH, Blackwood R, Pickard BJ, Thomson PA, Evans KL, Porteous DJ & Muir WJ (2007) Are some genetic risk factors common to schizophrenia, bipolar disorder and depression? Evidence from DISC1, GRIK4 and NRG.1. *Neurotoxicity Research* **11** (1) 73–83. New York: Springer.

Blows WT (2003) *The Biological Basis of Nursing: Mental Health*. London: Routledge.

Hendrick V, Altshuler LL, Gitlin MJ, Delratium S & Hammen C (2000) Gender and bipolar disorder. *Journal of Psychiatry* **61** (5) 393–396.

Hodgkinson CA, Goldman D, Jaeger J, Persaud S, Kane JM, Lipsky RH & Malhotra AK (2004) Disrupted in schizophrenia 1 (DISC1) association with schizophrenia, schizoaffective disorder, and bipolar disorder. *American Journal of Human Genetics* **75** (5) 862–872.

Hyman SE (1999) Introduction to the complex genetics of mental disorders. *Biological Psychiatry* **45** (5) 518–521.

Klar AJ (2002) The chromosome 1:11 translocation provides the best evidence supporting genetic etiology for schizophrenia and bipolar affective disorders. *Genetics* **160** 1745–1747.

Leibenluft E (1997) Issues in the treatment of women with bipolar illness. *Journal of Clinical Psychiatry* **58** (15) 5–11.

McClung CA (2007) Circadian genes, rhythms and the biology of mood disorders. *Pharmacology and Therapeutics* **114** (2) 222–232.

McGrath J (1999) Hypothesis: is low prenatal vitamin D a risk-modifying factor for schizophrenia? *Schizophrenia Research* **40** (3) 173–177.

Millar JK, Christie S, Anderson S, Lawson D, Hsiao-Wei Loh D, Devon RS, Arveiler B, Muir WJ, Blackwood DH & Porteous DJ (2001) Genomic structure and localisation within a linkage hotspot of disrupted in schizophrenia 1: a gene disrupted by a translocation segregating with schizophrenia. *Molecular Psychiatry* **6** 173–178.

Millar JK, Pickard BS, Mackie S, James R, Christie S, Buchanan SR, Malloy MP, Chubb JE, Huston E, Baillie GS, Thomson PA, Hill EV, Brandon NJ, Rain JC, Camargo LM, Whiting PJ, Houslay MD, Blackwood DH, Muir WJ & Porteous DJ (2005) DISC1 and PDE4B are interacting genetic factors in schizophrenia that regulate cAMP signaling. *Science* **310** 1187–1191

Moore T, Zammit S, Lingford-Hughes A, Barnes T, Lewis G, Jones B & Burke M (2007) Cannabis and risk of psychotic or affective mental health outcomes: a systematic review. *The Lancet* **370** (9584) 319–323.

Murali V & Oyebode (2004) Poverty, social inequality and mental health. *Advances in Psychiatric Treatment* **10** 216–224.

National Institute for Health and Clinical Excellence (July 2006a) *Clinical Guidelines 38 Bipolar Disorder: Presenter Slides*. London: NICE.

National Institute for Health and Clinical Excellence (July 2006b) *Bipolar Disorder: The management of bipolar disorder in adults, children and adolescents in primary and secondary care*. NCPG 38. London: British Psychological Society.

Parker G, Tully L, Olley A & Hadzi-Pavlovic D (2006) SSRIs as mood stabilisers for bipolar II disorder? A proof of concept study. *Journal of Affective Disorders* **92** (2–3) 205–214.

Persaud R (1997) *Staying Sane*. London: Metro Publishing Ltd.

Pendulum: The Journal of MDF The Bipolar Organisation **23** (2).

Pilgrim D (2009) *Key Concepts in Mental Health* (2nd edition). London: Sage.

Roberts RC (2007) Schizophrenia in Translation: Disrupted in schizophrenia (DISC1): integrating clinical and basic findings. *Schizophrenia Bulletin* **33** (1) 11–15.

Royal College of Psychiatrists (2011) *Bipolar Disorder* [online]. Available at: http://www.rcpsych.ac.uk/mentalhealthinfo/problems/bipolardisorder/bipolardisorder.aspx (accessed September 2011).

Roybal K, Theobold D, Graham A, DiNieri JA, Russo SJ, Krishnan V, Chakravarty S, Peevey J, Oehrlein N, Birnbaum S, Vitaterna MH, Orsulak P, Takahashi JS, Nestler EJ, Carlezon WA Jr & McClung CA (2007) Mania-like behavior induced by disruption of CLOCK. *Procedings of the National Academy of Sciences of the USA*.**104** (15) 6406–6411.

St Clair D, Blackwood D, Muir W, Carothers A, Walker M, Spowart G, Gosdeen C & Evans HJ (1990) Association within a family of a balanced autosomal translocation with major mental illness. *Lancet* **33** 613–616.

Stimmel GL (1996) Mood disorders. In: T Herfindal & D Gourlay (Eds.) *Textbook of Therapeutics*. Baltimore: Williams and Wilkins.

Walshe M & Murray R (2011) Obstetrics and schizophrenia. *Your Voice Spring* 14–15.

Whitehead M, Townsend P & Davidson N (1992) *Inequalities in Health: The Black report and the health divide*. London: Penguin.

Wilkinson RG (1996) *Unhealthy Societies: The Afflictions of inequality*. London: Routledge.

Further reading

Kendell R (1996) The nature of psychiatric disorders. In: T Heller, J Reynolds, R Gomm, R Muston & S Pattison (Eds) *Mental Health Matters: A reader*. Basingstoke: MacMillan.

Lopez AD & Murray CJL (1998) The leading causes of disability worldwide (years of life with disability). *Nature Medicine* **4** 1241–1243.

Pilgrim D & Rogers A (2008) Socioeconomic disadvantage. In: R Tummey & T Turner (2008) *Critical Issues in Mental Health*. Basingstoke: Palgrave MacMillan.

Shupikai Rinomhota A & Marshall P (2000) *Biological Aspects of Mental Health Nursing*. Edinburgh: Churchill Livingstone.

Chapter 3

Symptomatology

Key points

- The two essential features for a diagnosis of bipolar disorder are manic states and depressed states.
- There are also mixed states, cycles and variants of hypomania and cyclothymia.
- There are wide variations in the frequency, intensity, nature and duration of the symptoms.
- Labels can be harmful.

People who have experienced bipolar disorder describe the depressive episodes as being devastating but many of those who experience the manic phases describe them as being exciting and euphoric. However, the 'high' can escalate until the person is out of control and can reach psychotic proportions. The highest highs can involve extreme terror and can be as devastating as the lowest of the lows.

Case study: Linda

Linda's confused and worried husband describes the events which led up to her admission to an assessment unit.

It happened quite quickly, or at least it seemed to. I've never seen her like this before; it's just not her and I can't think why she'd suddenly act like this. Looking back, I can see it gradually got worse over about two weeks. She just became more and more active. I thought nothing of it, but then she started getting up at night and moving furniture about. She had this thing about needing to redecorate and she stripped the

---

wallpaper off the walls in every room, only she didn't finish it. She'd move to the next room halfway through the previous one, leaving them looking all torn and messy. Normally she'd be really fussy and put everything in its proper place, but now it's as if she doesn't care. She'd be like that with everything, starting something but not finishing it; she'd run a bath and then not have one because she wanted to do something else. She even let it overflow. She barely ate anything and all the time she was telling me how well she felt and that she'd never felt better. She kept saying that she had to sort things out.

After a few days of this it got worse and she ordered a new three-piece suite, carpets and other things we didn't need and couldn't afford. That really got me worried, but she was adamant that she knew what she was doing, even though I tried to say we didn't have the money for it all. Then things really came to a head when I got home and she was on the phone talking to someone about selling the house and she was offering it at a pittance, almost giving it away. I got really angry; I was upset and worried, but that just fired her up, she became irritated and angry, as if I was stupid and being unreasonable. It was then that I realised she might be ill because it was like she had changed completely, it just wasn't like her to act like this. She's normally fairly timid and reserved.

The next day she came home in a hire car and was wearing the most garish make up. At the time I had my brother round to help me to persuade her to go and see the doctor. I was astounded about the car and couldn't believe what I was seeing.

The manic phase

The following are some of the core symptoms that can occur in various combinations and degrees of severity during a manic phase.

Physical symptoms

- General restlessness and difficulty staying still for any length of time.
- A decreased desire for sleep or the inability to sleep, causing the person to have little or no sleep for days.

Bipolar Disorder: A guide for mental health professionals, carers and those who live with it
© Pavilion Publishing (Brighton) Ltd 2012

- Increased feelings of energy.

- A person may have no time for food or drink, and so physical complications can occur. They may feel that they do not even have time to go to the toilet. Constipation may occur or diarrhoea if there is a high level of anxiety with the mania.

Cognitive symptoms

- Insight is impaired. People in mania see no reason why their plans should be restrained or why extravagant expenditure should be curtailed. They seldom see themselves as ill or in need of treatment. They often fail to see any danger.

- Distractibility and difficulty concentrating are evident with the patient's attention easily diverted to inconsequential and unimportant details, making the performance of tasks difficult. Family and friends are likely to have noticed many new projects being started with nothing at all being finished in the lead up to mania.

- There can be expressions of unwarranted confidence and optimism alongside unrealistic beliefs in their ability. They may think that nothing can stop them from accomplishing any task. There is a serious lack of judgement with the person attempting to perform dangerous acts. Reckless driving is one such possibility.

- A flight of ideas occurs in severe forms. The person's thoughts race uncontrollably. When they talk the words come out in a non-stop rush, which changes abruptly from topic to topic, often before the previous one is finished. In its severe form the loud, rapid speech becomes hard to interpret because their thought processes have become so disorganised.

- Speech can be pressured, louder than usual, with no chance of interrupting them.

- Grandiose delusions can occur in which the person thinks they have a special relationship with God or the rich and famous.

Emotional symptoms

- Initially there can be a sudden onset of euphoria and elation, which can increase in a matter of days to a concerning level.

- Continued elevated mood or euphoria. This is way beyond the person's normal good mood. The person feels on top of the world even when confronted with bad news or difficult situations.

- At times people can become irritable, enraged and even paranoid when their plans are thwarted or their excessive social overtures are refused. Irritability can also arise when others do not share their optimism or enthusiasm. The person can switch very quickly between being very happy and very anxious.

Behavioural symptoms

- Hyperactivity is a common feature often accompanied by grand plans and participation in many activities. A person may try to cram everything into the day, for instance booking too many meetings or working excessive hours without a break. Overactivity is rarely productive since they seldom see things through before moving on to another scheme. Such hyperactivity coupled with an inadequate diet can lead to severe physical health problems. Death through exhaustion has occurred.

- Excessive use of alcohol and other drugs.

- Being overreactive to stimuli.

- Neglect. The person can neglect their appearance and personal hygiene, appearing dishevelled and poorly groomed. Conversely, they may smarten up as part of their grandiose plan.

- Added to the expansive mood is the real possibility of social and financial problems with the person indulging in spending sprees and foolish business ventures. Financial ruin can occur.

- Disinhibition is also often a key feature with the person being outspoken in their views and becoming overfamiliar with others or intrusive. Garish or provocative clothing and excessive make up are often chosen. Such disinhibition is often described as dramatic and flamboyant.

- Libido often increases leading to an increased interest in sex. Sexual disinhibition may also often be a feature with the person displaying inappropriate and out of character sexual behaviour. Unwanted pregnancies and criminal charges may be the outcomes of this feature.

Case study: Mania – the positive aspects, creativity and feelings of well-being

I remember one morning in March having coffee in a service station and noticing everything becoming more colourful. The daffodils were yellower, the sky bluer and all the advertising signs were so much brighter. I was waking up early and getting lots done. Work was going well and I even had a bonus for doing some exceptional work. All through April I lost weight, even though I was eating like a horse.

In May I bought new clothes, including jeans that I could not have imagined wearing a few months earlier. I celebrated by burning my old jeans and drinking champagne. It seemed appropriate at the time, but I thought it best not to mention this at work. I was now sleeping just two hours a night but I put my concerns about this aside.

I was the centre of attention everywhere I went with my continuous stream of witty thought-provoking remarks. Everyone loved me. I wanted to stay this way – energetic, enthusiastic, fun and slim!

Quite suddenly everyone around me seemed very inefficient. I spent a weekend at work and without asking anyone I rearranged everything from the computer files to the furniture. My boss was furious.

Somewhere on my runaway train journey I had lost touch with reality and started to believe I was more important than work, my boss, my friends. This was mania but now I wasn't going to listen to anyone.

Case study: Mania – the less favourable aspects of being manic

Once or twice I have benefitted from the energy that goes with mania but mostly my highs have been extremely unpleasant. Anxiety and paranoia kick in very quickly as my active mind latches onto all the worst possible scenarios, as in this example.

I was alone at home and as it was getting dark a car pulled into our cul-de-sac, parking with the two men inside facing our house. They sat there watching. I had not been sleeping and I was already very anxious.

I began to fear for my life. I believed they were checking if I was alone before they entered the house to kill me. I had to convince them I was not alone. Before putting any lights on, I ran upstairs drew the bedroom curtains, then switched the lights on. I stood in the hallway where they could see me and called up the stairs. I made two hot drinks and took these with biscuits up to a bedroom, making sure the two cups were clearly visible as I passed the hall window. I was terrified they would see through my deceit. It seemed like hours before they left.

Later I found out that my brother thought I was 'dangerously manic'. He had asked his friends to see if I was alright as my house was on their route home. My brother was right, I was dangerously manic – a danger to myself. My distorted thinking led on to severe self-harm.

It annoys me that the public see mania as a wonderful, happy state, when for me nothing could be worse. It was a terrifying and horrible experience.

DSM-IV criteria for a manic episode

A. A distinct period of abnormally and persistently elevated, expansive or irritable mood, lasting at least one week (or any duration if hospitalisation is necessary).

B. During the period of mood disturbance, three (or more) of the following symptoms have persisted (four if the mood is only irritable) and have been present to a significant degree:

- inflated self-esteem or grandiosity
- decreased need for sleep (eg. feels rested after only three hours sleep)
- more talkative than usual or pressure to keep talking
- flight of ideas or subjective experience that thoughts are racing
- distractibility (ie. attention too easily drawn to unimportant or irrelevant external stimuli)
- increase in goal-directed activity (either socially, at work or school, or sexually) or psychomotor agitation
- excessive involvement in pleasurable activities that have a high potential for painful consequences (eg. engaging in unrestrained buying sprees, sexual indiscretions or foolish business ventures).

(American Psychiatric Publishing, 1994)

If left untreated, a manic phase can last as long as three months. As it abates the patient may have a period of normal mood and behaviour, but eventually the depressive phase of the disorder will set in. The only exception to this pattern is unipolar mania.

> ### One man's madness: the manic depressive illness of Douglas
>
> '…when I am half manic I go in for wearing dark glasses … The dark glasses make me look more frightening and I enjoy, when I'm manic, looking frightening. It gives me a kick.'
>
> (The Listener 5/9/74)

The depressive phase

Though the key feature of bipolar disorder is the presence of manic or hypomanic episodes, depressive episodes are said to be more common in the course of the disorder (Judd *et al*, 2002). The major depressive episodes experienced in bipolar disorder have similar symptoms as in unipolar depression. The symptoms of depression are things we all experience from time to time, but it is the intensity and the persistence of the symptoms, alongside their impact upon daily life, which signifies a clinical depression.

Physical symptoms

- Difficulty sleeping; both early morning waking and the inability to get to sleep are common in depression.
- Decreased energy, feeling very tired all the time or 'slowed down'.
- Reduced appetite and weight loss. Occasionally there is weight gain arising out of comfort eating. This is more likely in bipolar than unipolar depression.
- Reduced libido and loss of interest in sex.
- Constipation.

> ## Question 1
>
> It is said that sleep is one way that depression in bipolar disorder differs from unipolar depression, as bipolar people will often sleep excessively during their depressive phases.
>
> List some reasons why this might be.

Cognitive symptoms

- Poor concentration, difficulty making decisions and remembering things.

- Loss of ability to experience pleasure (anhedonia).

- Decreased motivation.

- Approximately 17% of those with bipolar I and 24% of those with bipolar II attempt suicide (Rihmer & Kiss, 2002).

- Suicide is approximately 20 times more likely to be completed by those with a bipolar diagnosis than for the general population (Baldessarini & Tondo, 2003).

Emotional symptoms

- Depressed mood and prolonged periods of deep sadness and despair, which persist over time. The word 'despair' is accurate, meaning the absence of hope and the felt certainty of misery. These are not overly strong words as anyone who has been severely depressed will tell you that words to adequately describe the misery they have experienced do not exist.

- Feelings of worthlessness and guilt often lead to extreme self-criticism.

- Feelings of hopelessness and pessimism. People often use the word 'black' to describe their vision of the future and 'futile' to describe attempts to make things better.

Behavioural symptoms

- Far less activity/reduced range of activities.

- Inability to perform daily living tasks.

- Restlessness, irritability.

- Withdrawal and social isolation.

- Changes relating to eating and sleeping activities.

DSM-IV TR criteria for a major depressive episode

According to the *Diagnostic and Statistical Manual of Mental Disorders IV* (American Psychiatric Publishing, 1994) if five (or more) of the following symptoms are present during the same two-week period it indicates that a person is experiencing a major depressive episode.

1. Depressed mood most of the day, nearly every day.
2. Diminished interest or pleasure in all, or almost all, activities most of the day, nearly every day.
3. Weight loss when not dieting or weight gain.
4. Insomnia or hypersomnia nearly every day.
5. Psychomotor agitation or retardation nearly every day.
6. Fatigue or loss of energy nearly every day.
7. Feelings of worthlessness or excessive or inappropriate guilt nearly every day.
8. Diminished ability to think or concentrate, or indecisiveness, nearly every day.
9. Recurrent thoughts of death, recurrent suicidal ideation without a specific plan, or a suicide attempt or a specific plan for committing suicide.

American Psychiatric Publishing adds that the symptoms must cause clinically significant distress or impairment in social, occupational, or other important areas of functioning and that five symptoms need to include depressed mood or loss of interest or pleasure. See DSM IV for further details on diagnosis.

> ## Case study: Depression
>
> Depression is incredibly hard to describe to anyone who has not experienced it. For me, depression was like having my life force neutralised, with the removal of all hope. I had no anticipation of future events, good or bad. I wished I could stay asleep forever. I had no energy to engage with life at any level. I could not even shave or tie my shoe laces. I could see no beauty in the world or express any love. I felt so wretched the only answer was to leave this life. I have heard 'suicide is painless' but how do 'they' know? My friends told me 'it will pass and each day is another day nearer to getting better' – they were right but their sentiment was wasted as I was bereft of all logic. I could not simply 'reboot' my brain computer.

Other states

Mixed states

In mixed states the symptoms of both depression and mania are experienced. This seems incongruous but it is possible to have feelings of agitation and pressured thoughts alongside suicidal ideas and feelings of worthlessness. The DSM-IV criteria states that the symptoms of both mania and depression are present nearly every day for at least a week. Thus the person experiencing a mixed state will alternate quickly between euphoria and depression. As far back as 1896 Emil Kraepelin described six types of mixed state, each with variations in the symptoms of depression and mania.

Hypomania

The World Health Organization's ICD-10 criteria for hypomania describe it as a mild, persistent elevation of mood with increased energy and activity levels. It is a milder form of mania with similar but less severe symptoms. There is a feeling of physical and mental efficiency and well-being with increased talkativeness and sociability. Over familiarity, increased sexual energy, and a decreased need for sleep are present but do not necessarily disrupt work

Bipolar Disorder: A guide for mental health professionals, carers and those who live with it
© Pavilion Publishing (Brighton) Ltd 2012

or lead to social rejection. Irritability, conceit and boorish behaviour may be present but they are not accompanied by delusions. Diagnosis is possible if these symptoms are observed for at least four days, but it is probable that many hypomanic presentations go undiagnosed. Hypomania is so common that most people will see it as being busy, wanting to achieve a lot or simply as part of the person's personality. Even where it is quite apparent, health professionals will not readily wish to offer a diagnosis for something which is not harming the person or interfering with their life.

What is 'normal'

There is no clear division between 'normality' and hypomania and there is no clear division between hypomania and mania. The notion that mania is always more damaging than hypomania is not always true. A fully manic state will usually result in immediate help and ultimately, a resolution of the crisis. In a hypomanic state the person is unaware that their plans are unrealistic. They disregard the needs of friends, family and work colleagues and risky behaviour can continue for months without any professional help. This type of prolonged hypomania can wreck not only the bipolar person's life but the lives of many people around them.

Cycles

The episodic nature of bipolar disorder with periods of disorder interspersed with symptom-free periods is often referred to as being *cyclical*. This does not mean that any future episodes will follow a similar pattern or cycle to previous episodes. There is no such thing as a 'normal' cycle. The frequency, intensity and duration of episodes will vary enormously between individuals and with time for the same individual. Episodes may be several years or even decades apart. Some people can have frequent episodes and remain well in between while others will have frequent episodes with their moods remaining unstable in between. Rapid cyclers are those who have at least four depressive, manic, hypomanic or mixed states in a year. There are also ultra-rapid cycles in which the person can experience huge mood variations weekly or even daily. Some people with bipolar disorder are aware of their moods changing rapidly throughout the day on many days and this is described as an *ultradian* cycle.

Psychosis

Extreme mood swings may or may not involve psychotic symptoms such as delusions. Delusions are ideas that are firmly held despite evidence to the contrary. Grandiose delusions are common, for example believing you are God, a key politician, or very rich, and acting as such. Likewise, in severe depression delusions can form along the lines of personal ruin and worthlessness so that the person may believe they have committed a terrible wrong or are bankrupt. Delusions can be accompanied by hallucinations, increasing the chances of a misdiagnosis of schizophrenia. In the depressive phase psychosis can also take the form of psycho-motor retardation, a severe slowing down of speech, thought and movement that can also be seen as a symptom of schizophrenia.

Cyclothymia

A chronic disturbance of mood where there are numerous periods of mild depression and hypomania. This is sometimes referred to as mild chronic bipolar disorder. The depressive symptoms however do not reach the severity that would be classified as a major depressive episode. If this pattern persists for two years or more it can be classed as cyclothymia as it is likely to affect the individual's ability to function normally.

Question 2

Why might the word 'mild' in the above paragraph annoy people with cyclothymia?

Diagnosis, labelling and individuality

Diagnosis

It is not unusual for several years to elapse between first seeing a psychiatrist and receiving a diagnosis. Diagnosing mood disorders is difficult as both high and low mood can include a wide range of symptoms found in other disorders. For some, the diagnosis can bring a sense of

Bipolar Disorder: A guide for mental health professionals, carers and those who live with it
© Pavilion Publishing (Brighton) Ltd 2012

relief at being given a name for the disorder. Knowing what the disorder is enables people to find out about it and access support. For others, the diagnosis is only a medical label which, rather than offering them hope, brings with it a limited predetermined range of treatments and opinions and does little to focus upon individual needs.

Labelling

Many people with a diagnosis will often refer to it as a label. Labels can have positive and negative consequences. On the positive side, the diagnosis will allow a doctor to identify the treatment. It can tell a person what to expect and help them make plans for the future. A person can identify likely crises which might occur and plan to avoid them or deal with them. The diagnosis can also open doors to other forms of help such as support groups. As the label is medically derived, the assumption is that there is an underlying physiological malfunction. Thus labels can lead us to ignore the influence of social, psychological and environmental factors. It can also lead to an assumption that recovery needs to be medically derived.

Labels may be unhelpful for many other reasons.

- We can begin to look for signs and symptoms to fit the label.
- Behaviours can be misinterpreted as per the label.
- It can become a self-fulfilling prophecy.
- We can focus upon the disorder and not the person. Some people may interact with the person on the basis of the label rather than as themselves.
- Each label carries its own discrimination and stigma and the 'wearer' is likely to start to suffer from these.

Although it is illegal, employment discrimination against people with a mental health diagnosis continues to be widespread. Employers sometimes discriminate either deliberately or unconsciously against many people with mental health problems (Shaw Trust, 2006; Mind, 2011).

It is also worth knowing that from 1 October 2010 the Equality Act (2010) replaced most of the Disability Discrimination Act (DDA) (2005). However, the disability equality duty in the DDA continues to apply (Direct.gov, 2011).

Consideration points

- What do you think the average person imagines people with bipolar are like?
- What do you think the average person imagines people with mental health problems are like?
- Is the perception changing with increasing public education and awareness?
- Why might people with bipolar disorder who are managing the disorder make especially good employees?

A bipolar person's views on the diagnosis/label

A label can, to some extent, be hidden by people who have managed to eliminate the most severe mood swings from their lives. However, there are times when it can feel as if there is a big label stuck on your forehead, for example when applying for something as simple as travel insurance. The label can increase premiums because insurance companies consider all bipolar people to be 'high risk'. No account is taken of how long the person has been well, so even someone who has not had an episode for 20 years may find it too expensive to travel abroad.

Individuality

Having received the label it is natural for the person to consider how well the label fits. The reality is that no one is going to be the perfect BPI, BPII or any other diagnosis. There is likely to be a mixture of bipolar traits, but more importantly there will be far more traits not associated with bipolar. It is important for people not to 'become the label' or start behaving in the way someone with their diagnosis is 'expected' to behave. Public perception is changing slowly and in a perverse way it is a shame that those with mental health problems do not have their diagnosis tattooed on their foreheads so that the public can see that there are successful people with mental health issues who are getting on with their lives! The public's experience of people with mental health problems is usually when they are high-profile news subjects. Here the focus is usually on violence, which is actually quite rare.

Chapter 3: Symptomatology

Answers to questions

1. **It is said that sleep is one way that depression in bipolar disorder differs from unipolar depression, as bipolar people will often sleep excessively during their depressive phases.**

   List some reasons why this might be.

   Two reasons why bipolar people may sleep excessively during their depressive phases are:

   i. *If the depression follows a manic episode the person with bipolar is:*
       - *likely to still be taking a moderate dose of an antipsychotic, which will almost always induce extra sleep*
       - *simply exhausted after hardly sleeping at all during the manic phase.*
   ii. *A lack of sleep in depression may be due to the high levels of anxiety that often accompany it.*

2. **Why might the word 'mild' used in the paragraph annoy some people with cyclothymia?**

   - *Some people diagnosed with cyclothymia will experience suicidal depression but keep the diagnosis.*
   - *Some people with cyclothymia will remain moderately depressed for many years, and even for their lifetime. This can be severely debilitating, with a life devoid of pleasure and hope. Such a state is far from mild.*
   - *Some people with cyclothymia will have difficulty getting a diagnosis and feel that this limits the help they might otherwise receive.*
   - *Others with cyclothymia will be taking similar medications with similar side effects to those with BPI and BPII.*

References

American Psychiatric Publishing (1994) *Diagnostic and Statistical Manual of Mental Disorders (4th edition) (DSM-IV)*. Washington DC: American Psychiatric Association.

Baldessarini RJ & Tondo L (2003) Suicide risk and treatments for patients with bipolar. *Journal of the American Medical Association* **290** 1517–1519.

Direct.gov (2011) Disability and Equality Act [online]. Available at: http://www.direct.gov.uk/en/DisabledPeople/RightsAndObligations/DisabilityRights/DG_4001068 (accessed August 2011).

Judd L, Akiskal HS, Schettler PJ, Endicott J, Maser J, Solomon DA, Leon AC, Rice JA, Keller MB (2002) The long-term natural history of the weekly symptomatic status of bipolar I disorder *Archives of General Psychiatry* **59** (6) 530–537.

Mind (2011) *Workforce face the sack for admitting they feel stressed* [online]. Available at: http://www.mind.org.uk/news/5053_workers_face_the_sack_for_admitting_they_feel_stressed (accessed 18 August 2011).

Rihmer Z & Kiss K (2002) Bipolar disorders and suicidal behaviour. *Bipolar Disorder* **4** (1) 21–25.

Shaw Trust (2006) *Mental Health: The last workplace taboo*. London: Shaw Trust.

Short R (1974) *The Listener*. Septemeber 5 1974. London: BBC.

Further reading

Fink C & Kraynak J (2005) *Bipolar Disorder for Dummies*. New Jersey: Wiley. (See Chapter 2: Demystifying bipolar disorder.)

Frisch N & Frisch L (2006) *Psychiatric Mental Health Nursing* (3rd edition). New York: Thomson Delmar Learning.

Johnston S (2004) *The Naked Birdwatcher*. Helensburgh: The Cairn Publisher.

Shives L (2008) *Psychiatric-Mental Health Nursing* (7th edition). Philadelphia: Wolters Kluwer/Lippincott, Williams and Wilkins.

Thornicroft G (2006) *Actions Speak Louder*. London: Mental Health Foundation.

Thornicroft G (2006) *Shunned*. Oxford: Oxford University Press.

The last two reports explore in more detail the stigma and discrimination issues which derive from the application of labels to people with a psychiatric diagnosis.

Chapter 4

Assessment

Key points

- Each person's experience of bipolar disorder is different.

- A detailed assessment is necessary to obtain a thorough idea of the patient's circumstances.

- An assessment is a shared process.

- Assessment should be an ongoing process not just a snapshot taken at the acute phase of an illness.

- Rating scales and mood charts are useful.

Consideration point
■ How can you make an assessment as objective as possible, rather than it being just your own opinion of the patient behaviour and your interpretation of their words?

What to assess

Nurses develop plans of care by first undertaking a comprehensive assessment of their patient's presenting problems, personal circumstances and history. A good assessment will focus on the whole person and be holistic, covering psychological, social, and physical needs.

Each person's experience of bipolar disorder is different. Assessment seeks to gain a clear picture of the patient's unique experience, perspective and circumstances. It needs to examine current problems in the patient's life, highlight any risk, and identify the patient's strengths and resources. Care requires collaboration between a variety of health professionals, the patient and their family. Increasingly, assessments are shared and given due consideration to consent, thus saving the patient from having to retell their story to each and every health professional involved. Later in this section, best practice principles and methods of assessing are outlined after considering the areas of a thorough assessment in relation to bipolar disorder.

Assessment involves asking many questions. The following pages list the types of questions that need to be asked. Ideally questions need to be asked directly to the patient. Answers to these questions may come from other sources but in recording answers it is important to note who the answers came from. Patients experiencing mood swings may be slow to answer. If a relative is present you may need to ask them to give the person more time in order to hear answers directly from the patient.

Observation

The importance of observing the patient must not be underestimated. Everything from their posture, facial expressions, care taken over hair and any make-up, to the way they dress can give clues. However, often these clues can be misleading, particularly if you are not familiar with what is normal for a patient.

Pertinent assessment categories and useful questions

Safety/risk assessment

- **Suicide:** Have there been any past or recent suicidal thoughts/any specific plans in relation to suicide?

- **Self-harm:** Have there been past or recent occurrences of self-harm/ current thoughts of harming self?

- **Rest:** Are they having sufficient rest and sleep, or is there a danger of exhaustion?

- **Foods and fluids:** Are they getting enough nutrition and fluids, or is there a danger of undernourishment or dehydration?

- **Domestic:** What risks are there to home security and finances? Has the person been spending irresponsibly or leaving the house insecure?

- **Sexual behaviour:** Does it seem that sexual behaviour might put the person at risk of abuse or exploitation? Is there a high risk of an unwanted pregnancy or sexually transmitted diseases?

- **Work:** Are there risks to the person's employment?

- **Others:** Does the patient present a clear risk to others? For example, by driving dangerously?

Psychological/cognitive

Depressive elements
- Ask the person to describe how they have been feeling lately.

- Do they currently have hope/hopes?

- Do they *believe* they are achieving/completing any tasks at all?

- What are their current worries?

- Ask if they are experiencing anxiety and if so, how much anxiety compared to usual?

- How depressed do they get and how long has depression lasted in the past?

- Can they tell when they are getting low? What signs are there?

- How do they cope when they are depressed?

- Is there anything which helps?

- What makes it worse or increases the depression?

- How do they see the future?

- Do they have negative thoughts?

- Have they any thoughts of death or dying?

- Look for any feelings or verbalisations of worthlessness, hopelessness, despair and guilt.

- Is the person withdrawn and isolated?

- Do they experience negative thoughts about themselves and the future?

- Have they lost the ability to concentrate?
- Do they lack motivation?
- Do they get any enjoyment out of life or interests?
- Self-esteem: is it deflated and negative?
- Are there signs of anxiety?

Manic elements

- How do they feel about themselves?
- Do they have lots of energy?
- Do they experience highs and lows? How quickly do their moods change?
- Do they find they have to slow down to let others catch up with their thinking?
- Can they tell when they are getting high? What signs are there?
- Is the client euphoric, expansive and/or irritable?
- Do they seem to have an inflated sense of self-esteem?
- Do they display a low tolerance to others or being interrupted?
- Are they quick to anger? Are they irritable when plans are thwarted?
- Emotional lability; are they easily moved to tears and laughter?

Cognition

- Are they able to think clearly?
- Speech content: is it rational?
- Speech (rate and amount) rushed or pressured; is there evidence of a 'flight of ideas'. Patients in manic episodes will often be excited and overtalkative and can become irritable if interrupted.
- Lack of speech: do they just reluctantly mutter single word replies?
- Do they have difficulty concentrating for long periods?
- Is there any evidence of psychosis?
- Do they have delusions?
- Do they believe they have any special powers or associations and friendships?

Bipolar Disorder: A guide for mental health professionals, carers and those who live with it
© Pavilion Publishing (Brighton) Ltd 2012

- Is there any evidence of hallucinations?
- Do they hear voices, and if so how do the voices affect their life?

Thought disorder

- Do they have any thoughts which trouble them?
- How do these affect them?
- Does anything interfere with their thinking?
- How much insight does the person have into their disorder?

Behavioural elements

- How much energy do they feel they have?
- Is their posture slumped and reminiscent of dejection, or upright and alert?
- Patients with depressive symptoms may avoid eye contact. They may appear to be generally slowed down (psychomotor retardation).
- Are they overactive with an inability to sit still or sustain activity for any length of time?
- Have there been recent changes in libido – activity and interest?
- Are they disinhibited?
- Is their general behaviour intrusive, ignoring usual boundaries and invading personal space?
- Is behaviour impulsive?
- Have they lost interest in activities they usually enjoy?
- It is important to consider the relevance of the person's appearance. For example, look for excessive use of make up, jewellery, and garish dress that might suggest high mood. Patients with depression will often pay little attention to their appearance and personal hygiene; however, this can also be the case with manic episodes where the person has no time for what they perceive to be trivial pursuits. It is important to pause and think before asking questions about appearance. Perhaps consider how you would feel about being asked such a question and whether such a question needs to be rephrased to avoid possible offence.

Social networks and functioning

- How do they spend their free time?
- What are the important relationships in their life?
- What supportive relationships and networks do they have?
- How often do they see their friends?
- Have they lost interest in going out or meeting people?
- What are their hobbies and interests?
- Are they part of any other groups or clubs?
- What gives them pleasure?

Personal

- Values/beliefs
- Are there any aspects of their life which they feel they need to make changes in?
- Cultural needs and beliefs
- Is religion important to them?
- Do they go to a church?
- Religious and spiritual needs
- Sexuality needs/relationships/satisfaction

Domestic

- Where are they living?
- Do they like living there?
- Do they have enough money?
- Do they have debts?
- Any recent changes in economic status?
- Cooking, cleaning and washing
- Personal hygiene, any self-neglect?

- Shopping and budgeting.
- Neighbours and local community

Work

- Work satisfaction
- Hours worked on an average week and shift patterns
- Work stresses

Family

- Family/relationships (partners, parents, siblings, children, friends, main carers)
- Recent changes in family dynamics
- Dissatisfaction with roles and relationships
- Family needs
- Family history of mental illness

Physical

- When did they last eat and drink?
- How is their appetite?
- Do they usually have regular meals? Are they eating at the same/ different times now?
- Has their body weight changed recently?
- Are they taking any medication? Are they prescribed any other medications?
- Are there medications that have helped in the past?
- Do they experience side effects from these medications?
- Ask about alcohol use, smoking, illicit drugs, caffeine and other drugs. If used, explore the quantity and frequency of use. Is it social or an addiction?

■ Medical history and any physical problems/needs such as high blood pressure, diabetes etc.

■ Menstrual/gynaecological problems?

■ How much exercise, and how often?

Sleep

Sleep is both a warning sign and a trigger. Sleep is a key indicator of mood and changes in sleep patterns almost always result in mood changes. Understanding how the patient has been sleeping may tell you more about their mood than anything else, so ask plenty of questions to gain the best possible understanding of their sleep pattern.

■ Did you sleep well last night?
■ What time did you get to bed?
■ Did you get to sleep straightaway?
■ When did you wake up?
■ Were you awake much/at all during the night?
■ So that was X hours sleep then?

This is not an exhaustive list of questions. If the person is vague in their answers, it can be worth returning to questions about sleep later on.

History of presenting illness and current problem

■ Illness history, previous episodes/admissions

■ Previous medication and responses to it

■ How are they between episodes?

■ Current problem, nature, onset, duration, how has it progressed?

■ How long have symptoms persisted?

■ How frequently are these symptoms occurring?

■ Frequency of switching/cycling from depressed to manic

■ Precipitating events

■ Triggers to previous episodes

■ Current stressors/any recent significant life events.

Expectations of service

■ What does the person expect, want and need in the way of help and support?

Medical screening

Medical screening is important to be sure the disorder is not being caused by other physical conditions, which could produce similar symptoms and cause mood problems. Some common conditions to eliminate are:

Diabetes: Blood sugar tests will pick up on this illness which can result in mood swings.

Thyroid problems: Hyperthyroidism can occasionally present as hypomania or mania and is characterised by anxiety. Hypothyroidism can present with depressive symptoms.

Dementia: Depression is a common accompaniment to dementia. Insight into one's failing cognitive ability and frustration at not understanding what is going on around you understandably leads to depression.

Drug induced mood swings: These can be caused by the drug itself or the craving which comes with addiction and also by withdrawal syndromes. Alcohol is a natural depressant. Many stimulant drugs can cause 'highs' which may be similar to manic states. Antidepressants can also induce hypomania and antipsychotics can induce depression.

Hormonal changes: These can induce changes in mood with menstrual cycle and pregnancy being the most common causes.

Note: Any physical illness can cause you to feel mentally unwell and will often reduce your capacity to work, interact and look after yourself as well as making you feel miserable. This is normal. It is when the depressive symptoms are numerous, frequent and persist over time that a full depression is indicated.

The opinion of others

You will have your patient's words, the answers to your assessment and your observations with which to formulate a care plan. However, it is wise, and increases the objectivity of an assessment, if you canvass the opinion of others. If possible ask the patient for permission to do this. Close family and friends are an important source of information as are other health professionals who have been involved, such as the GP. A client in a manic state will also often not be capable of concentrating on your assessment agenda and it will be difficult to form a complete picture without the help of others. The same is true of the patient in the depths of a depression. Remember to clarify the opinion of others with the patient at the earliest opportunity.

With mood disorders, family and friends can be particularly useful in describing what the person's mood is like when they are well. If your patient is particularly unwell you may have no other way of knowing if they are normally quiet, like to be alone or perhaps are normally the life and soul of the party.

> ### Question 1
>
> What aspects of the assessment process can lead to a poor assessment?

How to assess

- The aim is to get to know the person, not the diagnosis. We want to know what is important to them and how the disorder stops them from enjoying life.

- Barker (1997) said *'Inadequate assessment is the biggest obstacle to the presentation of successful treatment'*. A care/recovery plan is only as good as the assessment it is based upon, get it wrong and all the care will fail to be relevant.

- There is a need to consciously avoid generalisations and jumping to conclusions/assumptions based on sex, age, ethnicity, class, occupation, appearance etc.

- Shared information is clarified information? The aim is to create a shared reality for the assessor, the patient, the family and the whole team so that each is aware of what the other thinks. There should be no deception. Elicit the patient's view and try to understand it. Feed that understanding back to the patient and inform them of the team's view and ensure they understand it.

- Don't rush. There is often no need to complete the assessment in one interview or within the first day. The process is ongoing and involves a degree of creativity and negotiation.

- It is important also to back up your assessment with observations of the patient's behaviour and words overtime, as this will change as they recover from the stress of admission.

- Any assessment checklist can be seen as a constraint, as they involve many 'closed' questions. Be ready to expand and clarify questions, especially if the patient seems stressed by the impersonal feel of a checklist approach. It is worth knowing how many times the patient has been through this checklist before or similar checklists. Are checklists already annoying them before you start?

- Use patient, family, friends, GP, other health professionals to add to the picture, with the patient's consent if possible.

- The assessment process is an opportunity to begin building up a therapeutic relationship so, if possible, the person who will be the patient's key worker should be the one who undertakes this.

- Be aware that if a person has been admitted to hospital, or even when being assessed at home, they are likely to be quite anxious and this will have an effect upon their ability to give accurate answers. You must spend time putting the person at ease first. Be aware that assessments can change moods.

- The process of assessment can help the patient to reflect upon and share their situation. This may lead to fresh insights for the patient.

- Assessment needs to focus on the patient's strengths as well as problem areas.

- During assessments you will often form ideas about what is happening with the patient. If these are simply feelings and hunches they should not be recorded, but can be shared with colleagues. Only observable facts and the patient's statements should be recorded.

- Rating scales. There are many rating scales for depression and anxiety, and a few for rating mania. You or your client can also use mood charts and diaries for rating and so add objectivity. Asking the patient to rate their mood will give you their view while involving them in their treatment. Mood Mapping is useful as part of an assessment, as it allows a visual representation of feelings, emotions and moods. Scales for anxiety, such as the Goldberg Anxiety Scale, can be useful because of their simplicity (Goldberg *et al*, 1988).

■ Be creative. If the client can self-assess, give them the form and a day or more to fill it in. Go through it together. Chat about it to reach a joint agreement. Share perspectives. This can create respect and empowerment and also gives you a far more valid assessment.

The Kipling questions

'*I keep six honest serving-men*
(they taught me all I knew);
Their names are What and Why and When
And How and Where and Who.'
(Kipling, 1902)

These six words provide many useful questions to ask and bear in mind when assessing a patient.

What?	What do you see as being your main problem?
	What helps and what hinders?
	What worries you most?
	What do you want to happen?
	What has helped before?
	What is the most important thing at the moment?
	What do you see as the cause of your problems?
Why?	Why do you think you have a problem?
	Why do you think you are unwell/struggling right now?
When?	When is the problem worse/better?
	When did you first start to feel something was wrong?
How?	How does it affect you?
	How do you relax?

How do you see the future?
How have you coped in the past?

Where? Where and in what situations is it worse?
Are there times and places where it is better?

Who? Are there people who help with your problems?
Are there any people who make things worse?

F.I.N.D.

These are four areas to explore to identify the impact of the disorder.

Frequency How often do these problems occur?

Intensity How intense is it? Can you say on a scale of one to 100?

Nature Can you describe it and how it affects you?

Duration How long does it last?

Case study: A person's recollection of being assessed

I was away from home when I needed to meet with a GP who arranged for me to stay at a psychiatric ward that I had never been to before. Some paperwork was being filled out and I was asked to wait on my own in the lounge. The news was on TV but I was too restless to take anything in. At the end of the news I went into the corridor and was told to return to the lounge.

No one spoke to me. I was in a right state as the slight paranoia I had been experiencing escalated when I heard nurses in the corridor talking about what to do with me. Just after midnight I was escorted to a small office where a psychiatrist had the notes that the nurses had been making.

He went through a long list of questions about my nationality and so on. When he asked if my first language was English, I said, 'No, it's Martian'. He muttered, 'hypomanic' under his breath. I had never heard the word before and resented that he was judging me without knowing what I had been through in the last few days. I then stuck to one word answers and refused to tell him my home address. Maybe I was in the wrong but in the state I was in this was one of the most traumatic nights of my life.

Self-assessment and mood scales

Sometimes we are obviously well and sometimes we are obviously unwell. With mood disorders there are times when things are not so obvious and it can be wise to accept the opinion of those close to us. Sometimes our moods are so low that we do not want to worry others, or so high that we have lost insight. Family and friends will almost certainly pick up on our moods because they spend a lot of time with us. They will probably be aware of whether we are generally active, calm, tired or anxious, becoming depressed or getting high. One way of monitoring or assessing mental state is to use a mood scale and construct a chart. The scale will have typical behaviours and ways of thinking ranked against words like hypomanic, mild depression and so on. An example of a mood scale is given in Table 4.1 along with several examples of completed charts (Figures 4.1 and 4.2).

Table 4.1: Mood scale	
Scale	Some typical experiences during mood disorder
10	No idea what is real Believing you are someone else Extreme paranoia Inability to make even simple choices Audio/visual/olfactory hallucinations
9	Most of your ideas are contrary to those around you Losing touch with reality Speech too fast even for friends Paranoia Money has no value at all Hardly sleep (maybe less than two hours in 24 hours)

Bipolar Disorder: A guide for mental health professionals, carers and those who live with it
© Pavilion Publishing (Brighton) Ltd 2012

Scale	Some typical experiences during mood disorder
8	Money means very little You know you are important Seeming to be thinking faster than those around you Talking louder or faster than those around you Disregarding safety Continue to start new projects but nothing being finished
7	Feeling very productive Able to charm friends and strangers Talking a lot (such as longer phone calls) Wanting to do more of everything Excessive spending
6	Needing less sleep Productive Feeling good about oneself Future looks bright Enjoy meeting people Fairly talkative
5	Awake and functioning well throughout the day, Sleeping well, life is OK, future looks OK
4	Sleep disrupted – perhaps wanting to sleep more Not so keen on crowds Concentration not so good A little agitated
3	Greater anxiety Difficulty concentrating Forgetting simple things Prefer to do routine rather than new tasks
2	Want to lay down a lot – whether able to sleep or not Slow thinking Some comfort in eating Desire to be alone Nothing is easy

Scale	Some typical experiences during mood disorder
1	Feeling worthless Almost no hope Suicidal thoughts Hardly doing anything
0	No hope at all Hardly thinking of anything but dying Not going anywhere or doing anything Seems like things have always been bad Seems like things *will* always be bad

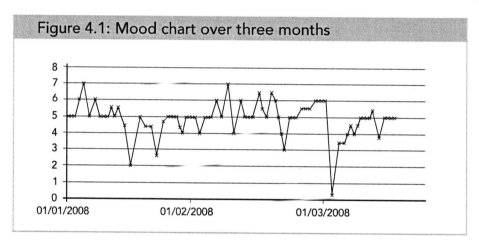

Figure 4.1: Mood chart over three months

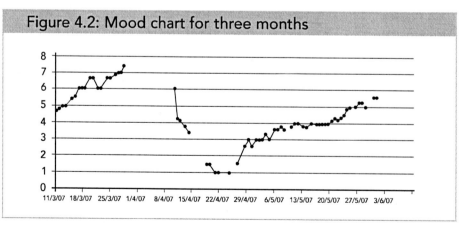

Figure 4.2: Mood chart for three months

Question 2

Why do you think there are gaps in the second mood chart?

Mood scales and charts will be examined in more detail in Chapter 21: Warning signs and relapse prevention.

Mental Health Act assessment

According to the Care Quality Commission (2010) there were 45,755 detentions under the Mental Health Act in 2009/10. The commission also reported that the number of psychiatric inpatients is increasing with 16,622 in 2010 compared with 14,625 in 2006.

The following is a brief outline of the three major sections of the Mental Health Act (2007) that can be used to detain people.

Section 2: Admission for assessment

Section 2 is the most common section and according to Mind the average length of stay under this section is two weeks.

Length: Under Section 2 you can be detained for a maximum of 28 days.

Application: The application can be made by an approved mental health practitioner, or your nearest relative.

Process: Two doctors must confirm that you:

- are suffering from a mental disorder that warrants detention in hospital for assessment
- should be detained in your own interests on grounds of health or safety, or with a view to the protection of others.

Section 3: Admission for treatment

Length: Under Section 3 you can initially be detained for up to six months. This is renewable for a further six months and thereafter for periods of a year at a time.

Application: This can be made by the nearest relative or an approved mental health practitioner where the nearest relative does not object or where it is not 'reasonably practicable' to consult the nearest relative.

Process: Two doctors must confirm that:

- the patient is suffering from a mental disorder of a nature or degree that they need medical treatment in hospital

- appropriate medical treatment is available for them

- it is necessary for their own health and safety or for the protection of others that they receive treatment and it cannot be provided unless they are detained.

Section 4: Admission for emergency assessment

Length: 72 hours maximum

Application: The application can be made by an approved mental health practitioner, or nearest relative. The applicant must have seen the person within the last 24 hours.

Process: One doctor must confirm that:

- there is an 'urgent necessity' for the patient to be admitted under Section 2 and there is no time to wait for a second doctor's opinion, or that

- it is undesirable to delay and wait for a second doctor's opinion.

Bipolar Disorder: A guide for mental health professionals, carers and those who live with it
© Pavilion Publishing (Brighton) Ltd 2012

Mental Health Act (2007) definitions

Approved mental health practitioner
These are usually social workers, nurses, occupational therapists or psychologists who have been approved by the local social services authority. Part of their role is to interview individuals to decide whether detention is the best way of providing appropriate care and medical treatment.

Nearest relative
This is usually a spouse, civil partner, cohabitee of six months or more, a child or a sibling. They can apply for their relative to be formally detained under a section of the act, although in most cases it is an approved mental health practitioner who makes the application.

Assessing mental capacity

The Mental Capacity Act (2005) exists to protect those who lack the capacity to make decisions for themselves in areas such as health care.

The act is underpinned by five principles.

1. **Presumption of capacity:** Everyone is assumed to have capacity unless it is proved otherwise.

2. **Right to be supported to make own decisions:** People must be given help before it is concluded they cannot make their own decisions.

3. **Right to eccentricity:** People have a right to make eccentric or 'unwise' decisions.

4. **Best interests:** Whatever is done for those without capacity must be in their best interests. It should take into account their values and beliefs. This may necessitate consulting their close relatives.

5. **Least restrictive:** Things done for those without capacity must be the least restrictive of their rights.

The act gives a test for assessing whether a person has capacity for decision-making at any one time. The act needs to be reapplied with every subsequent decision. Thus it is both time and decision specific. Importantly, this act tells us that *diagnosis alone does not denote incapacity*.

Capacity test

A person must be able to:

1. Understand the information
2. Retain the information
3. Weigh up the information (judge its pros and cons)
4. Communicate their decision

Answers to questions

1. **What aspects of the assessment process can lead to a poor assessment?**

Being rushed: *Rushing an assessment will lead to a lack of information and misinformation. The client will feel pressured and uncomfortable. The assessor is unlikely to give sufficient encouragement and support for the client to explore delicate and often painful issues.*

Diagnosis: *Focusing upon the illness and not the person will lead the assessor away from important information.*

Assumptions: *Try not to make generalisations or jump to conclusions with respect to such things as age, gender, race, class, appearance, occupation, etc. Be aware of your own prejudices.*

Not sharing the assessment: *Assessment must be shared. The assessor must get the opinions of others involved such as family, friends and other professionals.*

Formality: *Being restricted by a formal questionnaire sheet to fill in and not being creative with your questioning or adapting the tool to suit the client.*

Hunches: *These may be useful but should never be part of assessment. Assessment needs to be as objective as possible and the best way to achieve this is to share hunches.*

2. Why do you think there are gaps in this second mood chart?

Many people leave gaps in mood charts. There are days when people simply forget or generally do not feel like filling the chart in. Clients will go back and fill in gaps, but this may be of little use or even misleading as we are unlikely to remember our mood accurately. The most accurate recordings are ones that are made at the time.

On the example, the gaps early in April are likely to have been during a period of very high mood. At such times one can be just too busy to bother with the chart or feel so healthy and optimistic about the future that monitoring aspects of health seems unimportant.

The missing points in late April are likely to be times when the mood was exceptionally low. Moods below 2 will hardly ever be plotted as such low moods correspond to times of low energy where even picking up a pen can seem like a huge effort.

Some clients may choose not to plot points they feel indicate failure.

If this client's mood is not fluctuating widely each day, then the points missed towards the end of the chart while the mood is fairly steady are most likely to just have been through forgetfulness rather than extremes of mood.

References

Barker P (1997) *Assessment in Psychiatric and Mental Health Nursing: In search of the whole person*. Cheltenham: Nelson Thornes.

Care Quality Commission (2010) *Monitoring the Use of the Mental Health Act in 2009/10: The Care Quality Commission's first report on the exercise of its functions in keeping under review the operation of the Mental Health Act (1983)* [online]. London: CQC. Available at: http://www.cqc.org.uk/mentalhealthactannualreport2009-10.cfm (accessed 18 August 2011).

Goldberg D, Bridges K & Duncan-Jones P (1988) Detecting anxiety and depression in general medical settings. *British Medical Journal* **297** 897–899.

Kipling R (1902) *The Elephant's Child: Just so stories for little children*. London: MacMillan and Co.

Further reading

Craig T (2000) Severe mental illness: symptoms, signs and diagnosis. In: C Gamble & G Brennan (2000) *Working with Serious Mental Illness: A manual for clinical practice*. Edinburgh: Bailliere Tindall.

Fink C & Krynak J (2005) Getting a psychiatric evaluation and treatment plan. In: C Fink & J Krynak (Eds) *Bipolar Disorder for Dummies*. Hoboken, New Jersey: Wiley.

Shives L (2008) Assessment of psychiatric – mental health clients. In: L Shives (2008) *Psychiatric-Mental Health Nursing* (7th edition). Philadelphia: Wolters Kluwer/Lippincott, Williams and Wilkins.

Videbeck S (2009) *Mental Health Nursing*. London: Lippincott, Williams and Wilkins. (See Chapter 8: Assessment approaches.)

Useful websites

Department of Health information on the Mental Capacity Act (2005) at http://www.dh.gov.uk/en/SocialCare/Deliveringadultsocialcare/MentalCapacity/MentalCapacityAct2005/DH_064735

Mental Health Act (2007) at http://www.legislation.gov.uk/ukpga/2007/12/contents. This provides the official text of the Mental Health Act (2007).

Mind at http://www.mind.org.uk/help/rights_and_legislation. The Mind website has useful information on the Mental Health Act and mental capacity.

Section 2
Inpatient/acute care

Chapter 5

Inpatient case study

Prior to admission

Stephen is a 32-year-old form tutor for a mixed-sex class of 15 year olds. He is happily married and has two sons who are aged four and six. This is Stephen's first manic episode. He likes his job and is enthusiastic about his work and is committed to his family. Five months ago he took time off work for depression. He had become withdrawn and uncommunicative. He was not eating and he was sleeping all day. His GP prescribed him antidepressants. Stephen came out of his gloom within a few weeks and was back at work and fully functioning. However, over the last three weeks there has been a gradual onset of increasingly uncharacteristic and risky behaviour. There is now a real danger that he is putting his job at risk and he seems fixated upon what he describes as his 'schemes'. These schemes are grand plans. He has talked of emigrating without a job to set up a scheme to help people 'with life', but cannot explain it in detail.

Last week he started working longer and staying up at night to work on some unrealistic schemes for the school and money making. He had to be asked to leave the school several times by the caretaker, who wanted to lock up. Stephen submitted a report to the head at the school that made little sense and was derogatory about other staff members. When the head asked to see him about the report and the informal complaints from female staff about his overfamiliarity, Stephen became abusive. His speech became pressured and at odds with reality. He eventually stormed out, leaving the head with no option but to suspend him.

Stephen has recently been on an unusually large clothes buying spree. In the last week he has bought his children things they don't need such as skis and scuba gear. He has started ordering lots of unusual things from the internet and been spending large amounts of money.

He has recently been caught speeding and was cautioned. He has also taken to wearing a flamboyant suit as opposed to his normal drab clothes, wearing it for days without changing or washing. Last night he decided to redecorate and began clearing everything out of the house. He put things on the front lawn and began pulling up carpets. When confronted about it he made no sense. He was mostly talking in rhyme about irrelevant things. At this point the children were becoming scared and his wife called the GP out-of-hours service asking for urgent help. The on-call GP requested a psychiatric crisis visit and Stephen eventually agreed to go to the local admission ward to be assessed.

On admission

Stephen could not see what all the fuss was about and he was not ill. He felt 'great'. He was elated but also easily irritated. He would go very quickly from being 'over the moon' to being quite angry. He was displaying pressure of speech and talking loudly. He was expansive and using uncharacteristic gestures. His thoughts appeared to be racing and it was often hard to understand him. He was not making much sense at all; babbling quickly about his 'scheme' and the urgency. 'Everyone else is thick not to see what I see. It's a winner. It'll save the world.'

He was unable to stay still and was pacing around energetically, trying to talk to everyone to tell them that he had 'big celebrities on board'. His intrusiveness signalled a real danger that he would upset other patients who might react angrily to him and thus put him at risk. He was easily distracted but always returned to his scheme, often with a new slant. He showed no insight and came across as being very confident yet he looked dreadfully tired and drawn. His response to a suggestion that he might take a bath and change his clothes was: 'I look great. I feel great. I am great!'. He was not interested in eating and he looked dehydrated.

His wife said that Stephen hadn't been sleeping, because he was 'too busy'. He was not eating much either – all he had eaten was chocolate biscuits. She reported that he had been phoning people in the middle of the night and that he had been flirting with checkout girls at the supermarket. She was distraught and did not understand why he was behaving like this, but recognised that he must be ill.

Notes

This case study encompasses a number of fairly typical issues and behaviours relating to a patient experiencing a manic phase and thus being admitted to an assessment unit. The subsequent chapters outline key issues for health professionals, family members and carers to address during the acute phase of both high and low episodes.

Chapter 16: Care plans for the inpatient case study suggests a care plan for this client which covers these issues.

Chapter 6

The therapeutic relationship

Key points

- The role of the mental health nurse is diverse.
- At the heart of the role is the development of a therapeutic relationship with the patient.
- A therapeutic relationship underpins everything a nurse does.
- The therapeutic relationship is a partnership with the patient.

In order to provide treatment and support, a nurse seeks to promote the patient's independence and work in partnership with them rather than disempowering them and taking control. The nurse's role is to help the patient to recover.

Therapeutic relationships do not happen automatically. They have to be worked at and can often take weeks to develop sufficiently to be beneficial. Initially, the nurse and patient are strangers and it will take time before the patient feels comfortable enough to discuss their thoughts and feelings with the nurse. The acuteness of the disorder on admission may be a barrier to the development of the relationship. While the patient is acutely ill and lacking insight they will often feel antipathy towards the nurse as they are often cast in the role of the restrictor of liberty. Patient can display hostility because of their disorder in the acute phase. However the nurse needs to send out a powerful message of non-rejection by continuing to engage with the client and supporting them during the acute phase.

Building the therapeutic relationship begins with shared everyday activities such as discussing the news, taking a walk or sharing a coffee. These simple everyday human acts help to form the initial bonds and allow the nurse and the patient to get to know each other. Hopefully the patient increasingly feels that the nurse is a fellow human being who is there to help, allowing trust to gradually develop. The nurse will help this process by being a good listener and practising active listening skills and paying close attention to what is said. The key components of active listening are:

- giving time by simply listening and being there
- giving visual (nods) and other non-verbal ('uh-huh') feedback
- demonstrating interest and concern
- using reflection and paraphrasing
- reflecting the feelings as well as the content of what is said
- asking clarifying questions
- summarising.

The patient will be grateful to a nurse who has time to listen and demonstrates interest in their problems.

Reflection exercise: Basic listening skills

With a colleague, take it in turns to be a speaker and a listener. The speaker can talk about anything they wish to for five minutes. The listener practises active listening but is not allowed to say anything. Swap roles after five minutes and discuss how it felt not to be able to talk. What are the advantages and disadvantages?

This exercise can prove difficult as it is natural to want to interject and put your point of view across, however, in a therapeutic relationship you run the risk of hijacking the agenda and steering it away from the patient's concerns. There is the danger, too, of interrupting the patient just as they are getting the courage to discuss painful issues.

A good follow-up exercise is for the listener to report back to the speaker their version of the conversation to see if they have heard it correctly or misinterpreted it in any way.

It is useful to do these exercises with a third person as an observer to feed back upon aspects such as non-verbal behaviour and to give an objective overview.

Bipolar Disorder: A guide for mental health professionals, carers and those who live with it
© Pavilion Publishing (Brighton) Ltd 2012

Rogers' (1951) client-centred approach suggests that nurses need to display congruence, empathy and respect and be non-judgemental. Indeed, without such qualities it is difficult to build a workable therapeutic relationship. In being congruent the nurse needs to be open, honest and genuine in their communication and their words should reflect their thoughts and behaviours. Being empathic is gaining an understanding of what life must be like for the other person and communicating that understanding back to them.

Rogers suggests that the quality of the relationship itself plays a crucial role in helping patients to understand themselves, explore their resources, and manage their problems and lives more effectively. There is much evidence to suggest that it is not the form of therapy that is important in bringing about positive change, but the ability of the therapist to form a relationship with the patient.

There are many ways to define the therapeutic relationship but essentially it is a goal-directed relationship focused on helping the patient to overcome problems and move forward.

Characteristics of helping relationships

- The nurse recognises the patient as a co-worker and an equal.
- The patient begins to feel less isolated and more part of a team.
- The nurse wants to understand the patient's feelings and situation.
- Both the nurse and the patient realise the importance of common language. The nurse works towards understanding the patient's use of words about feelings and the disorder.
- Agreement on the interpretation of the problems and ways forward.
- Agreed goals and tasks are set.
- The relationship fosters a sense of hope for the future.
- The relationship recognises boundaries.
- The relationship avoids creating dependence.
- The relationship recognises the value of self-disclosure while avoiding social friendship.
- The relationship respects personal/cultural beliefs.

- The relationship recognises the role and value of challenging and confrontation.

- The collaboration understands that the patient must accept responsibility for working on their problems and not look to the nurse for answers.

- It should be empowering; the patient needs to feel they have some power.

- It recognises that change comes in small, realistic, achievable steps.

- It recognises that relapse is an acceptable and often frequent part of the learning process.

- The collaboration recognises that specialist help may be needed.

There are many other benefits of a good working alliance, which are more practical such as helping a patient prepare for meetings with health professionals, being an advocate and helping the patient understand their rights.

Self-disclosure

Self-disclosure can be useful in letting the patient know you have similar experiences and thus a degree of understanding of their situation. It also shows that you are human as well as a health professional. It is useful early on to help initiate the relationship, but it must never descend into a social friendship as to do so would jeopardise the goal-directed nature of the relationship. In this way a helping relationship may not always be therapeutic. When a nurse becomes over involved in a patient's life, the relationship is likely to lose its therapeutic value.

The therapeutic relationship in context

Davidson (1998) argues that a large part of the role of the psychiatric nurse is to get to know the individual behind the symptoms. He describes a view of psychiatric nursing that is both simple and empowering. From the base of the therapeutic relationship an initial part of the nurse's role is to provide *comfort* for the patient during disturbing and often frightening acute episodes. To be there with them as a 'co-presence', sharing their pain and not rejecting them.

Beyond this acute phase, as it fades naturally or as the symptoms are brought under greater control, another key role for the nurse emerges. This is to help the patient make sense of what is going on, *demystifying* the disorder, psychiatry and their predicament. This is done partly by exploring the patient's life situation and history with them, but also entails trying to explain what is happening regarding the disorder's symptoms and treatment.

Unfortunately, patients are often discharged once there is stability and symptom-control is achieved. In a poor care scenario little is done to examine the root causes of the patient's distress, let alone do anything about it. In a good care scenario once an understanding of the patient's predicament is achieved the next stage of the recovery process can begin. This entails the nurse working with the patient to examine just exactly what is causing them to have so much distress. This striving towards awareness can itself be a long process before a patient realises or admits what is effecting them. It is hard to admit such things as: 'I am an alcoholic', 'I am in a bad relationship', 'I lack confidence and assertiveness'. So this stage can take a long time, but having achieved this understanding it is still not the end of the story.

The next role for the nurse is to help the patient to translate this awareness into action to be able to overcome these difficulties. This may entail helping them to explore appropriate actions and supporting them in these, or helping them gain coping strategies. In this way it is hoped that future stress can be avoided or coped with so that it will not bring on another episode.

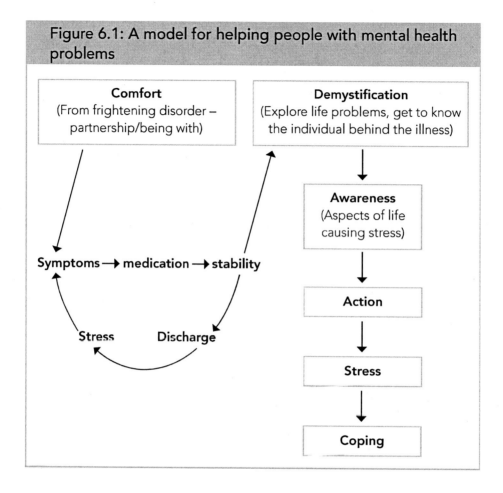

Figure 6.1: A model for helping people with mental health problems

Reflection exercise: The theraputic relationship

■ What do the nurse and the patient bring to a therapeutic relationship? Make two lists.

■ What gets in the way of a therapeutic relationship?

List as many hindering factors as you can and discuss with colleagues how to avoid or overcome these.

Note: Identifying how not to do something often helps us to see how we should do it.

Bipolar Disorder: A guide for mental health professionals, carers and those who live with it
© Pavilion Publishing (Brighton) Ltd 2012

References

Davidson B (1998) The role of the psychiatric nurse. In: P Barker & B Davidson (Eds) *Psychiatric Nursing: Ethical strife*. London: Arnold.

Rogers CR (1951) *Client-centered Therapy: Its current practice, implications and theory*. London: Constable.

Further reading

Barker P & Whitehall I (1997) The craft of care: towards collaborative caring in psychiatric nursing. In: S Tilley (Ed) *The Mental Health Nurse: Voices of practice and education*. Oxford: Blackwell Science.

Nursing and Midwifery Council (2002) *Practitioner–client Relationships and the Prevention of Abuse: Protecting the public through professional standards*. NMC: London. (This outlines the nurses' professional body's view on the boundaries of the nurse/patient relationship. It offers clear guidance and advice on the detection and prevention of abuse).

Repper J (1996) Creating effective relationships. In: R Perkins & J Repper (Eds) *Working Alongside People with Long Term Mental Health Problems*. Cheltenham: Nelson Thornes.

Reynolds B (2003) Developing therapeutic one to one relationships. In: P Barker (Ed) *Psychiatric and Mental Health Nursing: The craft of caring*. London: Arnold.

Speedy S (1999) The therapeutic alliance. In: M Clinton & S Nelson (Eds) *Advanced Practice in Mental Health Nursing*. Oxford: Blackwell Science.

Sundeen SJ & Stuart GW (1976) *Nurse–Client Interaction: Implementing the nursing process*. St Louis: Mosby.

Thomas B, Hardy S & Cutting P (1997) *Stuart and Sundeens' Mental Health Nursing: Principles and practice*. St Louis: Mosby.

Wright H & Giddey M (1997) *Mental Health Nursing: From first principles to professional practice*. Cheltenham: Nelson Thornes.

Chapter 7

Safety issues

Key points

- There are safety risks inherent in both the depressive and manic phases.
- Good risk assessment is the key to safety and support in hospital environments.
- Risk assessment is not a one-off process; it is ongoing.
- The observation of patients can be supportive and therapeutic.

Depressive phase

The risk of suicide must always be considered during a depressive phase. Low self-esteem and feelings of despair are prime drivers for suicide. The depressed person feels that they are a burden to others and that the future is hopeless and futile. In the depths of depression a person has too little energy to take their life and perversely, it is often when the individual is beginning to recover that the danger is greatest. At this stage they have regained the energy and motivation necessary to organise and carry out the act, while they are still profoundly depressed.

Other important risk factors to consider that might highlight an increased risk are:

- previous attempts
- social isolation, loneliness and social exclusion
- being single, widowed or divorced
- men have roughly a four times higher risk than women

- lack of a close intimate confiding relationship

- chronic physical ill health

- reliance upon alcohol or other drugs

- significant trigger events such as the loss of a close relationship, bereavement, failure or unemployment

- retirement, financial strains and other recent adverse life events.

Questions

1. Does the trigger/stressor need to be 'adverse'?
2. Can you think why positive events might be stressful?
3. Suggest examples of positive events that might be stressful.

Even in a hospital setting, where a person is under closer observation than in the community, there are still high risks for suicide. Indicators of increased risk of ward-based patients are:

- changes in normal behaviour patterns

- withdrawal

- self-neglect

- presence of suicidal ideas

- verbalisations and expressions of intent

- making preparations eg. writing a will and giving possessions away

- having a plan and a method in mind

- becoming more withdrawn

- writing suicide notes.

Suicide myths

People who talk about suicide don't do it

The assumption here is that it is the 'silent ones' who are most likely to commit suicide. However, most of those who have completed or attempted suicide have talked about it prior to the event. Such verbalisations offer vital opportunities to engage with the potential suicide in an attempt to offer support and alter the course of the person's actions. Much suicide management is about giving the person as many alternative possibilities and opportunities to reconsider.

People who talk about committing suicide are just attention-seeking

All verbalisations of intent need to be treated seriously. Most of those who complete suicide have talked about it. An attempt is an opportunity to recognise the seriousness of the individual's predicament and to engage with them fully and encourage them to discuss it further.

Talking about suicide will encourage it

Again, the reverse is true; it is crucial to talk to and engage with the person. Ignoring the subject will deny the person support and isolate them further as no one engages with them about it, giving the message that they aren't being taken seriously. The traditional wisdom which suggests that talking about your problems is the best way of dealing with them holds true here. Not discussing problems merely bottles them up, intensifying their severity.

All suicides are preventable

Unfortunately this is not the case, even with the best risk assessments and observation protocols, people will still find a way if they are determined. It is also often said that if someone wants to commit suicide they will and while that might be true, it does not mean that we should not try to prevent it. We need to seek every opportunity to provide the person with an escape route.

If a person is determined to kill themselves, nothing is going to stop them

This is not true. Even the most severely depressed person has mixed feelings about death, and most waver until the very last moment between wanting to live and wanting to die. Most suicidal people do not want to die; they simply want their misery to stop. The impulse to end it all, however, powerful, does not last forever.

Reducing the risk of suicide

We cannot prevent all suicides, but we can reduce the incidence

- Many people who attempt suicide are ambivalent about it as reflected in the number of people who seek help.

- With suicide, the intent to die fluctuates and passes, so it is important to provide as many 'get out' opportunities as possible ie. chances for the person to reconsider.

- The intensity of despair can fluctuate too. It is often time-limited and dependent on a range of environmental and social factors. These must be discussed and alternative possibilities explored in order to give hope.

What approach should be taken?

- Stay calm. The person will be anxious enough without picking up on your anxieties.

- Stay with them and validate their intention. Ignoring them will bring more anxiety and anger and push them away. It is helpful for the person to know that it is okay to talk and that you are not scared to do so openly.

- Merely giving the person time and listening to them will make them feel that they are being taken seriously.

- You need to convey a sense of safety. So be calm, slow and assured.

- Be non-judgemental as any other attitude will push people away from help.

- Use problem solving; state what the problems are and write them down.

- Brainstorm with the person possible alternative responses. Explore different ways of seeing and tackling problems.

- Look at each response and go through positives and negatives. Write them down and leave it with the person.

- If in a community setting, provide practical help and support to decrease their worry and increase feelings of being supported.

- Reduce access to means; take away drugs, encourage the person to stay with friends.

- Refer the person on to other agencies for other forms of help and support. If you think that help is needed urgently, be sure others know that you see this urgency.

Self-harm

There is a need to make a distinction between self-harm and suicide.

Self-harm is a method of coping with distressing feelings and thoughts rather than an attempt to take one's life, although occasionally it can go tragically wrong. It can take many forms but the most common are scratching and cutting, burning and inflicting blows to oneself, such as head-banging. Many people who self-harm describe it as being a tension relief mechanism which gives them respite from distressing feelings.

In self-harm there is no intention to die.

People who self-harm may have no thoughts of suicide at all and are usually in control of their actions in such a way as to have no great risk of accidental death. Although seemingly rare, self-harm can go wrong and lead to death that looks like a suicide. For this reason those who are consistently increasing the seriousness of their self-harming (such as making deeper cuts) need our fullest attention.

For further information relating to self-harm, see:

Self-injury information and support at www.selfharm.net

National Self-Harm Network at www.nshn.co.uk

Mind at www.mind.org.uk/help/diagnoses_and_conditions/self-harm

Manic phase

Safety and protection are just as important during a manic phase. It will often be necessary to use close observation and supervision, just as in the depressive phase, to protect the person from their own disinhibition and lack of judgement.

Common examples of harm in mania include:

- injury through rushed or ill thought out/careless acts/poor concentration/distraction/poor judgement/overconfidence

- physical exhaustion through overactivity and overexertion and lack of sleep

- loss of weight due to not eating, overactivity, and the patient being too busy with other concerns

- impulsive behaviour

- sexual disinhibition leading to unhealthy/unwanted encounters/unwanted pregnancies/sexually transmitted diseases

- financial extravagance

- legal risks such as law breaking eg. speeding

- retaliation against the person's intrusive behaviour, direct speech, invasion of personal space and ignoring of social boundaries/moral codes, such as interfering with property or intruding into social relationships.

- damage to reputation and ridicule.

The nurse and ward team have to set clear boundaries and limits to behaviour to safeguard the patient and protect others.

Case study: Disinhibition

'Oh Danny, can you come here please!'

As a male student nurse on a female admission ward, a patient in a manic phase following the birth of her daughter, who was on the ward with her, would frequently strip off and call for me by name to attend her. Her overtly sexual behaviour was very upsetting for her husband to witness as she presented as having no qualms at all.

It is imperative to provide a safe environment for the manic patient. This is a skilled task. In a manic phase the patient will have little insight and will not see the sense behind the restrictive measures you are likely to suggest. They may be easily moved to agitation and anger if their plans and desires are thwarted.

Risk assessment

Three main areas of risk can be identified as:

- risk to the patient from self
- risk to others from the patient
- risk to the patient from others.

There are many risk assessment tools. It is important to remember that risk assessment is an interpersonal process and not just a case of ticking boxes and ranking scores. The building of a therapeutic relationship, even without the benefit of much time, is the best risk assessment strategy. A good nurse will be able to clearly identify risk situations for their patients. As a starting point it is important to consider previous risky behaviour patterns and to enlist the help and insight of family/friends to ensure that the assessment is thorough.

Key areas of concern

Violence or injury to self (eg. suicide or self-injury): This could also be through accidents due to rushing or overconfidence.

Violence or injury to others: This may not be intentional or due to anger, but may arise through rushing and overconfidence.

Violence from others: This is likely to arise from the manic person's intrusive behaviour, persistence and lack of insight.

Sexual behaviour: The need is to protect the patient from their own disinhibition but also from exploitation of others who might take advantage.

Financial behaviour: As above, the risk is from both the patient's lack of judgement and manic vision, but also from being exploited by others.

Self-neglect: In relation to health such as diet and sleep, but also appearance, and personal hygiene.

Reputation: The patient needs protecting from damage to their reputation so that the actions of their manic episode do not have a negative impact upon their future.

A risk assessment needs to be used to generate a risk management plan. This in turn needs to outline clear actions, responsibilities and review dates.

Safe and supportive observation of patients at risk in hospitals

The Standing Nursing and Midwifery Advisory Committee report *Safe and Supportive Observation of Patients at Risk* (1999) brings together the best practice for trying to prevent inpatient suicides. The practice guidance is also useful for observation purposes for other risk situations, as in the manic phase. The committee recommended four levels of observation.

Level 1 – General observation: Minimum for all inpatients … at least once a shift a nurse needs to sit down and talk to each patient to assess their mental state and include an assessment of risk.

Level 2 – Intermittent observation: The patient's location needs to be checked every 15–30 minutes. This is agreed by the team and specified in their notes. This is appropriate for clients where there is a potential risk eg. depressed clients who have not openly expressed suicidal ideas, or those who have previously been at risk but who are now assessed as sufficiently recovered. This must be reviewed for each shift.

Level 3 – Within eyesight: For when the patient is likely to make an attempt to harm themselves. The patient needs to be kept in sight at all times. Any tools or possible implements of self-harm must be removed. It may be necessary to search the patient and their belongings. This is reviewed for each shift. A nurse should only undertake this level of observation for two hours at a time.

Level 4 – Within arms length: For those deemed highest risk. On some occasions more than one nurse may be necessary. Issues of dignity, privacy and gender and environmental dangers need to be carefully considered. This should be reviewed every two hours or so, though many would say that it should only be reviewed per shift as any improvements need to be proven overtime. Arguably, this level of observation should be rotated every hour, with each nurse having familiarised themselves with the case background and recent clinical events.

Such observations can be very intrusive with the patient resenting the nurse's presence. However, observations represent a golden opportunity for the nurse to interact with the patient in a supportive way and to build up a positive therapeutic relationship. Being with, and supporting a patient during their lowest moments can send a powerful message that you care.

Case study: Observation

They were watching me while they knitted. They would look up every so often, thinking that I did not know this was their role. When I asked them about observation they denied even looking my way. Thinking back, I can remember I was a little paranoid in the days leading up to my admission. This watching fuelled my paranoia. Fine, had they come over and talked to me every now and again or explained what sort of level of observation I was supposed to be on, I am sure I could have coped with that information. It was this covert observation… No, it was their attempts at covert observation that started to multiply what I call my 'non-standard thinking'. I came to believe they were not really nurses at all. I thought the real nurses had been abducted or kidnapped or something like that. Then the observing did not make any sense as while their backs were turned I walked out and around the building only to be greeted by: 'Where have you been? You know we are supposed to be keeping… Nevermind. Next time you go out, let us know.' The paranoia got worse. Did they really not know I had gone? Why did she stop halfway through that sentence? I decided never to ask about observation again. I sat in a corner in the sun and rocked. I had no idea why I was rocking but somehow it seemed the thing to do…

Most of us can think of a time when we felt uncomfortable because we were being watched or felt we were being watched, such as a teacher standing over your shoulder. This will often induce some anxiety.

Consider

- How could the nurses better carry out the observation described?
- Are you good at recognising when someone is feeling uncomfortable simply because you are looking at them or even just looking in their direction?

How observation can be made supportive

- Where possible, use a nurse who the patient knows or who they have a good relationship with. Otherwise, the nurse should be familiar with the patient's history, social context and significant recent events.

- Observation is an opportunity for one-to-one interaction. The nurse must show the patient positive regard. If a patient seems reluctant to engage and talk, the nurse can initiate conversation and convey a willingness to listen. The whole emphasis here is upon support and interaction rather than custody.

- A well-informed nurse with a grasp of the patient's history will be aware of their preferences eg. music, TV, reading, and can thus use the information to engage the patient.

- A well-informed nurse will also be aware of the patient's individual risk factors.

■ There are ways for the patient and possibly the carer to be involved. Instead of the nurse finding the patient every 30 minutes, ask the patient to report to the nurse. This and other ways of including the patient shift the emphasis and responsibility towards the patient and are no less safe.

■ Clearly the burden of responsibility should not be given to carers or family at times of high risk, only the nursing staff will know the environment well enough and only they will be able to appropriately restrain the patient if necessary. However, this does not mean that carers can never be involved, they might report to the nurse changes in status and behaviour, and they can be included in making evaluations and encouraging the patient to verbalise their feelings. Care must be taken not to alienate the carer from the patient or to damage the trust that has developed. If the patient sees the carer or relative as being in league with their 'captors' then this could happen.

■ If levels of observation need to be carried out for more than seven days, a full multidisciplinary team review should be carried out.

■ The necessity for placing the patient on observation levels is not a reason to stop them carrying on with routine ward life. They should be actively encouraged to join in any activities and groups which are occurring, having due regard to safety eg. environmental hazards.

The most important thing to remember is that the task of observation represents an opportunity to spend time with the patient and build up a therapeutic relationship.

Consideration point

■ Think about each of the levels of observation and generate as many ways as possible for the patient or family members to be involved.

Answers to questions

1. Does the stressor/trigger need to be 'adverse'?

This depends on how we use the words 'stressor', 'trigger' and 'adverse'. Certainly, any change can be a stressor/trigger. In themselves changes are not adverse, it is our interpretation of the change that determines whether we call it adverse or not. As Shakespeare's Hamlet said: '…there is nothing either good or bad, but thinking makes it so…'

2. **Can you think why positive events might be stressful?**

Although it may seem to us that there are positive and negative events, it is always how an event makes an individual feel and/or how the individual thinks about an event that determines whether the event is stressful. Reactions depend on many things including past experiences and the way the future is considered.

We also need to avoid focusing only on events as stressors. A lack of change, either in what the individual feels is an intolerable situation or simply when the feeling is one that something should be changing, can in itself be a stressor, which in turn may be a trigger.

3. **Suggest examples of positive events that might be stressful.**

The birth of a child, a wedding, birthday, party, Christmas, New Year, a holiday, job promotion, a family member returning from time abroad, moving to a new home.

References

SNMAC (1999) *Safe and Supportive Observation of Patients at Risk: Mental health nursing addressing acute concerns* (June 99). London: The Standing Nursing and Midwifery Advisory Committee.

Further reading

Alvarez A (1971) *The Savage God*. Harmondsworth: Penguin. (This is a personal study of suicide.)

Barker P & Cutliffe J (1999) Clinical risk: a need for engagement not observation. *Mental Health Practice* **2** (8) 8–12.

Barker P & Cutliffe J (2000) Creating a hopeline for suicidal people: a new model for acute sector mental health nursing. *Mental Health Care* **3** (31) 190–193.

Brimblecombe N (1998) Supporting clients with suicidal tendencies in the community. *Nursing Times* **11** (94) 10.

Cardell R & Pitula C (1999) Suicidal inpatient's perceptions of therapeutic and non-therapeutic aspects of constant observation. *Psychiatric Services* **50** (8) 1066–1070. (This is an excellent summary supporting the view that observation need not be a purely protective measure, but can be enhanced to be therapeutic.)

Cutliffe J (2003) Assessing risk of suicide and self-harm. In: P Barker *Psychiatric and Mental Health Nursing: The Craft of Caring*. London: Arnold.

Fletcher R (1999) The process of constant observation; Perspectives of staff and suicidal patients. *Journal of Psychiatric and Mental Health Nursing* **6** 9–14.

Hart L (1999) The reliable kettle. *Open Mind* **96** March/April.

Morgan S (2000) *Clinical Risk Management: A clinical tool and practitioner manual*. London: The Sainsbury Centre for Mental Health. (This is an extremely useful examination of risk assessment and risk factors. It gives good case examples and discusses the risk management issues relating to risk factors.)

Morgan S & Wetherill A (2009) Working with risk. In: I Norman & I Ryrie (Eds) *The Art and Science of Mental Health Nursing; A textbook of principles and practice* (2nd edition). Maidenhead: McGraw Hill/Open University Press.

Useful websites

Suicide Awareness Voice of Education at www.save.org

Chapter 8

Medication: the nurse's role

Key points

Nursing staff play a key role in administering and monitoring medication during a patient's admission to hospital. The key aspects of that role are:

- client education
- safe administration and record keeping
- monitoring effectiveness
- monitoring side effects.

It is vital that the nurse approaches medication in a spirit of true collaboration and partnership with the patient. The nurse must never assume that they know best. The importance of the role is underpinned by the Nursing and Midwifery Council: *'The administration of medicines is ... not ... a mechanistic task to be performed in strict compliance with the written prescription of a medical practitioner. It requires thought and the exercise of professional judgement.'* (NMC, 2008)

Before examining the nurse's role regarding medication, it is pertinent to examine attitudes to medication in general.

Consideration points

How true do you feel these statements to be?

- Medication can cure bipolar disorder.
- The main purpose of medication is to help the person with a mood disorder lead a healthier life.
- Medication improves a person's thinking.

A simplistic biological model might suggest that a person's moods are governed by chemicals, but the reality is that many external events and the way a person is thinking will affect mood. Medication must never be seen as the sole basis of effective treatment. It can provide a great degree of stability from which the person can begin to consider other aspects of treatment and thus aid recovery. Medication alone is rarely a complete cure.

Client education

There is much evidence that clearly explaining to the patient what their medication is for and why it is important increases the likelihood of treatment compliance. Hurried or complicated explanations may have been given by others, but it is the role of the nurse to give a clear and thorough explanation. It is important to ensure that the person understands the reasons for taking the medication, what it will do and the most common side effects. The patient cannot enter into a truly collaborative relationship with the team if they are not in possession of the facts. The education given by the nurse should also encompass general health promotion and inform the patient of lifestyle changes that might help them to stay well. While patients will vary in the amount of detail they want to know, nurses need to consider that many patients are very knowledgeable about their disorder and should be wary of sounding patronising. The nurse can also help carers and family to understand the role of medication and keep them involved in the treatment plan.

Question
A mother asks you: 'How long will my son need to take this medication?'
What is the best way to answer this question?

A nurse needs to know something about how long a patient may need to take a medication as it is a common question asked by patients and carers.

Safe administration of medication and record keeping

The consequences of taking the wrong dose of many psychiatric medications can be severe so it is imperative that the nurse follows the accepted procedure.

- The nurse must understand the action, dose range, contraindications and side effects of the medications given.

- Ensure the patient understands the need for the medication and consents to take it.

- Ensure the patient understands the instructions such as taking the medication with a meal or a drink.

- Verify the identity of the patient.

- Observe the patient and decide whether to administer the medication or to withhold it, according to the patient's condition. Side effects or other contraindications might necessitate withholding and these should be recorded in the patient's notes and the medical team should be informed.

- Check for any special requirements such as taking the patient's blood pressure.

- Check the route of administration eg. oral or intramuscular injection.

- Check the name, time and date on the prescription chart.

- Check the medication label and strength and expiry date.

- Calculate the correct dose.

- Observe the patient taking the medication. Do not leave it with them to be taken later.

- Ensure they have a drink to help them to swallow the medication.

- Sign the prescription chart.

- Subsequently monitor for effects and side effects.

It is not the purpose of this book to describe the correct procedure for the administration of intramuscular injections, but this is a common aspect of the nurse's role both in ward situations and the community. Strict adherence to policy and the correct procedure is essential as is the need for a good relationship based on partnership and honesty. The nurse must always check consent and not assume consent merely because the injection has become a regular event. The nurse must stay alert to the possibility of side effects and continue to monitor the effectiveness of the medication. The safety, comfort and consent of the patient remain the nurse's major concern.

Monitoring effectiveness

The nurse has a duty to monitor the effectiveness of the medicines they administer. The nurse can engage the patient in monitoring progress instead of just relying on their own observations. Ask the patient to keep a diary or to regularly record their mood and comments on a chart or rating scale. Meet with the patient frequently to jointly review and assess the impact of the medication alongside other treatments and events that will be influencing their mood.

Monitoring side effects

As psychiatric medications alter mood by making chemical and physical changes it is inevitable that there will be side effects. Sometimes side effects are mild and of no concern or not even noticed by the patient. At the other extreme side effects can be severe. It is imperative that these are checked for and monitored in partnership with the patient.

Remember the nurse's observations are of secondary importance to the patient's as only the patient can truly know the extent and impact of the side effects. Encourage patients to record, rate and chart side effects.

Lack of explanation can cause some patients to lose their faith in the teams looking after them and they may stop taking their medication. Nurses need to explain in plain language what the likely side effects will be and what to look out for.

The pharmacist

The pharmacist in the multidisciplinary team is an essential source of quality information. Where patients find it difficult to take their medication the pharmacist can often identify an easier alternative form. They are also a useful teaching resource for the ward team, keeping them updated on new medications and best practice. The pharmacist can give advice on difficult to manage regimes and may help with simplification.

Issues of compliance

The aim is for all decisions regarding medication to be mutually agreed between the patient and the team. The emphasis must remain on partnership even when full agreement is not possible.

If a patient stops taking medication it should be for a good reason and not because they have been ill-informed regarding the side effects or because they do not feel able to discuss their medication wishes with the team. Usually, ensuring bipolar patients take their medication is one of the simplest tasks a nurse has to perform as most people have the insight to realise that refusing medication is rarely a good route to wellness.

Occasionally, a patient will refuse their medication and it is important to explore the reasons for this with them. It could be because:

- the medication may be too strong and cause drowsiness
- they may feel that the medication is having no effect
- they may simply not understand why they need to take it
- they may be experiencing unpleasant side effects
- in psychosis they may feel they are being poisoned.

A lack of information may be the main reason why some patients do not comply. Recent evidence suggests that eight percent of patients were not told of the purpose of their medication and 24% did not receive a full explanation (Garrett, 2009). With respect to side effects the same survey found 44% were not told about the possibility of side effects. The nurse should ask the patient about their beliefs regarding medicine and the role it can play. Part of the ongoing care package is the regular reviewing of medication.

In psychosis there may be an element of paranoia which renders the patient suspicious of medication, they may, for example, feel that they are being poisoned. In the acute phase of the disorder there can also be a lack of insight with the patient not recognising their problems. The importance of a good therapeutic relationship becomes very apparent in this situation.

The nurse needs to avoid confrontation when trying to help the patient understand the benefits of the medication. The nurse may reiterate that medication is to help to reduce the symptoms and point out the benefits of compliance. This can be supported by highlighting the benefits and improvements the patient experiences compared to when not taking medication. It is important not to get drawn into an argument but to keep using any opportunity to point out the benefits you are sure about. The nurse can explain to the patient how medication might have prevented damaging behaviour in the past or even seemed to prevent manic or depressive episodes. Making the link with noncompliance and relapse is an important motivator.

Medication should not be given covertly unless in exceptional circumstances and only then following a team discussion and the involvement of close relatives, if possible. This decision should then be documented in the patient's notes with due regard paid to the Mental Capacity Act (2005). Occasionally patients can find themselves detained under the Mental Health Act (2007) and having to take medication against their will. The role of the nurse here is to participate in this with due regard and respect for the patient. The nurse should continue to explain the rationale behind the actions and offer ongoing support to the patient, acting as an advocate for their views within the multidisciplinary team. The nursing role extends to arranging for the patient to have representation from outside advocates and ensuring the patient is aware of their rights under the Mental Health Act.

Answer to question

A mother asks you: 'How long will my son need to take this medication?'

If you have no specific information about the prescription it is important not to guess. Opinions can give false hope and if you are later proved wrong the parent (and perhaps other supporters of the patient and the patient themselves) may trust you less.

Equally, not knowing and not giving an appropriate answer may give an impression that you are not keeping up with events or that you are withholding information. It is reasonable to ask the prescriber or a

Bipolar Disorder: A guide for mental health professionals, carers and those who live with it
© Pavilion Publishing (Brighton) Ltd 2012

qualified pharmacist. Even on hearing what the expert says, you will need to think about how to relay this information. Certainly few people want to hear, 'You will need to take this for the rest of your life', as this takes away so much hope and for many patients who have been told this in the past it has turned out not to be the case.

It is always best to tell the truth and say that everyone is different; some people do need to take medication for very long periods of time but others can reduce or come off medication if they have sufficient support and work towards recovery by utilising all the non-pharmacological approaches outlined in this book and elsewhere.

References

Garrett E (2009) *The Key Findings Report for the 2008 Inpatient survey: Acute co-ordination centre for the NHS Patient survey Programme*. Oxford: Picker Institute Europe.

Nursing and Midwifery Council (2008) *Standards for Medicines Management*. London: NMC.

Further reading

Bressington D & Wilbourn M (2009) Medication management. In: P Callaghan, J Playle & L Cooper (Eds) *Mental Health Nursing Skills*. Oxford: Oxford University Press.

Fleet M (2004) Supporting people and their families during psychopharmacotherapy. In: S Kirby, D Hart, D Cross & G Mitchell (Eds) *Mental Health Nursing: Competencies for practice*. Basingstoke: Palgrave Macmillan.

Harris N, Baker J & Gray R (2009) *Medicines Management in Mental Health Care*. Oxford: Wiley Blackwell.

Lehmann P (1998) *Coming off Psychiatric Drugs*. Berlin: Peter Lehmann Publishing.

Moncrieff J (2009) Deconstructing psychiatric drug treatment. In: J Reynolds, R Muston, T Heller, J Leach, M McCormick, J Wallcraft & M Walsh (Eds) *Mental Health Still Matters*. Milton Keynes: Palgrave Macmillan/Open University.

Chapter 9

The ward environment

Key points

■ The environment and atmosphere on a ward play a large part in helping a person to recover from an acute depressive or manic episode.

■ The nurse's role is to make the best possible use of the hospital environment to aid recovery.

As well as providing the treatments involved in an inpatient stay, the nurse has a crucial protective function to buffer the patient from the worst effects of the disorder. Much nursing is geared towards helping patients meet their basic needs, which may have been overridden by their mood. Consideration of rest, activity and diet are important in respect of both manic and depressive episodes and are dealt with in separate chapters. This chapter is about general principles that can be identified in relation to the ward and both manic and depressive episodes.

The patient's experience

We all experience our environment through seeing, hearing, feeling and smelling. How much attention is paid to each sense varies from person to person. It also varies according to our mood. In a manic state, particular senses can become more acute while others become less so. In depression we tend to think of all senses being dulled, yet perhaps a patient sitting or lying still in the middle of the day will experience the world in a very different way to other patients and busy nurses.

How might different patients experience the ward environment?

Seeing

■ As people experience extremes of mood, do they become more or less concerned by tidiness and cleanliness?

■ Does tidiness create a calm atmosphere?

■ Could pictures, posters or even just the way the ward is decorated affect mood?

Hearing

■ How might noise levels, music, TV and ward activities affect mood?

■ How can a very quiet environment be both beneficial and detrimental?

Feeling

■ Do moods influence how people experience and talk about pain?

■ How much impact does feeling warm or cold have on mood, and to what extent are experiences of temperature affected by mood?

Smelling

■ Are patients with high and low moods likely to be more troubled by smells?

■ What smells on the ward might irritate?

Tasting

■ How might taste be affected by extremes of mood?

■ How might mood be affected by tastes?

Sleep

Remember that sleep is a key factor in recovery from mood disorders. How might you help patients complaining about these sources of night-time noise?

■ Patients talking to themselves

■ Patients staying up late to talk

■ Other staff talking

■ Snoring from next bed/ bedroom

■ A new patient being admitted

■ Noise from outside of the ward

■ Arguments

■ A client setting off an alarm

■ Central heating

On listening to ex-patients' memories of being on a ward and relatives' memories of visiting the same ward, you frequently hear very different descriptions. This often highlights how patients may have been feeling eg. annoyed, frustrated or anxious.

The nurse can help by being alert for things on the ward that might cause irritation. When moods are fragile or extreme, reactions to small things can be untypical. It could be something as simple as a flickering light or a squeaky door but it will be in patients' interests to rectify it as soon as possible.

Atmosphere on the ward

The nurse's influence on the physical environment is often limited, whereas the atmosphere on the ward can be managed by the nurses. In inclement weather or for patients currently unable to leave the ward, the nurse needs to be especially aware of the effects of the internal environment – patients' surroundings. Generally, a calm and quiet atmosphere is best for recovery from mood disorders.

Consideration point

Barry is listening to classical music in the lounge when Roy walks in with his portable stereo playing something by the Rolling Stones. Barry storms out muttering: 'He does it on purpose. Every day he does it.'

■ How do you keep the peace in a confined space where residents are forced to live in close proximity?

Considering mania/hypomania

A calm and quiet environment with not too much going on will help to minimise risks of overstimulation. It is important to establish a strong routine with firm realistic behaviour boundaries. Large group activities for example, can be too stimulating.

As the person will be easily distracted the nurse can often use distraction to divert them away from unwanted or harmful behaviour. Having a confident and firm persona can help to set behavioural limits. The nurse's approach should be calm and unhurried to project that aura. There is a need to allow the patient personal space to express themselves without impinging upon others and thus protect them from embarrassment.

Clear and short communication is best as their attention span is likely to be limited. Reassure the person that you will think about requests or comments. Do not be drawn into arguments. It is vital that all members of staff adopt the same approach otherwise a patient can target the weakest link and undermine the efforts of the other staff. The patient needs a consistent response in order to establish any boundaries.

Nurses need to be prepared for patients in high moods repeatedly testing boundaries and to be able to 'soak up' this testing. In mania, patients are likely to display pressure of speech for long periods where the nurse may need to listen with patience while being careful not to reinforce outlandish ideas. Boundaries may need to be reaffirmed during these, mostly, one way conversations. Patients can become frustrated and angry as their unacceptable requests are rebuffed. The nurse needs to avoid argument and may have to withdraw attention in order to discourage unwanted behaviour.

Many patients will find the hospital ward restricting and not to their liking. They may want to leave and the Mental Health Act may need to be used to contain them for their own safety and recovery.

They may have grandiose ideas, lots of energy and know what is best for everybody else. The enforcement of restrictions upon such patients makes it difficult but not impossible to cultivate a therapeutic relationship. It is good to remember the value of spending time building bonds of trust even while restricting a person's liberty. When the patient is manic, short but frequent contacts can be the best way to avoid any animosity developing. Prolonged contact will be difficult to sustain and is likely to be counter-productive.

Consideration point

Think about the saying 'It's not what you do, it's the way that you do it'.

■ What might this mean for the nursing role generally, and how true is this when making short, frequent contacts with manic patients?

Bipolar Disorder: A guide for mental health professionals, carers and those who live with it
© Pavilion Publishing (Brighton) Ltd 2012

Eventually even the most truculent patient will develop a relationship with at least one nurse. You will need to accept that the patient will choose who they are prepared to work with.

The unacceptability of physical aggression may need to be reiterated and the patient helped to control their behaviour. The nurse needs to explain that they are rejecting the behaviour and not the person. The person may need to be nursed in a quiet area until the crisis has passed along with the anger and then debriefed as to why their behaviour was controlled, and reassured that they have not been rejected.

Creating a safe environment for a patient experiencing mania can be challenging as their overconfidence can place them and others at risk. For example, manic or even slightly manic patients can have so much energy and strength that anything that is not firmly screwed down can become a play thing. Close observation is necessary. Here the nurse runs the risk of irritating the patient. Observation need not be intrusive and done well can present the nurse with an opportunity to build up a relationship with the patient.

Another aspect of the protective function of the ward is to protect the patient from ridicule and abuse by the other patients. Awareness of the possibility of ridicule and abuse, educating other patients as to the nature of the disorder and setting firm boundaries along with good observation can be the best preventative measures.

Good observation will also be necessary to prevent the patient experiencing disinhibition during mania. It may be necessary for the patient to be closely monitored in their interactions with the opposite sex. It may be that the person has to be nursed in a single room, if available, to cut them off from the distractions and stimulus other people provide. Nursing away from others on the ward can reduce the risk of manic behaviour disturbing a calm ward atmosphere. Such approaches and ideas are to be shared with relatives of the patient who can help reinforce boundaries when visiting. Relatives may be able to help if you feel valuables and important items or documents the patient has would be better taken home in case the person were to give them away.

Considering depressive episodes

The depressed patient will need to have their self-esteem reiterated on a regular basis. Merely spending time with the person is suggestive of the fact that they are worthy of your time and company. The depressed patient will often reject such company but engaging a little at each contact can gradually build a relationship. A structured routine with firm boundaries and rules will help alongside a 'softly softly' slow approach to recovery. In this way the person can be encouraged to perform routine tasks and praised for doing so.

A slow reintroduction to interacting with others is wise as any rapid or forced attempt is likely to result in the patient withdrawing back into their shell. When depression strips away much of the patient's motivation the nurse may need to carefully lead with things such as conversation, with 'little and often' being a useful guide.

Remember

Pressurising a patient increases the risk of them rejecting you and withdrawing.

Suicide watch is a frequent necessity. As discussed in the chapter on safety, close observation is an opportunity to develop a close bond and need not lead to any antagonism.

Question

The nurse often treads a thin line in trying to protect the rights of individuals while at the same time administering the restrictions of liberty, which the Mental Health Act can bring. The nurse also has to maintain safety and take therapeutic risks.

For a patient who may be excited, irrational and overconfident, what safeguards can a nurse employ to help with these practice dilemmas?

Answer to question

For a patient who may be excited, irrational and overconfident, what safeguards can a nurse employ to help with these practice dilemmas?

The most important thing is to get the basics right and for the nurse to have built a good therapeutic relationship with the patient. The nurse must set firm boundaries so that the patient knows exactly what is and what is not acceptable. It is also important to ensure that everyone within the nursing team is acting in the same way. This consistency of approach is helpful to patients who may be unaware of boundaries and the appropriateness of their actions. The nurse must always give explanations for what they are doing so that when, for example, restricting a person's liberty the nurse must explain why they are doing this while still giving the message that they are acting in the patient's best interests. It can also be helpful to reduce stimulation and distractions for patients and try to engage them in calming pursuits.

Further reading

Aiyegbusi A & Norton K (2009) Modern milieus: psychiatric inpatient treatment in the twenty-first century. In: I Norman & I Ryri (Eds) *The Art and Science of Mental Health Nursing: A textbook of principles and practice*. Maidenhead: McGraw Hill.

Higgins R, Hurst K & Wistow G (1999) *Psychiatric Nursing Revisited: The care provided for acute psychiatric patients*. London: Whurr publishers. (This is a Department of Health commissioned study of the conditions in acute psychiatric wards. The case studies are particularly interesting.)

Sainsbury Centre for Mental Health (1998) *Acute Problems: A survey of the quality of care in acute psychiatric wards*. London: Sainsbury Centre for Mental Health.

Simpson A & Dodds P (2003) Acute inpatient nursing care. In: P Barker (Ed) *Psychiatric and Mental Health Nursing: The craft of caring*. London: Arnold.

Chapter 10

Education

Key points

- To a large degree knowledge is power and the more a person knows about something the less mysterious and the less frightening it becomes.

- It is not just the patient but also the family, other ward patients and staff who need explanations.

As with any disorder, the more a person understands it, the less they come to fear it, and the more its grip on them weakens. Education is a key feature in coming to terms with bipolar disorder, learning to live with it and making recovery possible.

This chapter describes the educational aspects necessary during acute episodes and relating to inpatient care. The patient, family, other patients and staff all need information. Education in the context of community care is described in Chapter 20: Education.

Knowledge empowers

Patients and family may prefer the term 'knowledge' to education. This knowledge is important to allow patients and family to appraise the severity of their disorder and to gauge the role or effectiveness of the treatment.

They need to understand choices and risks that are put before them. They need to know the what, how and why, in order to have a chance of understanding and controlling the disorder.

A lack of patient education can foster 'learned helplessness'. A person may give up hope and come to believe that the disorder is master over them; it is beyond their control and there is nothing they can do but succumb to its effects. For recovery to take place it is important that patients and their families do not fall into the trap of believing 'it just happens'. Hope comes from understanding that episodes do not 'just happen' and that future episodes are often preventable.

Client education

It is important that during acute episodes the person is not bombarded with too much information. During a manic phase a person will need protecting from overstimulation and during a depressive phase they may not wish to be informed. However, as the patient stabilises and is able to take on board information, they need to be helped to become aware of the nature of the disorder and their care.

A large part of the nurse's role is to demystify the disorder by explaining it in simple terms. For many, a basic explanation will suffice. Others may wish to go into more detail (causes and explanations, other treatments, etc.) and the nurse needs to be prepared to facilitate this by answering questions such as 'What is bipolar?', 'Is it genetic?', 'Is it permanent?', 'How will it affect my life?'. These are common questions from those newly diagnosed with the disorder. The nurse also needs to explain the treatment rationale and restrictions on liberty, which may have been applied and may still do so. Reasons for restricting liberty such as the use of the Mental Health Act must be explained at the time, but during an acute phase such explanations may often be meaningless or not fully understood. It is imperative that nurses fully explain such restrictions again to patients when they are more able to understand and discuss it.

Another educational feature of good nursing care is the involvement of the patient in drawing up and reviewing their care plans. Patients will need to know about methods for mood monitoring and the monitoring of the effectiveness compared with side effects of their treatment. The more the patient is directly involved in their own care, the more they will learn and move towards regaining their independence. Later on there will be a need for pre-discharge in-depth explanations regarding medication, how it is intended to work and side effects. Further post-discharge information can be found in Section 3: Bipolar in the community.

The need to make the patient aware of things they have done which might cause them some embarrassment (or even chaos) post-discharge is often overlooked. If they had been overfamiliar with their next door neighbour's spouse, for example, they need to know this, so that they can be prepared for when they next meet!

Other useful information will be how to ease back into work and deciding what to say and how much to say to their employer and colleagues, considering that stigma is usually a reality that has to be faced. It is pertinent to discuss with the patient and their family the concept of stigma and its consequences so that they might be better able to combat it, should they believe it is adversely affecting them (see Chapter 29: Dealing with stigma). Nurses need to explain the wider alternative range of treatment including discussion of talking therapies and support groups.

All of the following aspects of education are covered in Section 3: Bipolar in the community including recognition of moods, self-management of the disorder, avoidance of excessive stress, coping with everyday stress, how to combat depression, how to combat the resurgence of mania and general information on how to stay well.

Family education

Next of kin and loved ones are likely to be the patient's primary carers so it is important that family and friends are kept informed. A good nurse will sit down with the family and patient and go through key post-discharge issues and any common problems to look out for. Explaining the role of medication and the prevention of relapse will be important. All explanations need to be in everyday language and free of jargon. Giving information on where to find further help and support is important. The concepts of relapse and early warning signs need to be well covered with the patient and family, aiming to create a robust crisis management plan in the event of a relapse. Ensure that the family is introduced to the patient's community nurse.

The needs of other patients on the ward

Other patients often want or need explanations as to why the bipolar patient is behaving in certain ways. Explaining that it is part of their disorder and not personal will help other patients become more tolerant and they can be asked to modify their interactions with the bipolar patient. It is important that behaviours driven by extreme moods are not taken as a personal affront that could easily lead to conflict.

The mood on the ward plays a large part in the rate of recovery for those with mood disorders and patients on a ward will always affect one another's moods. This can work to everyone's advantage when patients help to cheer each other up or calm each other down. Many patients will say after a stay on a ward that another patient helped greatly with their recovery. The opposite can happen too. Patients can 'wind each other up' and tensions can arise. Bipolar people's moods are often influenced more strongly than we might expect by the moods of those around them. You may need to explain that the bipolar patient needs space. The bipolar patient also needs to be made aware of how their behaviour is affecting others.

Staff

Occasionally there may be a need to broaden the horizons of other staff members who might take a purely medical approach to bipolar disorder. Such an approach will deny patients the opportunity to explore different perceptions of the disorder and different forms of treatment and support.

Further reading

Dolman C (2009) How well do GPs detect bipolar? *Pendulum* **25** (1). (This article outlines the fact that many GPs have little training regarding bipolar and the nurse must not assume the patient or carer will get the information they need from their GP.)

Stevenson C (2003) Family support. In: P Barker (Ed) *Psychiatric and Mental Health Nursing: The craft of caring*. London: Arnold.

Chapter 11

Diet

Key points

- Diet can be radically affected by the manic and depressive phases of bipolar disorder.
- It is especially important to pay attention to adequate:
  - hydration
  - nutrition
  - elimination.

In both depression and mania maintaining an adequate fluid and food intake can be difficult. It is one of the most important safety aspects of care because it can cause a person to become dehydrated and malnourished.

A client's recollection

'When I was low I couldn't be bothered, it was as if I didn't deserve it, and when I was high it wasn't important; I felt I didn't need food.'

Consideration points

- What ways might a depressive episode impact a healthy diet?
- How might a manic phase lead to problems with nutrition?

Water

Dehydration is often the greatest risk and disturbed moods can affect a person's ability to hydrate adequately. In depression it could be as simple as not being bothered to get up and get a drink. Even making a cup of tea can be a huge effort for a depressed person.

Dehydration can occur very quickly in the manic phase when activity levels are high. The person in mania may be involved in obvious physical exercise such as walking long distances, running or gym work. They may appear not to be doing any formal exercise at all but could simply be very active nearly 24 hours a day and not feeling the need to rest. The high mood can override the signals that normally tell us it is time to stop, rest and drink. All this activity will be dehydrating.

Undernourishment

Depressive phases can cause a person to feel unworthy of food, which they feel would be better used if given to others who they feel are more deserving. People with untreated depression have died through a lack of nourishment. Similarly they may just be too depressed to have the energy to eat or their appetite may have altogether disappeared.

Manic phases lead to high energy levels, which often give rise to greatly increased activity and thus the need for increased nutritional intake. However, the need for sustenance is often overlooked as the individual has many other more urgent things to attend to or may simply not realise the need. They can be too busy to eat. In severe cases overactivity combined with a lack of nourishment can lead to exhaustion and collapse.

Excess in-take of calories

Manic episodes can also lead to overindulgence in food and drink. Weight gain can be an obvious concern but it may become especially dangerous if the person becomes too focused on alcohol. Depressive episodes can also lead to overeating rather than the more typical decrease in appetite.

Elimination

Extremes of mood almost always have an effect on elimination as the digestive system responds to changes in mood. For many, anxiety leads to frequent visits to the toilet with a persistent urge to urinate even though the bladder may not be full. Diarrhoea-like symptoms may also occur. Constipation may occur in both the depressed or manic phases of the disorder. Whether due to poor diet or changes to routine, there is a need to help the patient avoid this.

Care task 1: Ensure adequate hydration

Encourage a good fluid intake by ensuring that the patient has access to water and by frequently offering a wide range of drinks. Ask relatives what the patient's favourite drinks are and ensure these are available. Both tap water and bottled water need to be available in as many areas as possible. Bottled water can be more appealing and it can be easily carried around. You can leave a bottle in the person's room or by their favourite chair. High calorie, nutrient-rich drinks can also be offered to patients who are not eating well. Fruit juices can be promoted for anyone with constipation. (Always be aware of the possibility of increased anxiety from drinks with a high caffeine content.)

Care must be taken when offering 'hot' drinks as a person with mania or depression may not appreciate the temperature of the drink. In mania they may be in such a hurry that they drink it too quickly and are scalded.

Care task 2: Ensure adequate nutrition

Blood test results can help indicate the need for vitamin/mineral supplements.

Observe and if possible record the patient's weight and fluid intake. It will usually be possible to persuade a patient to stand on some scales for a brief moment, even if it is only now and again. This will give you a good idea of progress or urgency.

Patients may prefer snacks in favour of sitting down for a meal. In depression the patient may not have the energy or motivation to eat a full meal. In mania it may seem as if there is not time to sit still for a whole meal. Provide foods that are easy to eat or foods which can be eaten 'on the run' such as sandwiches, nutritious snack bars and fruit. It is best if you can hand the snack to the patient as they may eat it there and then. If they do, you will have an idea of how many snacks they are eating. If the patient will not eat anything they are given, another option is to leave snacks 'lying around' or in their room so that they can be picked up and eaten at any time.

Fortified drinks and supplements such as malted milk may be offered so that the person gains essential nutrients.

If you are in a hospital environment, find out about the patient's normal eating routines and their favourite foods. Ask relatives for their insights and if it is not possible for the hospital to provide such foods, encourage the relatives to bring in favourite foods. The patient may have a favourite snack bar or drink and while they may not sit down for a typical hospital dinner they may well devour a takeaway pizza or curry. (See the consideration point below.) Ask family and friends to encourage eating by sharing food together as part of their visiting routine.

In acute phases, allow the patient to sit on their own for meals if they want and to eat when they want, rather than trying to force them to adhere to institutional routines. In the depressive phase the patient may feel unworthy of sitting with others. You will need to accept this while not forgetting that eating with others is usually a part of recovery and that later on you will need to encourage this. Eating with others for the first time in a while can be a daunting experience but is a big step towards reintegrating with others.

Question
How might a nurse encourage a depressed client to eat and drink?

Be aware of any special dietary needs such as vegetarianism and religious or cultural diets.

Extreme cases

Occasionally a patient will not eat at all and high calorie, fortified drink supplements may be their only form of nutrition. In severe depression it may be necessary for the nurse to feed the patient with their consent. It may be that family members could help in this situation. In extreme cases mental health law has to be invoked as a life-saving measure and a nasogastric tube is occasionally needed to maintain life.

Case study: Jim

Jim is 76 and has been married for 53 years to Mary. Jim's depression has necessitated an inpatient stay. The antidepressants he has been taking are having no effect. Jim has been refusing to eat and has become extremely frail as a result. His physical state is very poor and the Mental Health Act is invoked to allow the team to give him a course of ECT. Mary is in agreement as it has worked once before when he did not respond to antidepressants. Before the ECT has any effect however, the team decide to pass a nasogastric tube to allow Jim to be fed against his will. He protests strongly, but the tube is passed and Jim is too scared to pull it out. Nurses now feed high calorie drinks through the tube to save Jim deteriorating physically any further. Often however, he protests briefly but violently, despite his depression, trying to push the nurses away and stop them feeding him. The nurses resist and persist, explaining what they are doing and why.

Consider

■ What are the ethical considerations in this scenario?

Care task 3: Ensure adequate elimination

It is important to record the person's toilet habits to guard against the possibility of constipation. The goal is to try and avoid the need for the use of laxatives, so take this into account by providing a diet which encourages bowel movements. Provide fruit juices and other high fibre foods. Apart from the patient not having the time or awareness in the manic phase to bother with elimination, the depressive phase can also bring with it the possibility of constipation. The lack of energy, exercise and poor diet all make the patient prone to constipation and this can be further complicated by the side effects of many antidepressant and antipsychotic medications. As well as a high fibre diet and the use of natural laxatives, the nurse should encourage gentle exercise, such as walking, to stimulate the bowel.

Care task 4: Ensuring the person does not overeat or drink alcohol

If a patient is rapidly gaining weight you may need to limit their access to food by giving smaller portions and monitoring them closely at meal times. Encourage the patient by letting them know that they are doing well and use their distractibility to move them onto a focus other than food. It may be that clear limits have to be set, and again, the positive encouragement of a carer who has a good therapeutic relationship with the patient may pay huge dividends.

It can also be useful to seek the advice of a dietician who can devise a diet plan which will limit weight gain, and educate relatives and other visitors so that they do not unwittingly undermine the plan.

A range of aerobic exercises can be encouraged to combat weight gain. The depressed person may not want to exercise so plenty of encouragement will be important. Perversely, one usually looks to limit the activity of someone in the manic phase but in this case one should encourage activity. Such opportunities for shared activity can help the nurse and patient develop the therapeutic relationship to a more effective level.

Bipolar Disorder: A guide for mental health professionals, carers and those who live with it
© Pavilion Publishing (Brighton) Ltd 2012

Alcohol

Given the likelihood of the patient being on antidepressants and/or mood stabilisers it is important that alcohol is avoided completely. It may increase manic behaviour, cause a switch to depression or deepen existing depression by inducing the morose contemplation. Ensure that you make all relatives and visitors aware of the dangers of alcohol. Also, bear in mind statistics which show that alcohol is a large factor in suicide attempts.

Consideration points

- During manic phases it is likely that the nurse will be encouraging the person to eat. It is also likely that the patient has been prescribed an antipsychotic medication. What are the likely effects of this medication on their nutrition?
- How realistic is it to advise that alcohol should be avoided completely?
- What would it do to your mood if you were told that you had to give up alcohol or another favourite drink or food, such as chocolate?
- Sometimes carers may be overcautious and exaggerate the need for strict adherence to advice. What is the likely outcome of insisting patients follow strict guidelines and enforcing difficult lifestyle changes?

Answer to question

How might a nurse encourage a depressed patient to eat and drink?

- *Ensure the nurse has a good relationship with the patient and spend time with them even though they may not be very responsive. Show you care!*
- *Be sure the patient knows food and drink are available.*
- *Be sure the patient knows how to access it and that they are allowed to access it.*
- *If the patient is missing at a drink or meal time, find them. It may be necessary to wake a patient who may be sleeping, or to ensure that they are provided with food when they wake up.*
- *Find out what their favourite foods are and ask relatives to bring in some of these if they are not readily available.*

- Talk about the drink and food in a natural way. Being overly positive such as saying, 'Rice pudding! My favourite!' is likely to be perceived as false by the patient if it is not true. Honesty is essential.

- Don't be overly insistent as this will likely have the opposite effect to what you want.

- Talk about the nutritional content of the drink and foods. Perhaps more importantly listen to patients' views on nutrition. Bipolar patients can be very 'clued up' on such things when they have been looking to nutrition as part of their well-being plan.

- Use food supplements and fortifying drinks if necessary.

- Be aware of the patient's needs.

- Listen carefully and ask clarifying questions when they tell you about suspected food intolerances and digestive problems.

Further reading

Frisch N & Frisch L (2011) *Psychiatric Mental Health Nursing (4th edition)*. New York: Delmare/Cengage. (See the nursing care plans outlined in Chapter 14 and 15.)

Nash M (2010) Assessing nutrition, diet and physical activity. In: M Nash (Ed) *Physical Health and Well-Being in Mental Health Nursing*. Maidenhead: McGraw Hill/Open University Press.

Schultz J & Videbeck S (2005) Care plan 22: major depressive disorder. In: *Lippincott's Manual of Psychiatric Nursing Care Plans*. Philadelphia: Lippincott, Williams and Wilkins.

Schultz J & Videbeck S (2005) Care plan 23: bipolar disorder manic episode. In: *Lippincott's Manual of Psychiatric Nursing Care Plans*. Philadelphia: Lippincott, Williams and Wilkins.

See further reading in Chapter 27: Food and mood.

Chapter 12

Supporting the family

Key points

■ The patient does not exist in isolation from the rest of the world.

■ Supporting family and close carers is important for recovery.

Family members of a person with bipolar disorder can be faced with a great deal of uncertainty, worry and even bewilderment. Changing moods, extravagant behaviour, sudden irritability or extreme generosity might be some of the things that are hard to understand. Financial flippancy and inappropriate sexual overtures may add to the worrying picture and be a major source of concern.

During an acute episode the family may ask many questions about the disorder to further their understanding and will be doing lots of care tasks to support the person. Therefore education is one of the most important ways of supporting the family. The nurse can demystify the disorder by giving jargon-free explanations. Explanations may include:

■ what bipolar is

■ causes

■ medication

■ behaviour problems

■ what the future may hold.

The nurse needs to listen to the family and help them to deal with their feelings of fear and anxiety.

Families may be fearful because they have read or been told about the genetic element of bipolar disorder and will be worried about the likelihood of other family members developing the disorder. We know that people with mood disorder will often have relatives who experience mood disorder, making it important not to assume that they are the only person in the family who experiences mood swings. Equally, there may be no history at all of mania/bipolar in the family. It is therefore essential to avoid making assumptions. You may want to ask questions about the family's experiences. Listening to family members will make your role easier, as it will become clearer what they do not know.

The nurse's clear explanations and support will also allow the family to prepare for the future by outlining the difficulties which might lie ahead. Building this relationship with the family encourages family members to be proactive rather than just bystanders in the treatment of their loved one. It will be comforting for relatives to know what the disorder is, what treatment there is and how they can help. This may involve partners, parents, children and others. The nurse needs to seek the consent of the individual as to whom they wish to be informed and involved.

Case study: Meena

Meena's parents, Amin and Golma, were worried about her for years and were relieved when she agreed to spend a few days on an assessment ward where she received a diagnosis of bipolar. Two weeks later Meena was still on the ward. Staff could only say that Meena did not want to see any visitors at all, not even her parents. Amin used the internet to find a bipolar self-help group and went with Golma to the group's monthly meeting where they discovered that other relatives said they were often left 'out of the loop' and given very little information.

Consider

■ What is the minimum information that needs to be given to relatives?

The nurse can also support the family with how best to support their bipolar member. This can involve looking at the way the family communicates, their attitude to the disorder and encouraging their involvement in the treatment programme. This is covered in Section 3: Bipolar in the community. The nurse should also give the family details of any local and national support groups that they can access.

Further reading

Aiken C (2010) *Family Experiences of Bipolar Disorder: The ups, the downs and the bits in between*. London: Jessica Kingsley Publishers.

Johnston J (2005) *To Walk on Eggshells*. Helensburgh: The Cairn Publishers.

Johnstone M (2010) *Living with a Black Dog*. London: Constable and Robinson Publishers.

MDF The BiPolar Organisation (2008) *Manic Depression Bipolar Disorder Information for Family and Friends*. Available from www.mdf.org.uk

MDF The BiPolar Organisation (2008) *Bipolar Disorder in Children and Young People*. Available from www.mdf.org.uk

Stevenson C (2003) Family support. In: P Barker (Ed) *Psychiatric and Mental Health Nursing: The craft of caring*. London: Arnold.

Pendulum (2006) Winter **22** (4) (This volume contains six interesting articles on families and bipolar disorder)

Useful websites

Bipolar Significant Others at www.bpso.org
Canadian bipolar significant others website with some useful information

Carers UK at www.carersuk.org
Information and advice generally about caring

MDF: the Bipolar Organisation at www.mdf.org.uk

Chapter 13

Personal care

Key points

- In both depressive and manic states people are less able to meet their own self-care needs.

- The depressed person will have no motivation while the manic person may have outlandish ideas about what is acceptable, or may have no time to bother with what seems to them to be the trivia of personal hygiene.

Mania

In a manic state a person can dress in a bizarre or overtly sexual fashion and thus attract unwanted and potentially damaging attention. Dress can be flamboyant and accompanied with excessive make-up or jewellery. It is important that the nurse does not give reinforcing attention to the bizarre appearance and gives positive feedback when a more subdued mode of dress is worn. Engaging with a patient in the process of dressing or applying make-up, and providing a moderating influence by suggesting and praising more appropriate clothing choices is helpful. Try and use the influence of family and friends who may be able to bring in less garish but favourite clothes for the patient to choose. This is important in preserving the patient's dignity and protecting the patient from ridicule and even abuse. Similarly the patient may have no time or inclination to attend to their personal hygiene and again the nurse can use gentle encouragement and praise to ensure adequate personal care is taken to prevent either physical complications or the patient becoming ostracised.

> ## A patient's recollection
>
> In August we had a man brought in drunk and without a shirt. I lent him a T-shirt and he wore it day and night for the next four weeks. When I was discharged he insisted on taking it off and giving it back to me. It wasn't quite as dirty and smelly as I had expected as the nurses had persuaded him once a week to take it off and wash it. I saw him some weeks later with a different shirt. It turned out that a relative had brought him one much earlier but it had never crossed his mind to change.

Depression

A person can be too depressed to be concerned with their appearance or personal care needs. Their personal hygiene may deteriorate to such an extent that they put themselves at risk of developing physical complications.

Excessive body odour and unclean appearance may repulse other patients and even the person's best friends. Establishing a routine which is encouraged by a nurse can be effective as it eliminates the need for decision-making for the depressed patient. The nurse may need to encourage the patient to get up and physically help them with their personal hygiene, all the time giving praise for small efforts. Once the routine is established the nurse can begin to encourage the patient to make small improvements. It is important to enforce this routine as it will set limits to the time spent lying in bed ruminating and it also provides an interaction point when the nurse can provide positive encouragement and praise. Gradually the nurse can withdraw and encourage more self-care.

Organising time for a warm bath with scents and trying to make a special occasion out of it can help, as can engaging the help of family and friends to bring in favourite soaps or deodorants and other personal care products.

All interventions in relation to appearance and hygiene revolve around the nurse trying to persuade the patient to do something they do not feel like doing. Therefore, the better the therapeutic relationship with the patient the better your success with this task is likely to be. Once gains are made the key to building on them is not to rush the patient into submission but to proceed gradually.

Case study: Indifference to attention

The first day after Adrian's admission gave the student nurse occasion to reflect on the severity of depression. Adrian, being newly admitted, was not known to any of the ward team and had not been there long enough to get to know any of the nursing staff. He was too depressed to be bothered about anything and felt unworthy of the attention of the student who was trying to encourage him to change his clothes. Adrian was dishevelled and in need of a change of clothes and bath. The other patients on the ward were becoming a little offensive towards him because of the smell. Despite their best encouragement the nurses could not persuade Adrian to change and wash; he just lay on his bed almost in a stupor, saying nothing and giving no eye contact. Gently two nurses persuaded Adrian to let them help him to bathe, but it took them the best part of the day, and throughout the procedure Adrian uttered not a word but just let the nurses do what they needed to do.

Further reading

Frisch N & Frisch L (2011) *Psychiatric Mental Health Nursing (4th edition)*. New York. Delmare/Cengage. (See the nursing care plans outlined in Chapters 14 and 15.)

Johnstone M (2009) *Living with a Black Dog*. London: Constable and Robinson Publishers.

Schultz J & Videbeck S (2005) Care plan 22: Major depressive disorder. In: *Lippincott's Manual of Psychiatric Nursing Care Plans*. Philadelphia: Lippincott, Williams and Wilkins.

Schultz J & Videbeck S (2005) Care plan 23: Bipolar disorder – manic episode. In: *Lippincott's Manual of Psychiatric Nursing Care Plans*. Philadelphia: Lippincott, Williams and Wilkins.

Chapter 14

Activity, rest and sleep

Key points

- Activity levels and patterns of activity are disrupted in both manic and depressive states.

- In depression a person needs to be coaxed gently back into activity whereas in mania a person's activity levels may need to be restricted and monitored for safety.

Mania

Manic patients can feel very powerful and are likely to overestimate their abilities. They can be impulsive and react quickly to stimuli. Their high energy levels may make them very demanding in comparison to those around them.

In mania the client needs a safe and structured environment. As a rule the nursing aim is to create a quiet, calm and relaxed atmosphere that is free from loud noises, distraction and stimulation. This can be a hard task on a busy acute admission ward! The attention and presence of others also serves to attract the manic patient whose 'entertaining antics' might easily be encouraged by an attentive audience. It is usually best to initially ensure that the client does not have too many social contacts.

Poor judgement puts manic patients at risk physically, socially, financially and sexually. Nurses need to be on hand to intervene if the patient looks like they might do something they later regret. This protective function is important until the patient has regained the ability to make sound judgements. Nurses also need to monitor and be aware of the reactions of other patients on the ward who may become irritated by the manic patient's pestering and insistence. It may be necessary to explain to the manic patient how their behaviour is impacting upon others. This is likely to need careful thought and skill on the part of the nurse with the patient having a short attention span and so much going on in their overactive mind.

Likewise, other patients need to be informed that the person's behaviour is part of their disorder and of the importance of tolerance. Nurses will occasionally have to redirect the manic patient away from an activity or situation if they are acting inappropriately or becoming overexcited. As the patient is once again nursed in a calmer environment feelings can be discussed and therapeutic relationships built upon. As the patient gradually recovers from the manic phase, the impact of their behaviour can be discussed more fully.

Sexually disinhibited behaviour may range from overfamiliarity and flirting, to stripping off in public areas, and unprotected sex with strangers. Nurses need to ensure that patients do not dress or act too provocatively in order to protect them from embarrassment and exploitation. The nurse needs to handle these situations with delicacy by gently suggesting an alternative activity and distracting and steering the patient away from danger. A capable nurse will be able to use the manic patient's short attention span and distractibility to steer them towards a safer activity. Nurses are often criticised for restricting freedom as they try to balance the patient's human rights and protect them from their disorder. Remember that it can be difficult to distinguish between disordered behaviour and 'normal' behaviour, especially if the patient's pre-morbid personality is not known.

Sometimes the patient will need time out from others to allow them to calm down and forget the ideas and activities they were getting overexcited about. Good observation will tell the nurse when the patient is becoming too excited and when the other patients are nearing the end of their tethers and becoming irritable. A nurse who has taken time to build the beginnings of a therapeutic relationship is likely to be successful in removing the patient from awkward situations.

It can often be a useful diversionary tactic to engage patients with a fairly strenuous activity to change the focus of their attention and use up their excess energy, but be wary of doing this with a patient who is on the go all the time because there is a danger that they become exhausted. Although a rare occurrence, people in mania have died of exhaustion. Having some quiet, unenergetic time in which to recuperate is important. Often manic patients will be restless and it is good to try to get them to help with small tasks which the nurse has to do, such as getting a room ready for a meeting or group, setting up art materials or helping with toast or tea making. Other useful diversions are simply taking a walk or if you are lucky enough to have a garden, tidying it up. Competitive activities may need to be avoided as these can raise levels of excitability and irritability.

Case study: A recollection – How I calmed down

Every evening Jake and I competed. One night it was press-ups; I did 86 and he just kept on going. Another evening we went out in the car park and raced from one end to the other again and again with other patients timing us and egging us on. The nurses looked on in horror. They wanted us to 'CALM DOWN!'. Their efforts to stop us were futile as the more they tried to stop us, the more competitive we became. I had never been so fit in my life and I had never had so much energy.

A new nurse arrived on the ward on the evening we had planned our 24-hour table tennis match. She watched us for a while then asked if she could join in. After a few minutes she said that what she really needed was some help washing the dining room tables. Jake and I did the best table washing ever. We did the tops, legs and even got the chewing gum off from under the edges. We forgot about the table tennis and moved onto the chairs.

It was like this from then on. We stopped competing and worked as a team on getting the ward shipshape. The ward became a better, calmer place for everyone and for me this channelling of energy into something both mundane and practical helped ground me, and some of my crazy ideas dissolved away. I realised my future was not to be a hospital cleaner and it was time to focus on wellness and discharge.

At times the nurse must also soak up some of the manic patient's activity and conversation by listening respectfully and without getting drawn into unusual views. Tactful responses which do not encourage unrealistic thoughts are useful. These may be considered to be 'tactful disagreements' where the nurse needs to bear in mind the manic patient's irritability and recognise that it is a fine line between 'grounding' and 'irritating'! In general the nurse needs to be relaxed and calm and skilled at mediation, avoiding being drawn into an argument.

> ### Reflection exercise: Distracting a manic patient
>
> Write a list of ways you could quietly distract a manic patient.

Depression

In depression the person is in need of a structured routine whereby they are gradually reintroduced to both social and solitary activities. The ward can provide low key social interactions such as eating with others and sitting with others to watch television. The nurse can gradually build on the degree of interaction required of the depressed patient. There is a risk in the nurse being too keen to see progress and causing setbacks by encouraging too much too soon.

Solitary participation in everyday activities of living are important stepping stones towards more social interaction and these can be encouraged by the nurse in a one-to-one relationship, with the nurse gradually withdrawing overtime. Merely spending time with the depressed patient is a first step towards becoming active again. Being with the patient demonstrates your interest and concern for them. It is important to show them that you consider them to be worthwhile. If the patient is willing to talk, the nurse needs to use active listening skills to demonstrate their regard for the person (see Chapter 15 on Supportive counselling).

The depressed patient may have a tendency to sleep for a lot of the day because of depression. Thoughts and feelings of 'it's not worth it', 'there is only misery and gloom' and, 'I am not worthy', can strip away all motivation. The depressed person may not want to do anything. These feelings are likely to change according to the time of day. When a daily pattern is recognised there is the possibility of acting accordingly, encouraging activity and self-care when the patient is most receptive to encouragement.

In depression, as in mania, the patient's attention span is likely to be short. Here, and in the early stages of recovery, the patient should be offered simple but meaningful (not patronising) activities. Short successful bouts of activity are useful in providing the nurse with the opportunity to give praise for success and thus boosting the patient's self-esteem. The patient can draw satisfaction from having completed the activity and this will be underscored with the nurse's positive comments.

Going for a walk or helping on the ward are helpful options. A good nurse will get to know much of their patient's background and can tap into their personal interests and hobbies in order to try and rekindle some spark and engage them in an activity that has special meaning. It is useful to draw up a weekly timetable of activity for the patient as a prompt to remain active. Encouraging the patient to chart their feelings about these activities allows monitoring, engages the patient in their own therapy and creates useful talking points. The patient can alter the programme according to its success or failures.

The nurse may organise events on the ward for fun. The therapeutic value of humour is well documented, yet greatly underestimated (Smith *et al*, 2010). If the nurse encourages the patient they can draw out the humour of the individual, forcing them to laugh despite themselves and their depression. Shared humour is also a good way of helping to build up a therapeutic relationship. It is good to have activities that are not strictly related to the person's problems or diagnosis but are just normal daily activities.

Consideration points

- In what way can the patient/patient relationship be beneficial and therapeutic?
- Think about the proverb: 'All work and no play makes Jack a dull boy!' What fun activities can you think of which you might do on a ward to engage the patients?

Rest and sleep

While the patient with depression will be encouraged to sleep less the patient experiencing a manic state can often reach a state of physical exhaustion and will need to be encouraged to rest and sleep as much as possible. In general the manic patient needs to be nursed in a quiet environment with little stimuli and ideally provided with their own room rather than sharing.

No matter how overactive a patient is it can be useful to encourage them to join in less frantic, supervised physical activities which might help to tire them for sleep. Manic patients will find it hard to sleep because of their racing brain and pressing thoughts urging them on to do things. They may not want to sleep or will wake up after only a short nap, feeling ready to go again.

Extra medication to induce sleep is often necessary. This needs to be seen as the last resort as the risk of addiction can be high. Start by focusing on methods used by millions of people at home when they need to improve their sleep. Examples include avoiding caffeine and other stimulants, not eating a big meal before bed, avoiding excitement near bedtime and the use of subdued lighting in the patient's room.

Despite the best efforts, some manic patients still will not be sleeping enough during the night. For these people having a nap during the day can make all the difference between mania escalating or lessening. It is important to be aware of patients who have not been sleeping and ensure they have opportunities to nap – even five minutes can make a big difference. As the mania gradually wears off, a more regular sleep pattern can be established. Nurses will need to be aware of the other patients at night and ensure that they are not disturbed by the nocturnal activities of the manic patient.

References

Smith M, Kemp G & Segal J (2010) *Laughter is the Best Medicine: The health benefits of humour and laughter* [online]. Available at http://www.helpguide.org/life/humor_laughter_health.htm (accessed September 2011).

Further reading

MDF The Bipolar Organisation (2010) Spring. *Pendulum* **26** (1). (This issue has four useful articles on walking and mental health.)

Frisch N & Frisch L (2011) *Psychiatric Mental Health Nursing (4th edition)*. New York: Delmare/Cengage. (See the nursing care plans outlined in Chapter 14 – The client experiencing depression and Chapter 15 – The client experiencing mania.)

Nash M (2010) Assessing nutrition, diet and physical activity. In: M Nash (Ed) *Physical Health and Well-Being in Mental Health Nursing*. Maidenhead: McGraw Hill/Open University Press.

Schultz J & Videbeck S (2005) Care plan 22: Major depressive disorder. In: *Lippincott's Manual of Psychiatric Nursing Care Plans*. Philadelphia: Lippincott, Williams and Wilkins.

Schultz J & Videbeck S (2005) Care plan 23: Bipolar disorder – manic episode. In: *Lippincott's Manual of Psychiatric Nursing Care Plans*. Philadelphia: Lippincott, Williams and Wilkins.

Smith M, Kemp G & Sega J (2010) *The Health Benefits of Humor and Laughter*. Available at: www.helpguide.org/life/humor_laughter_health.htm

Chapter 15

Supportive counselling

Key points

- Communication skills like active listening are important aspects of building therapeutic relationships and thus being able to offer support to patients.

- Demonstrating concern for the patient and merely 'being there' for them are important.

During acute phases the patient, whether depressed or manic, needs a supportive presence and someone to listen to them. When the acute phase has passed and moods are more stable it is possible to explore psychological treatments such as cognitive behavioural therapy.

The nurse builds a therapeutic relationship with the patient as they are there in times of both distress and elation. As the acute phase subsides the nurse will be helping the patient understand the disorder and the client will need someone they can talk freely with and whom they trust with the many questions they have. In depression nurses need to be comfortable with sitting in silence with a patient. This demonstrates that the nurse is available for the patient and that the patient knows they are worthy of the nurse's attention. When the patient is ready to talk the nurse needs to demonstrate good active listening skills.

Active listening

This is a combination of verbal and non-verbal communication techniques which help you to focus more closely upon what is being said and thus gain a greater understanding of its meaning. It also demonstrates to the patient your close attention to them and willingness to understand.

Verbal active listening skills

- **Reflection.** This is putting back to the person what they have just said in order to clarify meaning and understanding. It helps the patient know you have understood them and gives them the chance to correct you if you have not. Remember, it is important to reflect your understanding of the feelings underpinning what the patient has said as well as the content of what they have said.

- **Paraphrasing.** A useful form of reflection where you put back to the patient what you have heard in your own words.

- **Silences.** These need to be tolerated as they give both you and your client time to reflect and think about what has been said. Many of us are uncomfortable with silences and all too often bring them to a premature close. Silences are an important part of communication.

- **Open questions.** These require the person to open up and explore their situation with more than a 'yes' or 'no' answer. Open questions can include 'How did you cope with that?' and 'What else do you think could have been done?'

- **Clarifying questions.** These are to allow you to check that you are right in your assumptions about what the patient has said. 'What do you mean by that?' 'You said you did… was that because…?' Here the tone of the questioning is crucial. Be sure to ask in a non-threatening uncritical manner.

- **Probing questions.** 'Can you tell me a bit more about…?' These questions help you to find out more detail.

- **Summarising.** No one has total recall and every now and again it is important to stop and summarise what you have heard so far. This will tell the patient how well you have been listening and give them the opportunity to clarify if you have misunderstood.

Non-verbal active listening skills

- **Posture.** See Gerard Egan's SOLER below for demonstrating attentiveness.

- **Body language.** Reading the patient's body language tends to underpin your thoughts as to how they are really feeling. It is hard to disguise your true feelings non-verbally.

- **Facial expression.** Ideally, show you are relaxed and smile while demonstrating concern, worry, surprise etc. when appropriate. Be sure to read the patient's facial expressions too. Facial expression can be said to provide a window into the emotional state of the speaker. Such awareness allows you to feed this back, 'you look quite angry about that' and get some clarification.

- **Tone of voice.** This usually gives an insight into the speaker's feelings. Your tone needs to demonstrate concern and sincerity.

- **Gesture.** Nodding is an important gesture. It is so natural that sometimes we are unaware we are nodding. If you notice yourself nodding then keep doing it, but do not overdo the nodding! Hand and arm gestures can help to give emphasis to important points.

- **Proximity.** Respect the patient's personal space but do not create a barrier out of the distance you are apart.

- **Utterances.** These are the 'mmm' and 'uh uh' type utterances we tend to make often alongside nodding our heads. They signal to the patient that we are interested and listening. If you catch yourself doing this a lot it is likely to be a good thing, so do not stop. Equally deliberately doing a lot more of this could be off putting for the patient.

Carl Rogers

Carl Rogers' core conditions for counselling, which are empathic understanding, unconditional positive regard and congruence, underpin active listening skills (Rogers, 1957). It was important for Rogers that not only was the counsellor able to achieve these conditions but how they were perceived by the patient.

Empathy

It is important to identify with your patient's world and see their life as closely as you can from their point of view. In this way can you achieve the fullest understanding of your patient's communication, or your patient's inner world and what life is really like for them, being aware of both their thoughts and feelings.

Unconditional positive regard

This is having positive feelings for the patient, feeling warmth towards them and being non-judgemental. It is also seen as accepting their uniqueness and difference. You can display and feel this without necessarily agreeing with the patient's behaviour. In this way it is possible to offer counselling to someone who has abused another person; you accept the person but reject the behaviour. This is important as often in counselling situations the counsellor will challenge the patient's behaviour.

Congruence

Sometimes referred to as genuineness, congruence means being self-aware, being yourself and above all being honest with the patient. There will be consistency between what you say and your non-verbal behaviour.

The Skilled Helper

In *The Skilled Helper* Gerard Egan (2002) describes a SOLER framework of skills for 'tuning in' to patients.

Sit facing the patient squarely and do not turn your body away from them. This demonstrates that you are ready and focused on them. Do not sit directly facing them as this will often be intimidating if you are close together. Most people will be comfortable with the chairs at a slight angle to each other.

Open your posture. Folded arms and crossed legs can be signs of disinterest whereas a more open posture demonstrates availability. If you are uncomfortable with uncrossed legs ensure that you are confident that your posture still demonstrates your attention and openness to the patient.

Leaning forwards also suggests to the patient that you are interested and alert to what they are saying and are focused on them.

Eye contact should be maintained. Lack of eye contact is a sign of distrust in western society and too much eye contact can be interpreted as aggressive, so look away occasionally but maintain the contact. This again demonstrates that you are interested and listening.

Relax. This may be the most important factor. Try to be yourself. There is a danger that you will concentrate too much on SOLER and other counselling 'guidelines' that you become an automaton and not a real person. Being comfortable with the way you are sitting means you will be less likely to fidget and send out other signals that you are not totally attentive. Your being relaxed will also help to put the patient at ease.

References

Egan G (2002) *The Skilled Helper: A problem-management and opportunity-development approach to helping* (7th edition). St Paul, MN: Brooks Cole.

Rogers CR (1957) The necessary and sufficient conditions of therapeutic personality change. *Journal of Consulting Psychology* **21** (2) 95–104.

Further reading

Videbeck S (2009) *Mental Health Nursing*. Philidelphia: Wolters Kluwer Health/Lippincott Williams and Wilkins. (Chapter 6: Therapeutic communication)

Wilkin P (2003) The craft of psychiatric mental health nursing practice. In: P Barker (Ed) *Psychiatric and Mental Health Nursing: The craft of caring*. London: Arnold.

Chapter 16

Care plans for the inpatient case study

Key points

■ Care plans are useful tools for involving the patient in their own care. They are shared, team plans which ensure that the right approach is consistently taken.

■ While many problems will be common, patient care plans need to be individually tailored to each patient's unique needs, presentation and circumstances.

■ With regular reviews, care plans allow us to measure progress.

There are many different ways in which nurses can construct care plans. They all identify areas of concern (problems) and detail the nursing interventions (actions) to overcome them. In this chapter major problems are listed with the suggested nursing actions. Notice how therapeutic relationships underpin and enhance the success of all the nursing actions.

Common problems

Problem: Patient is overactive and cannot keep still.
Action: Communicate in a calm voice and use short sentences. Involve the person in controlled activity such as sport, which requires physical effort and distracts them. Encourage frequent rests and naps if the patient cannot stay still for long. Maintain a calm environment and avoid stimulation. If the person is at risk of injury then increase the levels of observation to ensure no harm ensues. Provide a structure and routine. Consider the use of sedation if necessary to ensure rest.

Problem: Patient is not sleeping and looks tired.
Action: Suggest short daytime naps. During the night, minimise interaction with a patient who cannot sleep. Provide a private room with minimal stimulation. Dim the lights and turn off the television. Encourage rest and explain its value. If necessary stay with the patient while they rest and keep conversation to a minimum. Use relaxation techniques. Remind them that a warm bath prior to going to bed can be helpful. Sedation may be necessary if all else fails and the patient's health is at risk from extreme exhaustion.

Problem: Patient is irritable and intrusive to others.
Action: Communicate in a calm voice and use short sentences. Do not be drawn into an argument. Observe for signs of frustration and intervene early. Set firm limits for behaviour which is distressing for others. Keep the patient occupied. Remind the patient of the need to respect the personal space of others.

Problem: Patient has grandiose ideas.
Action: If the person is at risk of injury, increased levels of observation are recommended to ensure no harm occurs. Listen but keep interactions short so as not to indulge the ideas. Explore the reality of ideas as the patient gets better. Protect from ridicule. Try to distract to other activities. Keep an open mind, in that psychiatric patients' grandiose ideas have sometimes turned out to be achievable objectives.

Problem: Patient has pressured and loud speech, and is making demands on others.
Action: Communicate in a calm voice. Listen. Try to distract with simple activity. Ensure all staff respond in a similar way to ensure consistency. Listen and soak up the verbalisations. Ask the patient to speak more slowly. Explain that you cannot understand them if they speak too fast.

Problem: Patient lacks insight.
Action: Build a therapeutic relationship and use this to help the patient gain the insight necessary for their recovery.

Problem: Patient is in need of a bath and fresh clothes.
Action: Encourage the patient to indulge in all aspects of self-care and matters of personal hygiene and grooming. Give praise and help them. Organise a 'special' bath, ask family to bring in favourite grooming products.

Problem: Patient is dressing in out of character, flamboyant clothes.
Action: Clothes can both reflect and affect our mood. Minimise attention given to bizarre appearance and behaviour. Encourage less garish clothes and ask the family to provide favourites from home and possibly to take away any outlandish clothes. Be with the patient and help them choose and dress and give praise and encouragement in choosing appropriate clothing.

Problem: Patient is not eating or drinking enough.
Action: Encourage the patient to partake in meals, serve them in their own room to avoid them being distracted from eating. Offer food frequently. Give snacks if they cannot sit still. Ask the family to bring in favourite foods. Use snacks and finger foods which can be carried around such as high calorie cereal or chocolate bars. Put food in their hands. Give bottled water to carry around. Use fortified drinks. Put favourite drinks in their room. Consult the dietician. Place on a weight chart if necessary. Monitor for possibility of constipation.

Problem: Patient is hypersexual.
Action: If the person or others are at risk then increase the levels of observation. Explain the dangers of risky behaviour. Keep the patient otherwise occupied. Use distraction to another activity. Reduce the opportunity for socialisation and nurse in a separate area for a while if necessary. Explain to other patients the nature of the disorder.

Problem: Patient's family are worried and do not understand the disorder.
Action: Educate the family about the disorder, prognosis, and treatment plan. If the patient wishes include family in discussions, planning and treatment. Discuss how to deal with problems and give them contact details of support groups. Inform how to access help in a crisis. As the patient recovers discuss these aspects together as a family or couple and move on to discuss medication issues and relapse prevention.

Problem: Patient liable to leave the ward.
Action: Increase levels of observation if necessary and explain the reasons to the patient. Communicate in a calm voice and listen. Give simple clear explanations. Try to distract with simple activity if the patient is insistent. Be firm but do not argue. A firm structure and clear boundaries can be reassuring for the patient.

Problem: Patient is medication non-adherent.
Action: Be aware that side effects can feel worse than the disorder. Encourage compliance and educate the patient as to the need and purpose of the medication. Involve family and friends to support this. Explain possible side effects and try to engage patient in self-monitoring. When patients tell you of extreme side effects ensure the prescribing doctor is aware of what the patient is experiencing and talk about the medication with them.

Problem: Patient's behaviour is having an impact on other patients.
Action: Observe for signs of frustration and intervene early. Distract the patient to activity away from others. Explain to other patients the behaviour is a result of the disorder. Reduce opportunity for socialisation and nurse in a separate area for a time if necessary. Observe and intervene to protect the patient from embarrassment.

Consideration point

Re-read each of the above problems and consider which ones may have been created or enhanced by detention on the ward.

In what ways does hospital admission 'bring things to a head' and turn difficult behaviour into nearly impossible behaviour requiring quicker nursing intervention than had the patient remained in the community?

Reflection exercise: Nursing problems

- List some further nursing problems.
- List a range of nursing actions or responses for dealing with these problems.

Further reading

Frisch N &Frisch L (2011) *Psychiatric Mental Health Nursing (4th edition)*. New York: Delmare/Cengage. (See the nursing care plans outlined in Chapter 14 and Chapter 15.)

Schultz J & Videbeck S (2005) Care plan 22: major depressive disorder. In: *Lippincott's Manual of Psychiatric Nursing Care Plans*. Philadelphia: Lippincott, Williams and Wilkins.

Schultz J & Videbeck S (2005) Care plan 23: bipolar disorder manic episode. In: *Lippincott's Manual of Psychiatric Nursing Care Plans*. Philadelphia: Lippincott, Williams and Wilkins.

Chapter 17

Drug treatment

Key points

- Medication helps to alleviate symptoms and stabilise mood variation.

- Medication is not a cure for bipolar disorder.

- Drugs are only one part of the treatment package. They can help the person live a normal life in conjunction with other non-drug treatments.

- Stopping medication often increases the risk of relapse.

This chapter explores the medication used to help control bipolar disorder. The key drugs are mood stabilisers, antipsychotics and antidepressants. This chapter uses the generic drug name rather than the brand name for ease of reference.

In a nutshell

Mood stabilisers are used to lessen mood swings.

Antipsychotics and **antidepressants** are used to moderate manic and depressive phases of the disorder. Sometimes these can be important in ending a current episode.

Benzodiazepines are given to help calm people, reduce anxiety and help with sleep.

Mood stabilisers

Lithium and anticonvulsant drugs are used try to stabilise mood and stop the cycles of mood swings.

Lithium

The mineral lithium carbonate had previously been used to treat mania prior to it being used to stabilise mood and help to prevent relapses. Many mechanisms have been suggested for how this mineral stabilises moods.

Lithium is said to have a narrow therapeutic range. Too little and it may be ineffective, while too much causes toxicity and can be fatal. Therefore blood tests are essential. Early blood tests determine the dose for the individual and then less frequent monitoring allows the doctor to consider changes and ensure that no more lithium is taken than necessary. Patients taking close to the therapeutic maximum report feeling 'flat' and 'a little low', which may be part of lithium's greater effectiveness in preventing mania compared with preventing depression (see Schatzberg *et al*, 2010).

When lithium does not give the required effect it is often used in conjunction with an antidepressant or antipsychotic.

Side effects

Some common side effects are increased thirst, gastrointestinal irritation (this may include vomiting and diarrhoea), sedation, tremor, a metallic taste in the mouth and weight gain.

Lithium toxicity

Overdose can be fatal, and the patient, family and nurse need to be vigilant for the signs of toxicity. If these are apparent the drug must be stopped and medical aid sought. Detoxification is most effective in a hospital setting where levels of lithium and other salts in the blood can be monitored. The stomach may need to be pumped. If the person appears prone to toxicity, is an unreliable drug taker or is unwilling to undertake regular blood tests, then the drug should not be reconsidered.

Lithium toxicity (continued)

Signs of toxicity
Tremor of the hands, nausea and vomiting, blurred vision, unsteadiness, drowsiness, ataxia (difficulties with co-ordination, balance and speech), agitation, dysarthria (poor or slurred speech), nystagmus (involuntary side to side eye movement), confusion, thirst, diarrhoea, rashes.

Severe toxicity is indicated by convulsions, low blood pressure, irregular heartbeat, muscle jerks and reduced consciousness.

NB. Toxicity can occur at lower levels in older adults.

It is clearly important that patients and their families are well-informed about toxicity and the need for regular blood tests. Patients may need to remind their GP that they are on lithium as it interacts with many other drugs. They should also check with a doctor or pharmacist about any over-the-counter remedies they may want to take.

Dehydration raises the concentration of lithium in the blood and so can increase the risk of toxicity. Those on lithium need to pay attention to how much they drink and not go for too long without drinking. Travelling/being away from home is a time when particular attention is needed as routines change and it is possible to not realise dehydration is occurring. Hotter weather/increased ward temperatures will increase the rate of dehydration. Dehydration may be accelerated by caffeine (see Chapter 27 – Food and mood).

When taking lithium, patients also need to avoid overindulgence in sodium in the form of dietary salt. This salt blocks some of the same receptors as lithium and so reduces its impact. Conversely, on rare occasions people on lithium can drink so much as to significantly lower lithium levels.

Lithium is treated as a toxin by the kidneys, which need to work hard in removing it. This means that the more lithium that is consumed the greater the risk of damage to the kidneys. Kidney function tests are required several times each year with special attention needed for those on higher doses or with reduced renal function.

Lithium affects thyroid function and therefore thyroid function tests are required.

Anticonvulsants

Roughly 25% of people will not respond to lithium or cannot take it because of side effects or other complications and some researchers (eg. Soloman *et al*, 1995) put this figure as high as 64%. Several anticonvulsants effective in stabilising mood are also available.

Carbamazepine

Carbamazipine is frequently used for patients who cannot tolerate lithium. It is another mood stabiliser requiring regular blood tests. Tests are for agranulocytosis (a dangerous lowering of the white blood cells).

Side effects
Dizziness, sedation, blurred vision, lethargy, headache, hypotension (lowering of blood pressure), ataxia, gastro-intestinal problems.

Carbamazepine can also reduce the effectiveness of oral contraceptives.

Sodium valproate

Sodium valproate has increased in popularity in recent years with fewer side effects being reported. It is said to be particularly effective in preventing manic relapses and in rapid cycling bipolar. Patients need to be monitored when changing brand in case of changes in response.

Side effects
Weight gain, tremor, dizziness, ataxia, drowsiness, weakness, confusion, nausea, indigestion, temporary hair loss and diarrhoea.

Lamotrigine

Lamotrigine is a newer anticonvulsive drug which has been found to be effective in stabilising mood. Goldberg *et al* (2009) suggest that lamotrigine is particularly successful in controlling rapid cycling and mixed bipolar states in people who have not received adequate relief from lithium, carbamazepine and/or valproate, and that it has greater antidepressant potency than either carbamazepine or valproate.

Side effects

Dizziness, headache, double vision, unsteadiness, nausea, blurred vision, sleepiness, rash, vomiting. Although rashes are not the most common side effect, they are frequently the reason given for discontinuing lamotrigine.

Combinations

Doctors may choose to prescribe lithium with carbamazepine, or lithium with valporate, or lithium with lamotrigine, with usually each drug used at a lower dose. For some patients who have not remained stable on a single drug this can be far more effective and may reduce some toxicity risks.

Antipsychotics

Antipsychotics (also known as neuroleptics) tend to be used to induce sedation and have a calming effect upon the manic patient who is in danger of exhaustion. They are in effect 'depressants' acting by blocking dopamine receptors curtailing the effects of excess dopamine. They are also used for the actively psychotic patient in either the manic or depressed state who is a danger to themselves or others. The calming effect will occur quickly but the antipsychotic effect can take up to a few weeks. Antipsychotics are classed as older 'typicals' and newer 'atypicals'. In general, the newer drugs tend to have fewer reported side effects.

Typical antipsychotics

Chlorpromazine, thioridazine, haloperidol, flupentixol, sulpiride, trifluoperazine, pimozide, loxapine, fluphenazine and benperidol.

Atypical antipsychotics

Clozapine, amisulpiride, olanzapine, quetiapine, risperidone.

There are also intramuscular injections of antipsychotics that are usually referred to as 'depot injections'.

Depot injections

These long-acting drugs are suspended in an oily substance and given via intramuscular injection for slow release over a period of days or weeks into the bloodstream. These are useful for maintenance therapy as they reduce the need for taking many tablets and thus increase compliance. Several of the oral antipsychotics are available as depot injections and the profile of side effects remains as for the oral drug, though there is some evidence that they give rise to more extrapyramidal side effects than their oral counterparts.

Examples of depot preparations are:

Depixol (flupenthixol)
Haldol (haloperidol)
Modecate (fluphenazine)
Piportil (pipotiazine)
Clopixol (zuclopentixol)
Risperdal consta (risperdone)

Nursing considerations for depot injections

- Ensure informed consent is given, not just assumed.
- Reiterate the reason for the injection and discuss any patient concerns.
- Ensure comfort and dignity.
- Patient can choose their position (usually lying or standing).
- The Z track technique is to be used.
- No more than 3ml should be injected in any one site.
- An initial test dose needs to be given to check for side effects.
- Monitor for adverse reactions, side effects and effectiveness.
- Injection sites need to be rotated.

Remember: Poor technique means a painful injection.

Side effects of antipsychotics

Antipsychotic medications can have many side effects and not everyone will experience them all. The side effects tend to increase with the dose and the length of time they have been taken. Some are minor and can be tolerated while others are disturbing and therefore need careful monitoring. The drugs target a wider range of receptors than those associated with illness allowing the side effects to be grouped accordingly.

Extrapyramidal side effects

These tend to occur more with the typical antipsychotics. Observe the patient for Parkinsonian symptoms such as tremor, a shuffling gait and stooped posture. Excessive salivation can also occur.

Dystonia: Abnormal face and body movements. Rigid eyes.

Tardive dyskinesia: Involuntary movements of tongue, face and jaw, typically with the jaw moving as if constantly chewing and the tongue going in and out. It is very disabling and embarrassing. Alternative treatment needs to be found to avoid these involuntary movements becoming irreversible.

Akathisia: This includes restlessness especially in the legs, feelings of pins and needles and an inability to sit still.

Other side effects

Antimuscarinic symptoms: Dry mouth, blurred vision, constipation and difficulty passing water.
Cardiovascular: Low blood pressure, tachycardia (rapid heart rate) and arrhythmias (abnormal heart rhythm).

Impotence: Patients may not want to tell you about this, yet it can often be the major reason for non-compliance for many who find this difficult to tolerate.

Weight gain: Most people taking antipsychotics will gain some weight. How much weight gained depends on the exact drug and dose. It also varies greatly between individuals. Some people hardly seem to be affected while others gain weight at an astonishing rate. Suddenly finding out clothes that fitted well no longer fit at all can be alarming for patients. There is much non compliance with antipsychotic use related to weight gain with patients choosing to regain their previous healthier weight and slimmer body image rather than continuing with the medication.

Drugs used to combat side effects

There is a range of antimuscarinic/anticholinergic medications used to relieve the abnormal movements and other side effects produced by antipsychotics. Common ones are procyclidine, orphenadrine, benzatropine, benzhexol and biperiden.

Antipsychotics can have long-term health effects. For example, the increased risk of diabetes among those taking some atypicals.

Consideration point

■ Which of the above side effects for antipsychotics are likely to impact on a patient's ability to interact effectively with others?

For example, rigid eyes: almost everyone moves their eyes as they talk, naturally making and breaking eye contact with the listener. When you have a conversation with someone affected by 'rigid eyes', how does this unnatural stare make you feel?

Antidepressants

These are used to help alleviate a severe depressive episode. Usually antidepressants can take up to three weeks before they begin to have an effect on mood and their full effectiveness can take longer still. It is important that the patient understands this if they are to give the drug a chance to work. It is also worth mentioning that the effectiveness of antidepressants can be impeded by alcohol consumption.

There is a range of different antidepressants.

Tricyclics (TCIs)

These are older antidepressants. The most common ones are amytriptyline, clomipramine, dothiepin, doxepin, imipramine, lofepramine, trimipramine and nortriptyline. They have a higher incidence of reported side effects than the newer ones, which include dry mouth, dizziness, headache, drowsiness, nausea and increased appetite.

Selective serotonin reuptake inhibitors (SSRIs)

These are newer antidepressants such as fluoxetine (Prozac). Others include citalopram, fluvoxamine, paroxetine, sertraline and related drugs are venlafaxine and trazodone. These increase the level of the neurotransmitter serotonin in the brain to improve mood. They should not be stopped suddenly.

Monoamine oxidase inhibitors (MAOIs)

These are often avoided as they can interact dangerously with certain foods, especially cheese and yeast-based products such as Marmite, which contain high levels of tyramine. The combination raises blood pressure to high levels accompanied by a severe headache, which can be fatal. All alcohol should be avoided. MAOIs will also interact with some over-the-counter remedies and some hayfever treatments. Less severe side effects are drowsiness, constipation, dry mouth and occasionally swollen ankles. Common MAOIs are phenelzine, isocarboxazid and tranylcypromine.

Benzodiazepines

These are used for calming, reducing anxiety and helping with sleep. Examples are diazepam, chlordiazepoxide, flurazepam, oxazepam, lorazepam, nitrazepam, temazepam and alprazolam.

Side effects

These are likely to be minor such as tiredness, feeling light-headed, and occasional confusion. It is important to remember that benzodiazepines are highly addictive and should only be used for short-term relief.

Electro-convulsive therapy

Electro convulsive therapy (ECT) is a last resort treatment for those who do not respond to drug treatments and other therapy. It can work much faster than drugs. Many people argue that it should only be used in life threatening situations, such as an immediate risk of suicide. However, if a person is developing a disabling chronic condition,which is untouched by other means of treatment, or they are refusing food and drink and are severely distressed, it is likely to be tried. It has certainly proven to be an effective treatment in many cases of intransigent depression and helped shorten acute manic episodes. In depression it is used as a short-term treatment while waiting for other treatments to have an effect.

NICE guidelines for bipolar disorder (2006)

Acute phase
Consider an antipsychotic if:

- manic symptoms are severe
- there is marked behavioural disturbance.

Consider valproate or lithium if:

- there has been previous response and good compliance with one of these drugs.

Consider lithium if:

- symptoms are less severe.

Long-term treatment
Base choice of lithium, olanzapine or valproate on:

- previous response
- risk and precipitants of manic versus depressive relapse
- physical risk factors
- patient preference and history of adherence
- cognitive state assessment.

NB. Valproate should not be prescribed routinely for women of child-bearing potential.

If continuing symptoms or relapse
Use alternative monotherapy or add second prophylactic (preventative) agent:

- lithium and valproate
- lithium and olanzapine
- alproate and olanzapine.

If this proves ineffective
- Prescribe lamotrigine or carbamazepine.

References

Goldberg J, Calabrese J, Saville B, Frye M, Ketter T, Suppes T, Post R & Goodwin FK (2009) Mood stabilization and destabilization during acute and continuation phase treatment for bipolar I disorder with lamotrigine or placebo. *Clinical Psychiatry* **70** (9) 1273–1280.

NICE (2006) *Clinical Guideline 38. Bipolar Disorder. The management of bipolar disorder in adults, children and adolescents in primary and secondary care.* London: National Institute for Health and Clinical Excellence.

Schatzberg A, Cole J & DeBattista C (2010) *Manual of Clinical Psychopharmacology* (7th edition). Arlington: American Psychiatric Publishing.

Solomon D, Keitner G, Miller I, Shea M & Keller M (1995) Course of illness and maintenance treatments for patients with bipolar disorder. *Journal of Clinical Psychiatry* **56** 5–13.

Further reading

Dougherty L & Lister S (2011) *The Royal Marsden Hospital Manual of Clinical Nursing Procedures* (8th edition). Chichester: Wiley-Blackwell.

Goodwin G & Sachs G (2004) *Fast Fact: Bipolar disorder*. Oxford: Health Press. (All useful and well-written but see especially Chapters 6 and 7 relating to medication.)

Healy D (2002) *Psychiatric Drugs Explained (3rd edition).* Edinburgh: Churchill Livingstone. (See Section 2 Management of Affective Disorders.)

Okuma T (1993) Effects of carbamazepine and lithium on affective disorders. *Neuropsychobiology* **27** 138–145.

Rodger M & King L (2000) Drawing up and administering intramuscular injections: a review of the literature. *Journal of advanced Nursing* **13** 574–582.

Videback S & Acott K (2009) Mental Health Nursing. London: Wolters Kluwer / Lippincott Williams and Wilkins. (See Chapter 15: Mood disorders for a clear overview of bipolar disorder generally and the nursing aspect in relation to medication.)

Wilbourn M & Prosser S (2003) *The Pathology and Pharmacology of Mental Illness.* Cheltenham: Nelson Thornes. (See Chapter 3: Altered mood.)

Young A & Newham I (2006) Lithium in maintenance therapy for bipolar disorder. *Journal of Psychopharmacology* **20** (2) 17–22. (This is an interesting review of the role lithium plays in preventing relapse.)

Useful websites

MDF The Bipolar Organisation at http://www.mdf.org.uk/?o=56892. (This site gives information about medications and treatment and is regularly updated.)

Rethink at http://www.rethink.org/living_with_mental_illness/treatment_and_therapy/medication/benzodiazepines/ (This page gives information specifically about benzodiazepines.)

Section 3
Bipolar in the community

Chapter 18

Case study in the community

Patricia, 52, was diagnosed with bipolar disorder 25 years ago. She had hospital admissions for what seemed to be symptoms indicating mania when she was 19, 23 and 27. Since this time she has been taking lithium and up until last year attended a surgery for blood tests every four months. Her blood test results were indicating acceptable levels within the therapeutic range.

You have been asked to visit Patricia at her house to assess what support she may need. This is an unusual visit for you because she is not a client of your recovery team and you have not been told of any specific problems. This seems to have been through a request from Patricia's GP after he received worrying information from Patricia's brother, Matthew, who also has a bipolar diagnosis. Matthew is well known to the recovery team.

The only other information you have is that Patricia lives with her husband and her children have left home.

You are let into the house by her adult son, who says, 'Mother is in court but might be back in 10 minutes or so.' As he makes you a cup of tea he explains that Patricia's current husband moved out after an argument six months ago. He says that his mum has been late for everything he can remember since his fifth birthday party, so if she is only 10 minutes late this is normal. She walks in exactly 10 minutes late.

She is dressed very smartly with what seems to be appropriate make up. Patricia explains that she is a magistrate and things have become very busy recently with a colleague off sick. She is talking fast and fairly loudly but very clearly and is explaining herself very precisely.

You ask why her GP is concerned. Patricia knows that Matthew has seen the GP and their concern is because she has supposedly stopped taking all medications. She explains that this is not true but she has reduced her lithium gradually from 800mg/day to 200mg/day over a six-month period starting from the day her husband left. She says that she has no plans to take any less and shows you a seven-day tablet dispenser containing 200mg for each day.

Patricia's explanation for this change is that she now believes that all her past problems were due to men. Her first admission was after a row with a boyfriend. Her second was after two years of bullying by her first husband and the third was related to a problem with a man too. Now her husband has moved out she says that she does not need as much medication.

You ask how she is sleeping. She is quite embarrassed to tell you that she now goes to bed at 9.30pm and wakes up at 4am. She adds that she feels it is just enough sleep and if she were waking up any later she would never be ready for her court and charity work.

As you get up to leave Patricia certainly now seems overexcited as she shows you her food and mood diary detailing everything she has eaten over the last six months. She has this idea that certain foods were adding to her anxiety and so far has identified five food types that cause immediate and rapid changes in her mood.

Patricia tells you that she does not want to see her GP and does not want blood tests. She says that she agreed to this meeting purely to reassure everyone that all is well and that she is not going to suddenly become manic. She shakes your hand vigorously and walks you to your car still talking about her food diary and how food is more important than medicine.

You drive away feeling that it was nowhere near enough time to assess someone's mood and dreading having to write a short report with a recommendation.

Consideration points

- Using a mood scale, where would you judge Patricia's mood to be?
- Using a mood map, where would you put Patricia's mood and using the map can you show any mood change(s) during the meeting?
- Are you reassured by Patricia's explanation of what she is doing with her medication?
- Do you think Patricia should have a routine blood test for lithium?

Bipolar Disorder: A guide for mental health professionals, carers and those who live with it
© Pavilion Publishing (Brighton) Ltd 2012

- Is Patricia putting herself at risk of a mood swing by sleeping too little and apparently working very hard?
- Is her food diary a sign of an obsession or simply a case of logical thinking?
- Would you recommend a follow-up visit or would you say that Patricia is coping well in her own way and recommend that the team focus on their core activity of helping those currently/recently in crisis?
- Whether or not your team is to support Patricia, give some suggestions about the sort of preventative support someone like Patricia might benefit from.

Chapter 19

Principles of recovery

Key points

- Recovery is about having a satisfying life.

- It does not mean the absence of disorder.

- Each person will have their own understanding and targets for recovery.

- Some key concepts which aid recovery are having hope, taking personal responsibility, using strengths, learning about the disorder and having good support.

Recovery is a personal concept that has no rules – just guidelines. There has been much written on recovery in recent years and this chapter examines some themes which have emerged. Every attempt to define recovery produces new ideas and confirms that there is no single best way to view recovery.

Making Recovery a Reality suggests that *'recovery is about building a meaningful and satisfying life, as defined by the person themselves, whether or not there are ongoing or recurring symptoms or problems'* (Shepherd *et al*, 2008). The Mental Health Foundation suggests that recovery is about staying in control of your life despite having a mental health problem.

Reflection exercise: Defining recovery

Write your own unique definition of recovery in less than 100 words.

In the previous quote, a key point is that recovery is *'defined by the person themselves'*. Health professionals cannot define recovery for an individual. It is necessary that health professionals listen to the person's hopes for the future in order to understand their ideas about recovery. It is also worth noting that recovery can happen without the help of health professionals and in some cases not everyone aims to recover.

It is often useful to think of recovery as being a journey rather than a destination – a process rather than a place. Bipolar people who have had many episodes may not see themselves on a journey of recovery. They may see their life as more of a journey of discovery. However much you believe in recovery, such alternative views need to be respected and appreciated because they are just as valid. What others call discovery, self-management or another name is likely to have the same principles as recovery.

Wellness Recovery Action Plans

The National Institute for Mental Health issued a Guiding Statement on Recovery in 2005, which set out the principles for recovery-based work. Principle 9 stated that *'Users of services with the support of clinicians, practitioners and other supporters should develop a recovery management or wellness recovery action plan'*. These 'written' plans derive from the work of Mary Ellen Copeland in the 1980s and include the following.

Tools: identifying tools to help develop a healthier lifestyle. Things the person has done in the past or which they could do to help them move towards wellness.

Maintenance: things the person needs to do in order to maintain wellness, such as ensuring a good diet, sleep and exercise.

Triggers: identifying what could cause stress and relapse and identifying what to do about such triggers.

Early warning signs: identifying signs such as irritability or anxiety which tell the person their symptoms are getting worse. This will include self-monitoring of symptoms.

Crisis management plans: for when all else fails, these outline the person's wishes, what they want others to do for them and how they want to be treated and cared for.

WRAP plans also include ideas for building self-esteem and self-management.

Bipolar Disorder: A guide for mental health professionals, carers and those who live with it
© Pavilion Publishing (Brighton) Ltd 2012

Wellness Recovery Action Planning

Copeland's research in the 1980s identified five concepts for recovery that have stood the test of time and are easy for both health professionals and clients to remember. These are the concepts taught on Wellness Recovery Action Planning (WRAP) courses. These concepts apply when recovering from all kinds of crisis whether work-related, accidental, financial or relationship issues etc.

1. Hope

When something traumatic happens people can temporarily lose hope. For a while we may not be able to imagine how we can ever rebuild our lives. Hope can ebb away gradually each time things do not work out. Hope can also disappear in an instant if, for example, you are diagnosed with an illness that you are told is incurable. For recovery to happen we must believe that it is possible; we must have the hope that life can be different.

Questions

1. How much hope is needed to start recovering?
2. How can a nurse inspire hope?

2. Personal responsibility

This concept is linked to overcoming both dependency and loss of control. After a crisis a client is likely to have become dependent upon health professionals and others to a degree and will need to start regaining more control of their life. Others may see ways to help with this and can create opportunities for them to take greater responsibility. However, it will always be the client's choice as to when to start taking more control and responsibility.

Like hope, surprisingly little personal responsibility is needed to aid recovery. Often when people are seen to be making an effort to recover, those around them become more prepared to help, and with greater enthusiasm.

Are there special considerations for bipolar people when we talk about personal responsibility?

- Many bipolar people quickly take on more responsibility than is good for them. This may in part be a conscious or unconscious attempt to make up for a feeling of lost time from when they were unwell.

- Too much personal responsibility too soon can risk developing feelings of 'everything depends on me', leading to increased anxiety.

- Feelings of excess responsibility can create a desire to escape. This could, for example, lead to 'escape' into the use of drugs/alcohol with associated mood changes.

Personal responsibility is needed for positive mental health but extra care is needed when encouraging bipolar people to take on more. Your role is likely to be one of helping them achieve a balance in what they feel they are responsible for and what they need to be leaving to others (see Chapter 34: Achieving balance).

3. Self-advocacy/agency

In depression very few people can effectively self-advocate ie. say what they need. Recovering this ability can take a long time.

Case study: The partner

It is your first visit to see a client diagnosed with bipolar disorder. You have read through notes and understand that they have had several short manic episodes, which were each followed by long depressions with no recognised periods of 'normal' moods for more than three years.

On arrival you ask the client: 'How are you feeling today?'
Her partner answers: 'She's not too good today.'
You ask: 'How did you sleep last night?'
Her partner answers: 'She slept about four hours. Twelve to 2am and then 6am to 8am. She spent most of the night in the kitchen. I don't know what she was doing.'
You say: 'So your sleep is not ideal. While you are not sleeping, are you able to get on with useful activities?'

Her partner steps in just as quickly as before: 'Well I couldn't see much difference in the kitchen when I got up this morning. I think she put a few things away but the worktops hadn't been wiped down.'

Consider

- How frustrating would you find this conversation and why?
- Do you think this type of conversation might be common?
- How did things ever get this bad?
- How do you politely/appropriately ask the partner to stop answering?
- How quickly do you think the bipolar person might answer your questions if given a chance?
- At this stage do you have any idea about this client's mood? (Depressed? 'Normal'? Hypomanic?)
- If available, would a week of respite care help the client regain some self-advocacy?

It can be useful to think of self-advocacy as self-agency. Self-agency it is not just about speaking up but it is also about being able to choose from a range of options. The recovering bipolar person needs to have choices and not have someone telling them which option to choose.

Supporters can help with this. First, by making sure more than one option is put before the person in recovery, then by supplying enough information about each option. This is not as easy as it might sound.

- If our only experience of this person is someone who has been lacking capacity then we may find ourselves resisting the idea of offering choices.

- If the person is in a low mood they may not be taking in the information we are giving them.

- If they are in a high mood one possibility is that they will flit between options, saying, 'Yes, I'll do that… oh, on second thoughts, the first option must be better, or then again…'

Consideration point

■ It is often debated whether a patient needs to be stable before they can begin recovery. Why might this be said and what is wrong/right with this idea?

Providing you are not adding to the person's anxiety and hypomania by supplying options and information, then it is still likely to be the best thing to do.

Self-agency may be further expanded to 'Using your strengths' and recognising that recovery not only involves speaking up and choosing what to do, but often progresses best when people choose to do what they are best at rather than continuing to struggle with activities that others such as parents, partners or health workers have advised them to do.

Encouragement can be given when interest is expressed in trying different activities, especially if they are talking of retrying activities they were once good at and enjoyed doing. Again care is needed when listening to someone in a state of hypomania – consider whether their plans are realistic.

4. Education

It is a common belief that most bipolar people are of above average intelligence, however there is little evidence to confirm this and many people have missed out on educational opportunities as a result of the disorder. This concept is about the person with the diagnosis learning about the disorder and general self-care.

Learning about the disorder

People with the disorder should be encouraged to find out more about it. Books, magazines, newsletters, websites, online forums, self-help groups and conferences can all be recommended as good sources of information.

Bipolar Disorder: A guide for mental health professionals, carers and those who live with it
© Pavilion Publishing (Brighton) Ltd 2012

> ### Consideration points
>
> - Are there any risks associated with education?
> - How might people who are in hypomania or are still depressed cope with new information?
> - Could there be adverse effects from giving information?

There has been a lot written about bipolar disorder and much has been written by those who experience it. Often this is in the form of autobiographical works, which give a good insight and contain potentially useful ideas. There are many other aspects of education such as medication, side effects, triggers, relapse prevention etc. (See Chapters 10 and 20 for a further discussion of education)

Learning more about general self-care

This chapter has discussed how the disorder is related to lifestyle and how episodes are brought on by stress/life events. This provides good opportunities for bipolar people to learn about lifestyle choices and how to avoid or overcome much of the stress that has caused previous episodes.

With this concept in mind, remember that education about self-care comes from a much wider range of sources than just bipolar literature. There are many documentaries and radio programmes about related subjects, such as sleep, nutrition, exercise and mental health conditions. These can be useful but be aware they are not all based on good evidence.

5. Support

Support is a subject covered in more detail in Chapter 22: Support and networking. Everyone needs support in many different forms and amounts. Support can make the difference between falling into a crisis and being able to take events in our stride.

Getting support may be difficult. The disorder may well have driven some family, friends and potential support away. After an episode or series of episodes it is likely that effort needs to be made in rebuilding support networks. It has been said that this is about becoming part of your 'tribe' again (Murray & Fortinberry, 2004).

Case studies

David: Rebuilding support in the workplace

Before I had my troubles I never thought about support. I simply had friends. I helped them and they helped me. It was only when I returned to work after five months off sick that it struck me how my support network had changed. A few people reacted very differently towards me. I am not blaming those who did not speak to me because they did not know what to say. I was in the same boat – I did not know what to say to them either!

The number of colleagues I found I was now able to consider to be friends had dropped from too many to count to five or less. My concern now was that I might lean too heavily on these few true friends. I decided that no matter how low I felt I would only ever tell one friend about my feelings in any one day. It was an idea that worked most days, but on the worst days I would sit quietly with the work's occupational health nurse and have a little cry. I had never needed to speak with her before my crisis and now she was a key supporter, simply because she was there and I did not feel she was judging me.

It took a long time to adjust, but now I feel the crisis did me some favours. There is something to be said for knowing who your real friends are and knowing who you can turn to in a crisis.

Barbara: From rock bottom to feeling supported

Before the internet I felt alone in a way that I think most people will struggle to imagine. I had a dual diagnosis of bipolar II and severe agoraphobia, and I feared just about everyone. I was like a prisoner in my little flat.

At one time the depression and the fears were so bad that I did not go out of the door or see anyone for a week. I do not know if I would have starved if my neighbour had not knocked and said she had not seen me for a while. That day was a turning point as for the first time I told someone other than a health professional just how bad things were for me.

This neighbour was an angel. My food cupboard and fridge were empty and she went out and bought me some essentials. Soon after she more or less dragged me around to her place. It will sound odd to some youngsters but that was the first time I had seen anything at all on the internet. The idea that I could chat with people with similar problems to me – well, it was very liberating.

Each time I went to use my neighbour's computer she seemed to have a friend or relative of hers there and they became my friends. I have never asked if maybe it was a set-up. If I was tricked into coming out of my shell, I don't care. This was exactly the support I needed. Am I cured? The agoraphobia is now at a point where I get out and about. OK, I don't do the big supermarkets, but I have always preferred the corner shops anyway. I still have the bipolar II diagnosis but now I am wondering if the main problem with my moods was because I wasn't mixing. I didn't have supporters and now I do.

Other concepts and principles

As well as the concepts discussed above, you will come across more principles of recovery such as staying active and building social contacts. Remember that recovery is possible and that key indicators of it include the person having meaningful occupations and valued roles. These make explicit the link between recovery and the principle of social inclusion. In fact one could argue that you cannot have recovery without social inclusion. The nursing role does not stop at medical recovery but needs to embrace wider aspects of life such as housing, finances, work and play.

Tips for recovery-oriented practice

- Listen
- Help the person with personal goals, not your professional ones
- Demonstrate belief in the person and their strengths
- Inspire hope
- Combat the 'sick role'

- Try to use non mental health resources
- Encourage self-management
- Discuss and respect the person's wishes regarding treatment and therapy
- Work in partnership
- Maintain hope in the face of setbacks

(Shepherd *et al*, 2008)

Answer to questions

1. **How much hope is needed to start recovering?**

Just one tiny spark! In helping people recover, the tiniest bit of hope is often all that is needed to help people move on.

2. **How can a nurse inspire hope?**

- *By having hope and communicating it*
- *By believing in the potential and strengths of the person, and valuing them*
- *By listening*
- *By sharing the journey despite the setbacks*

References

Copeland ME (1997) *Wellness Recovery Action Plan*. Dummerston: Peach Publishers.

Murray B & Fortinberry A (2004) *Creating Optimism: A proven, 7-step programme for overcoming depression*. New York: McGraw-Hill.

NHS & National Institute for Mental Health (2005) *NIMHE Guiding Statement on Recovery*. London: DH.

Shepherd G, Boardman J & Slade M (2008) *Making Recovery a Reality*. London: Sainsbury Centre for Mental Health. Available from www.centreformentalhealth.org.uk.

Further reading

Ajayi S, Bowyer T, Hicks A, Larsen J, Mailey P, Sayers R & Smith R (2009) *Getting Back into the World: Reflections on lived experiences of recovery* [online]. London: Rethink. Available at: http://www.rethink.org/mental_health_shop/products/rethink_publications/getting_back_into_ th.html (accessed September 2011).

Ajayi S, Bowyer T, Hicks A, Larsen J, Mailey P, Sayers R & Smith R (2010) *Recovery Insights: Learning from lived experience*. London: Rethink. Available from: www.rethink.org/ recoveryinsights

Slade M (2009) *100 Ways to Support Recovery*. London: Rethink. Available from: www.rethink. org/100ways

Thomas J (2006) *Taking Leave*. London: Timewell Press Limited.

Useful websites

Copeland Centre at www.copelandcenter.com

Mental Health Foundation at www.mentalhealth.org.uk

Wellness and Recovery Action Plan at www.mentalhealthrecovery.com

Chapter 20

Education

Key points

- Education has long been established as a major aspect of mental health recovery.
- One of the key features of remaining well is learning as much as possible about the disorder and how to stay well.

Much can be done to help people make adjustments to the way they live in order to avoid severe episodes of depression or mania. Helping the client to learn more about the disorder and recovery is an important part of the role of the mental health nurse. The nurse can work in partnership with the client by empowering them to take charge of their lives. The amount of help needed will vary from client to client.

Bipolar disorder pervades many areas of a person's life. As such there can be no one solution or overreliance upon one form of treatment. There needs to be a comprehensive range of interventions and tactics that an individual and their family can draw upon to help them counter the impact of the disorder in different areas of their lives. Such an approach is often referred to as being holistic and it is important that the mental health nurse incorporates these aspects of recovery and does not become overreliant on a medical solution.

Some key areas of education include:

- relapse prevention and warning signs
- getting support
- medication management
- identifying and managing stress
- assertiveness

- healthy thinking
- healthy eating
- lifestyle issues (sleep, alcohol, fitness, activity and work)
- family support.

These areas are explored in detail in subsequent chapters. This chapter is about understanding the importance of the role of education and examining the sources.

As the client and their family come to know about the disorder it will help them overcome some of the mystery and their fears. It is healthy and natural to want to know as much as possible about a disorder in order to be able to make informed judgements about treatment options. Mental health professionals need to be objective in supporting clients. Many people are not easily convinced and hang to long-held beliefs. It may be that the health professional will have to help the client follow a path that they do not feel is the best one, as sometimes we need to experience a failure before we are convinced of the wisdom of a different course of action. Often too, despite their initial frustration, the mental health professional will be surprised to find that a certain course of action they were sceptical about actually worked and that the client was in the best position to make a judgement.

The supporter's role is one of pointing out possibilities to the bipolar person and their family/friends. Start by thinking about how much each of the people involved already knows. This initial knowledge is going to vary immensely from knowing nothing at all about the diagnosis to those who may have been involved with mental health matters for all their life.

Consideration point

Education is not just about introducing new ideas. It is often about helping people challenge false or outdated beliefs. For example: 'Manic depression is about being depressed in a manic way.'

- What common misconceptions can you think of in relation to mental illness in general?

Bipolar Disorder: A guide for mental health professionals, carers and those who live with it
© Pavilion Publishing (Brighton) Ltd 2012

Leaflets

Everyone is likely to struggle with reading when their mood is high or low or if they are in an anxious state. This means leaflets with few words are often a good starting point. The quality of information and quality of presentation varies greatly between leaflets from different sources. Sometimes the glossiest and most abundant leaflets are produced by commercial organisations. These are likely to be short on helpful information and biased towards their sponsor's point of view. For example, leaflets promoting the benefits of caffeine paid for by coffee/tea producers.

The best leaflets often come from national charities. MDF The Bipolar Organisation produces a range of leaflets on bipolar disorder. Most of the organisation's local groups will keep copies of them so it may be possible to read them there before obtaining particular ones for your clients. Other charities producing good leaflets include Rethink and Mind.

Books

Many books have been written about the disorder in recent years and the majority of them appear to supply some very useful information. The main types are:

- self-help
- personal accounts (some by celebrities)
- novels
- textbooks.

As with leaflets it may be detrimental to recommend those you have not read. Remember stressed people and those in low or high moods will often struggle to read more than a sentence at a time.

TV documentaries

In the two-part BBC documentary The Secret Life of the Manic Depressive, Stephen Fry was able to bring bipolar disorder to the attention of many people (Wilson, 2006). Although very much focused on celebrities, the programme goes a long way towards normalising the disorder and showing that many people who have experienced it go on to achieve a great deal.

Other documentaries about famous bipolar people (historical or contemporary) have included:

- Steward Goddard (who became the 1980s pop idol Adam Ant) (Moulson, 2004).
- Patty Duke (Cates, 1990).
- Vincent Van Gogh (Hutton, 2010).

When looking for documentaries to help bipolar people and their supporters you should also consider any that deal with stress, sleep, diet and ways of generally improving lifestyle.

Radio discussions

Where radio stations have a 'listen again' feature this can be useful when you hear something you feel will help clients or their supporters.

Websites

Most websites where bipolar disorder is discussed contain some useful information. Be cautious when using websites as all the information needs to be verified for its authenticity. It is worth considering that just because information is published by a large organisation it does not mean it is necessarily true. Some useful websites are listed at the end of the chapter.

Newsletters and e-zines

There are some good newsletters on bipolar/mood disorder. The challenges of finding the better ones and ones that are consistently good are perhaps even greater than finding good websites. This is also the case with e-zines where you can subscribe for free for information emailed to you on a regular basis.

Charities

All the main national mental health charities provide information on bipolar and depression on their websites and in leaflets. Currently, the only national charity specifically for bipolar disorder is MDF The Bipolar Organisation (formerly the Manic Depression Fellowship). Membership of this charity is inexpensive and something worth recommending to bipolar people and their supporters. The charity's magazine, *Pendulum*, has been published four times a year for more than 20 years. It is a good source of information on all matters about diagnosis, research, latest publications, locations of self-help groups and much more. Local groups of MDF will have back issues of *Pendulum* in their library.

Online forums

MDF The Bipolar Organisation has a forum which is available to members on the website (www.mdf.org.uk). One of the larger forums is on the international site www.bipolarsupport.org. See useful websites for others.

Self-help groups

There are over 100 local groups of MDF The Bipolar Organisation in England and Wales, with more in Scotland. Most cities have one or more groups. It is likely that the majority of UK citizens live within 10 miles of an MDF group. Most groups meet once a month. There are also local bipolar self-help groups that are loosely affiliated with MDF or may be completely separate from the main charity eg. 'Mood swings' groups based in Manchester and Chorley. (See further reading for details).

A local support group is likely to be a good place to pick up a lot of useful information quickly. You will be able to hear firsthand what is working and not working for bipolar people in your area. They are likely to have a library allowing you to flick through leaflets and books before deciding whether to buy your own copies and ask about membership and borrowing books.

In learning about bipolar it is important to listen to both experts by education and experts by experience. Where the information from these sources seems to differ there is a long and gradual process of weighing up which you believe to be more accurate. You will almost certainly need to pay attention to both types of information, realising both are likely to contain a lot of truth. It takes time to learn which information to use and when.

The phrase 'experts by experience' could be used to describe anyone who has had experiences and learned from them. Many, perhaps most bipolar people, are likely to feel they are experts on mood disorder based on what they have been through. This fits in with the philosophy of the MDF's Self Management Training Programme that says: *'People with manic depression can become the experts on their own mental health'*. Not everyone is able to tell their story to an audience whether on stage or in a book. For this reason meeting these experts in a workshop situation or one-to-one can be very useful in understanding what it is that they have learned and are keen to share.

Local/national conferences

Local conferences about mood disorders are rare but conferences about mental health in general occur in most regions from time to time. The MDF annual national conference gives a chance to hear experts speak, meet experts by experience, visit the bookstall and take part in workshops. A few of the past subjects for these workshops have been CBT, food and mood, photography, balance, creative writing and mood mapping.

Films

Not many people will immediately think of films when hoping to learn about mental health but films can be very useful. Films that show people coping well with mental illness or going on to great success can be educational and inspirational, such as A Beautiful Mind and Shine (see further reading). However, some popular films, driven by commercial need, may be anything but helpful and can sensationalise mental health issues and increase stigma through inaccurate portrayal.

Consideration point

For robust recovery education is essential and almost certainly requires lifelong learning.

Sir Francis Bacon said 'Knowledge is power!'.

■ Why might this quote be particularly relevant for nurses and for clients?

References

Cates G (Director) (1990) Call Me Anna: The Patty Duke Story. USA: Call Me Anna Company. (Actress Patty Duke portrays herself in this autobiographical film that details her long-time struggle with mental illness.)

Moulson J (Director) (2004) The Madness of Prince Charming. Manchester: Scarlet Television.

Hutton A (Director) (2010) Van Gogh: Painted with words. London: BBC.

Wilson R (Director) (2006) The Secret Life of the Manic Depressive. BBC Documentary: IWC Media. (A two-part television documentary directed by Ross Wilson and featuring British actor and comedian Stephen Fry. It explores the effects of living with bipolar disorder, based on the experiences of Fry, other celebrities and members of the public with, or affected by, the disorder)

Further resources

Books

Goddard S & Ant A (2007) Stand and Deliver: The autobiography. London: Pan Books.

Greive B (2001) The Blue Day Book. London: Robson Books.

Johnstone M (2009) Living with a Black Dog. London: Robinson Publishing.

Wooton T (2010) Bipolar in Order. San Francisco: Bipolar Advantage Publishers.

Film

Howard R (Director) (2002) *A Beautiful Mind*. Hollywood: Universal Pictures. (A film based on the life and schizophrenia of John Forbes Nash Jr – a Nobel Laureate in Economics.)

Hicks S (Director) (1997) *Shine*. Sydney: Australian Film Finance Corporation. (This is an Oscar-winning film inspired by the life of David Helfgott, an Australian concert pianist diagnosed with schizoaffective disorder.)

Useful factsheets and leaflets

Bipolar Affective Disorder by Royal College of Psychiatrists, Leaflets Dept, 17 Belgrave Square, London, SW1X 8PG tel: 0207 2352351 leaflets@rcpsych.ac.uk

Rethink's mental health shop leaflets: mhttp://www.rethink.org/mental_health_shop/factsheets_az.html

MDF The Bipolar Organisation factsheets: http://www.mdf.org.uk/?o=56959

Useful websites

Best content in bipolar disorder at http://groups.diigo.com/bipolar/bookmark A resource put together by the co-ordinator of the Cambridge bipolar self-help group.

Bipolar for All at www.bipolar4all.co.uk

Bipolar Happens at www.bipolarhappens.com.
A long running, US-based, email series from Julie Fast, author of Bipolar Happens.

Bipolar Recovery at www.bipolarrecovery.org
Email series and blog regarding recovery from bipolar disorder.

Channel 4 at
www.channel4.com/health

Mind at
www.mind.org.uk/help/diagnoses_and_conditions/bipolar_disorder_manic_depression

Mood Swings Network at www.moodswings.org.uk

NHS Clinical Knowledge Summaries at http://www.cks.nhs.uk/bipolar_disorder

National Institute of Mental Health at www.nimh.nih.gov/health/publications/bipolar-disorder

Rethink at
www.rethink.org/about_mental_illness/mental_illnesses_and_disorders/bipolar_disorder

Royal College of Psychiatrists at
http://www.rcpsych.ac.uk/mentalhealthinfo/problems/bipolardisorder/bipolardisorder.aspx

Chapter 21

Warning signs and relapse prevention

Key points

- The understanding of warning signs for depression and mania is essential for the prevention of relapse and promoting recovery.

- Relapse prevention also involves learning helpful strategies to allow appropriate responses to these signs.

Warning signs of impending relapse may be referred to as 'prodomes'. Most bipolar people are able to identify a range of signs that indicate to them and others they are becoming unwell (Smith & Tarrier, 1992). The recognition of early warning signs allows early intervention in the hope of preventing relapse. People can control the disorder by instigating their own relapse prevention strategy. They become empowered and can avoid the need for hospitalisation by adjusting their stresses, lives or medication accordingly. It is also invaluable for families and carers to be able to recognise signs that the bipolar person may not be aware of. When family recognise the warning signs they can make efforts to reduce stresses upon the patient.

Language

Contemporary thinking in relation to recovery suggests that clinical, medical and diagnostic language should be avoided (Copeland, 1997). For example 'prodomes' should be referred to as 'warning signs'.

Consider

- What alternative words or phrases can you think of for 'relapse' and 'symptoms'?

Reflection exercise: Triggers

Which of these might be triggers?

- Pressure and stress
- Lack of adherence to medication
- Work
- Family (too high expectations, pressure)
- Social factors
- Poor relationship with health professionals
- Unrealistic goals
- Not being involved in your own care
- Stigma

What are some other possible causes?

Self-monitoring by clients is crucial. Clinicians work with clients to help them identify warning signs and devise effective strategies for dealing with them before things become worse.

Most warning signs are likely to be seen within these broad categories:

- increased anxiety
- changes in energy level
- sleep disturbance
- changes in appetite
- changes in mood
- indications of unusually negative or unusually positive thinking such as gloomy or grandiose ideas.

Specific warning signs

Warning signs can be many and varied. For example:

- spending longer in bed
- talking too much
- stopping listening to music/stopping hobbies
- work deterioration
- poor concentration/attention span
- not doing the washing up
- increased/decreased sex drive
- worsening hygiene
- not changing clothes
- irritability.

Consider

- What else could you add?

It is useful to be able to distinguish between triggers and warning signs.

Trigger or warning sign?

It can be difficult for clients to see their lives in clear cut ways where one event is clearly leading to another. Life is often (maybe usually) too complex to always be able to see which things are triggers and which are warning signs.

For example, lack of sleep is a well known warning sign, yet a client may say that their lack of sleep is not a warning sign for them, but their number one trigger. Your focus will still be on understanding why they are not sleeping and helping them to overcome this.

A crucial part of recovery depends on the individual gaining understanding of their warning signs. Everyone will have their own unique set of personal warning signs for mood swings with some signs being far more significant than others. Some health professionals refer to this as their 'relapse signature'.

> ## Reflection exercise: Personal warning signs
>
> We all have a personal mix of warning signs for increasing pressure and the effects of stress.
>
> From your own experiences, create a list of your warning signs relating to mood changes. For example, what do you notice when you start to become more anxious, more motivated or your mood begins to lower?
>
> Looking at your own list, do you feel it will be unchanging through your adult life, or do you feel that with time your warning signs may change?

In group settings, the above exercise highlights that people often have similar warning signs. This can counteract the feeling of being strange or of being the only one. At the same time this exercise emphasises how different everyone is in their experiences of changes in mood.

Being able to distinguish between warning signs for low mood and those for high mood is very useful, although there can be changes in thoughts or behaviours that simply indicate that mood is changing without clearly indicating in which direction.

Having established that there are many warning signs it is important to appreciate which are the earlier and later signs. For most purposes a simple split between early and late signs is sufficient, although an appreciation for the intensity of these is useful. Looking at the mood scale in Table 21.2 it could be said that the further a warning sign is from experiences most people have on most days, the stronger the indication is of a significant mood swing. For example, 'slight withdrawal from social situations' is common for many people, while 'extreme paranoia' is far less common in our everyday lives.

The role of the recovery worker/carer is to help the bipolar person appreciate their own early warning signs and to help them start to recognise these as soon as they start to occur. Initially, early signs tend to be difficult to recognise. Often a person or their relatives can believe episodes just happen without warning. The reality is that in almost every case there are early warning signs. Unfortunately, sometimes it seems to be necessary to go through several episodes to become familiar with warning signs and triggers.

> ## Case study: Taking action on a warning sign
>
> Fran often became depressed for several weeks at a time. Fran and her mother said the depression always came on suddenly without warning. After a few meetings with the recovery worker Fran is able to say with certainty that the first thing she knows about each depression starting is that she wakes up and does not want to draw the curtains back or switch the light on. She agrees that this is one of her earliest warning signs.
>
> The ensuing discussion concludes that Fran should contact the recovery worker if ever this becomes a pattern. The recovery worker then explains that one way to avoid future depressions is to act on your earliest warning signs and this can mean doing the opposite of what you feel like doing. She tells Fran that the next time she wakes up feeling even the slightest bit down and not wanting to draw the curtains back, she must quickly draw the curtains back or switch the light on.
>
> **Consider**
>
> ■ How realistic are the above approaches?

Common areas in which warning signs are observed

Mood

Mood changes are an obvious warning sign and can be reported by the client or by those close to them. It is useful to reflect here upon the psychiatric terms 'mood' and 'affect'. 'Mood' is what the person feels and states, and 'affect' is what the person portrays. Thus someone could be quite depressed but appear relatively happy.

Anxiety

This is another key indicator that all is not well. Anxiety is a common accompaniment to depression. It can also be a trigger.

Sleep

Relatively small changes in sleep patterns are often one of the earliest warning signs. Responding to changes in sleep pattern and restoring sleep quantity and quality is an important factor for many people in averting episodes.

Eating habits

Mood is closely linked to food and even slight shifts in mood can result in changes in eating habits. This might be something as simple as a desire to drink more or stronger coffee, or perhaps for someone who regularly has tomato sauce with fish and chips not bothering to get it out of the cupboard. More generally a person who is depressed commonly loses their appetite, though in some cases they will overeat for comfort. A person becoming manic might start to eat foods that they don't usually eat. They can also become too busy to eat and begin to lose weight.

Withdrawal

This is common with a developing depression, but it cannot be ruled out as an early warning sign of high mood, particularly if the client has previously cut themselves off to focus on projects that then become part of a manic episode.

Tiredness/lethargy

One of the clearest indications of low energy is sleeping in the daytime. Coupled with other signs, this may well be a warning sign of depression. It will often be clear to family members and friends that the person has lost their usual spark.

Overhappy

This can be an awkward warning sign. After diagnosis and when others close to the person have some knowledge of bipolar disorder, every time the bipolar person smiles or laughs they can be jumped upon with: 'Are you sure you are alright? You're not going high again are you?' It is important to realise that there is no link between happiness and mania. Mania is not necessarily a happy experience.

Overenthusiasm/many plans/big ideas

These warning signs are associated with over-optimism. The belief behind these warning signs is that everything is going to work out right this time and however difficult or unrealistic the task, the bipolar person believes they will succeed. Often these will not be regarded as problematic to the person with the disorder but will be clear evidence to the family. However, do not forget that everyone needs to dream a little and sometimes have hopes beyond the norm.

Overspending

This affects many but not all bipolar people. As a warning sign this is likely to be a gradual increase in spending and so may go unnoticed until a surprisingly expensive or uncharacteristic purchase has been made. Those who overspend when in a high mood include those who make:

- many small purchases over a period of days or months, gradually going into debt
- a few outrageous purchases (often on credit/with money they do not have), such as an expensive holiday or a sports car.

Overactivity

Overactivity is seen in many of the above warning signs. Generally this refers to a person trying to do too much or trying to do too many things at once.

Talk of discomfort and pain

As the mood lowers people are more inclined to talk about aches and pains, however, later when in a very low mood people may stop talking about the pain they are in.

> ### Creativity as a warning sign
>
> Creativity can be difficult to spot unless you know the person. Maybe they are a writer, gardener, painter, potter, sculptor, singer, decorator, builder, model builder etc.
>
> **Consider**
>
> ■ Do increases in creativity always indicate higher mood, and does reduced creativity mean a lower mood?

Irritability

This is often cited as a key indicator of an encroaching manic episode as the person becomes increasingly irritated by those around them and unable to understand or agree with them. Can we see irritability? Family and friends are certainly likely to notice a shorter than usual temper.

Rapid speech

Changes in the speed of speech can be difficult to identify until you know a person fairly well. Initially it is going to be difficult to know whether this person naturally speaks fast. If someone is speaking so fast that it is difficult to understand them you may want to ask them to slow down. If, within a few moments, they are talking too fast again this may well be a warning sign of high mood.

Excessive speech/communication

As with rapid speech you may need an idea of what is normal for the individual before you can say what is abnormal. These days this excess is as likely to be on the phone, by email, on an internet forum, a blog or a social networking site.

Bipolar Disorder: A guide for mental health professionals, carers and those who live with it
© Pavilion Publishing (Brighton) Ltd 2012

A home visit

Liam has written in his private diary for years and in recent times has begun spending 30–60 minutes a day typing his latest thoughts in an anonymous blog. When you next visit his flat you notice that it is so untidy that it is difficult not to tread on the papers all over the floor. He says he cannot offer you coffee this time as he has been too busy to wash any cups. At first he is reluctant to share what it is he has been busy doing. Then he tells you that the diary and blog are taking so much longer each day and he loses track of time while being 'creative'.

While you wash a couple of cups and make drinks, he tells you more. 'Two weeks ago I decided to let some friends read my blog. They said it was amazing and persuaded me to open it up to anyone and put a link on their forum. Then things went crazy! I've got readers from Canada to Australia and most places in between!' Liam is so loud that you want to ask him to talk quieter but do not want to interrupt the story. He goes on, 'This is the biggest thing I have ever done. I bought in a whole load food to save time going out anywhere and I have just been so focused. I know I am supposed to sleep but talking to people in so many countries, there's only ever an hour or two between California logging off and my new mate in New Zealand asking questions about my latest work.'

You notice you are standing on a bill. 'Oh, that's OK', says Liam, 'It's only the gas. I'll wait 'til the red one comes through.'

Consider

- What warning signs can you see here?
- Many other communication channels might be used to excess such as email, Facebook and Twitter. Some of these can be open public forums. What dangers do they present, and how can exploitation and unwanted attention be avoided?

Appearance

This is probably the easiest warning sign for carers and it is often easy for clients to identify with. In the example of a man who normally shaves and then does not, this could be because his mood is higher and he is now too busy or in a lower mood and can't be bothered. Consider if a client normally dresses casually in clean clothes when you visit them at home and dresses smarter when they come to see you at your place of work. If they then come to an appointment in dirty scruffy clothes, there is clearly something going on, but is it a warning sign? Then you visit them at home and they are having breakfast in their best suit. We have to be careful here as everyone changes their appearance from time to time. Any small change in appearance could be a warning sign or could be an indication of a return to normal mood. It is usually very unwise to judge a person's mood on appearance alone.

Other warning signs

The following often appear in lists of warning signs.

- Poor concentration
- Loss of enjoyment
- Loss of/increase in libido
- Reduced physical health

- Negative thoughts
- Paranoia
- Suicidal ideas

Consider

- What would each of the above warning signs tell you about a person's mood?

Any kind of warning sign can be useful for your client when monitoring themselves. For signs to be useful for health professionals and carers, these must be signs that can be recognised. Reconsider the list in the above box. These are signs that many/most bipolar people will recognise, however, these are signs that are unlikely to be immediately obvious to the observer. Remember it is essential to know quickly about early warning signs if they are to be useful for controlling mood or avoiding future episodes.

Bipolar Disorder: A guide for mental health professionals, carers and those who live with it
© Pavilion Publishing (Brighton) Ltd 2012

Examples of warning signs

Tables 21.1 and 21.2 were created by a bipolar client on a recovery course. They are not exhaustive lists of warning signs. These were the signs the client was aware of during the course. In Table 21.2, the grouping 'waking up early', followed by 'can't get to sleep', followed by 'can hardly sleep at all' are common sequences but others will report early and late symptoms in different orders – once again remember that we are all different.

Table 21.1: Warning signs for depression

Earliest...	Later...	Later on...
Sleeping more	Dragging tiredness	Wanting to sleep all the time
Desire to drink alcohol		Bingeing
Slow on feet	Feeling extra tired	Not reacting
Talking less	Muttering to myself	Not talking at all
Feeling cold and unaware	More pain in shoulders, neck and back	Aches and pains inc. teeth
Moping/not believing	Desperation	
Wanting to be alone		
Body 'closing down'		
Thinking of same problem all the time		
I know that after a high I have a greater risk of depression		

Table 21.2: Warning signs for mania

Earliest...	Later...	Later on...
Waking up early	Can't get to sleep	Can hardly sleep at all
Not drinking the right stuff		Drinking the wrong things
More activity than usual	Not being able to sit still	Endless activity
Talking a lot	Talking loud	Rapid speech leaving others cold

Earliest...	Later...	Later on...
Teeth frequently clenched or grinding	Not feeling pain	Wanting to feel pain
Breathing fast	Jerky breathing	
Contacting people I do not normally see		
Easily provoked into having an argument		
More animated facial expression/hands		
Fear of annihilation of self		
I know that after a low – I have a greater risk of a high		

Mood charts

Mood charts can be enormously helpful in identifying early warning signs by keeping track of signs and responses to events. A numbered system, often called a mood scale, as shown below in Table 21.3, suits a lot of people, especially when a few other measures are recorded alongside the number. For example, hours slept and medication taken or a particular drink, food or incident that the client feels could be giving rise to mood changes.

Table 21.3: Example of a mood scale		
Comments		Some typical experiences during mood disorder
If experiencing several of these for some time this could be described as **mania**	10	no idea what is real believing you are someone else extreme paranoia inability to make even simple choices audio/visual/olfactory hallucinations
	9	speech too fast even for friends paranoia losing touch with reality money has no value at all most of your ideas are contrary to those around you hardly sleep (maybe less than 2hrs in 24hrs)

Comments		Some typical experiences during mood disorder
People can live in a state of **hypomania** for quite long periods with behaviours and beliefs like these	8	money means very little you know you are important talking louder or faster than those around you disregarding safety seeming to be thinking faster than those around you continue to start new projects but nothing being finished
	7	feeling very productive excessive spending able to charm friends and strangers talking a lot (such as longer phone calls) wanting to do more of everything
These experiences/ behaviours could be said to all be part of **'normal moods'** experienced at times by almost everyone	6	needing less sleep productive feeling good about oneself future looks bright enjoy meeting people fairly talkative decision making is easier than normal
	5	sleeping well, awake and functioning well throughout the day, life is OK, future looks OK
	4	sleep disrupted – perhaps wanting to sleep more not so keen on crowds concentration not so good a little agitated
Several of these for some time may indicate **moderate depression**	3	greater anxiety difficulty concentrating forgetting simple things prefer to do routine rather than new tasks
	2	desire to be alone nothing is easy, want to lie down a lot – whether able to sleep or not slow thinking some comfort in eating

Comments		Some typical experiences during mood disorder
If experiencing several of these for several weeks help may be needed to overcome **depression**	1	feeling worthless almost no hope wishing you had never been born suicidal thoughts hardly doing anything
	0	no hope at all not going anywhere or doing anything hardly thinking of anything but dying seems like things have always been bad seems like things will always be bad

Action plans

Action plans outline what a client wishes to be done in the event of warning signs emerging. They are usually worked out with the family and medical team in advance and include:

- personal coping strategies
- relaxation
- contacting key worker
- identify medication changes to be made
- what to do more of
- what to do less of
- what family and friends can do
- list of things they find helpful
- list of people they find helpful.

These will be explored in more detail in Chapter 30: Advanced statements.

Having looked at warning signs, the following chapters in this section are largely concerned with acting on them and the practicalities of what to do when signs are noticed and how someone can look after themself ie. relapse prevention.

References

Copeland ME (1997) *Wellness Recovery Action Plan*. Dummerston: Peach Publishers.

Smith JA & Tarrier N (1992) Prodomal symptoms in manic-depressive psychosis. *Social and Psychiatric Epidemiology* **27** 245–248.

Further reading

Shaw B (2009) *Wonderfully Strange*. Woodstock: Writersworld.

Stuart Goddard/Adam Ant (2006) *Stand and Deliver*. London: Pan.

Thomas J (2006) *Taking Leave*. London: Timewell Press Ltd.

Websites

Bipolar Recovery at http://www.bipolarrecovery.org/warning-signs/index.html

Copeland Centre at http://www.wraptraining.co.uk/pdf/values-and-ethics-copeland-center.pdf

Chapter 22

Support and networking

Key points

- Having a network of support is very helpful to someone who is in recovery from bipolar disorder.

- The greatest source of support for most people is their family, partners and friends.

- There are many other forms of support worth accessing.

Support

The level of support needed and how this support is offered will vary according to the phase/stage of the disorder as well as from individual to individual. Often mental health problems can reduce a person's social networks and this increases vulnerability to life's stresses. Emotional and psychological support is hugely important for recovery and it is helpful if such support comes from outside as well as inside the family. It is sometimes easier to speak to someone you do not know very well (or at all) and there is great comfort in sharing experiences with others. Meeting with others goes a long way to combat the sense of isolation that can be felt if no one else seems to really understand what it is like to live with a mood disorder.

What do we mean by support?

It is worth thinking about what is meant by support. It will mean different things to different people. It is important that individuals each have a clear idea of what they want when they say they want support.

Reflection exercise: Your support needs

Make a list of your own needs so that when you seek support you are fully aware of what it is you want.

Many national organisations will have good education and information departments. They may well also have local branches and many will run self-help or support groups locally. These will provide opportunities to meet with others in a trusting environment to share experiences, difficulties, coping strategies and tactics for self-management of the disorder and give each other encouragement. Such groups can also combat feelings of powerlessness and isolation while boosting confidence and self-esteem with members drawing strength from each others' experiences and insights.

Groups can be a safe place to vent feelings of frustration about treatments or anything else in life that is not right, with others who may understand these frustrations. Membership of self-help groups can also involve helping each other to feel more in control and overcoming the disorder. The opportunity to get involved and help others through your own experiences and skills is also therapeutic in its own right. Such contact and experiences can help the bipolar person to become more of an expert rather than being passive or a patient. The mental health nurse's role includes providing information about groups, including contact details. The nurse may also need to encourage and support the client's attendance.

Self-help groups are not for everyone. Many bipolar people can have times where they struggle with social situations. Those who have been in a patient role, not expecting to help themselves for many years, can struggle with the self-help concept. It is important for the mental health professional to be familiar with the venue and meeting time of any nearby groups so that they can pass this information onto clients and their families.

If the person you are supporting is not enthusiastic about visiting a self-help group you may wish to go along and see for yourself what happens at a meeting. Each group decides on its own format for meetings and whether/when special activities such as guest speakers are to be. In general, groups welcome visits from supporters and membership is open to all carers. As a mental health professional it is essential to tell the group co-ordinator in advance about your role, as there are likely to be confidentiality issues and some group members may prefer not to have health professionals present.

Bipolar Disorder: A guide for mental health professionals, carers and those who live with it
© Pavilion Publishing (Brighton) Ltd 2012

Many self-help groups organise activities that help the members with their recoveries. A popular activity is often walking as a group. This can be a huge benefit, helping with exercise, increased daylight and a chance to talk with others about the disorder or life in general. (Green, 2010)

Case study: Disillusioned

Bill has been on the committee of a local self-help group for a few years. Recently he has become disillusioned. He tells you: 'For most meetings one or two new faces turn up. They collect a few leaflets, tell us some of their troubles, say it is great to meet people like themselves and the meeting has done them the world of good. Then we never see or hear from them again.'

Consider

■ Why might it be that many seem to only want to attend once, even though Bill's group has a great atmosphere?

■ Can you think of anything you might say to Bill in response to him becoming disillusioned with self-help?

The case of the smiling depressive

When people are depressed the need for support is usually clear to staff, close family and close friends. However, the need for support may not be at all obvious to those who are slightly more removed. Family not at the same address may not be aware of the depression. Similarly, colleagues who ask if all is okay are likely to receive an automatic response of 'Yeah, fine'. The phenomena of the 'smiling depressive' can in this way reduce possible support. As Stephen Fry said in his documentary '*I may have looked happy. Inside I was hopelessly depressed*' (Wilson, 2006). Many potential supporters can be easily fooled by the slightest smile. They can see many warning signs of depression but disregard them because the client is smiling.

Why is networking part of mental health recovery?

The Rethink Recovery Narratives Project (Ajayi *et al*, 2009) is one of many projects to identify support as a fundamental theme in recovery (see reading list). The data and analysis involved in this project allowed researchers to further conclude that one of the 'mediators' underpinning the interviewees' recovery was the restoration of the balance between dependence, independence and interdependence.

Dependence is associated with one-way support. Typically, the dependent client is constantly looking for help and either unable or unwilling to help others. Traditionally, services have wanted clients to be more independent yet in doing so they can become more isolated, which can later be detrimental to their mental health. A challenge is to better understand the concept of interdependence and help clients develop this.

Dependence

'I can become dependent like a baby in four hours in a psychiatric setting … you have to be able to receive what is useful and to discard what is damaging'. Interviewee on Rethink Recovery Narratives Project (Ajayi *et al*, 2009)

Consider

In what ways do you think this rapid shift to dependency might be:

- useful for staff
- damaging for the client.

What might staff do to minimise this?

In the early stages of recovery clients become increasingly dependent on mental health services, family and friends. It is then seen as a good idea for them to become independent again. Greater independence is something to be encouraged, but caution is required.

During a manic phase the bipolar person may well have been acting extremely independently and not feeling any need for support. They could have been making numerous choices without listening to any advice. This extreme independence will have been part of the disorder/part of the problem. During a depressive phase the bipolar person may again have been acting independently by virtue of not feeling worthy of support, perhaps rejecting/rebuffing the support of others.

Reflection exercise: Support

How do we support people:

■ Who want to be independent?

■ Who do not believe that we understand their needs?

■ Who may consider they are coping alright even when their mood is drifting down or creeping up?

Can you see an argument against promoting independence here?

While independence is to be encouraged, many consider interdependence to be a healthy state for mood stability. This is a mindset where people can readily accept help while not desperately needing it. It is where we improve our self-esteem by helping and developing networks while not feeling we are totally dependent on them. This avoids the extra anxiety that can be created when others seem too dependent.

Networking is a good way of developing interdependence. Before encouraging networking it is important to understand the client's current network(s). Have they been able to maintain friendships with everyone they knew before their latest episode? Will they be returning to the same roles (paid work, voluntary work, social life…) and so be seeing the same people? Or has their episode caused them to change their routines? Are all their contacts local? Perhaps they sometimes travel a long way to visit relatives and friends? Do they network online and if so how important is this to your client? Without knowing a lot of this background information, it is possible to offer implausible suggestions and you risk alienating the client.

> ### Reflection exercise: Internet and social networking
>
> For clients who use the internet, consider the advantages of joining a social networking site.
>
> Could there be a healthy maximum number of regular online contacts?
>
> Are all relationships on social networking sites likely to be interdependent in terms of being mutually beneficial?
>
> Could their online contacts be more likely to understand their challenges than people they meet locally?

Socialising

> ### Consideration points
>
> Consider the following statements.
>
> - Depression is a symptom of underlying social problems.
> - We are a relationship-forming species – a highly social animal.

In their 7-Step Program for Overcoming Depression, Murray and Fortinberry (2004) suggest that learning to socialise again is the key to leaving depression behind.

As a starting point in understanding a client's view of who their supporters are and who they network with, they may be happy to draw a diagram with them at the centre and the names of their contacts around them (see Figure 22.1). The person may feel they have very few contacts, possibly having driven friends and even family away with their mood swings. They may need to be reminded of support such as their GP and other mental health workers.

Note: Most clients are likely to benefit from seeing their network in this way. However, for some this exercise can be distressing.

Figure 22.1: A social network

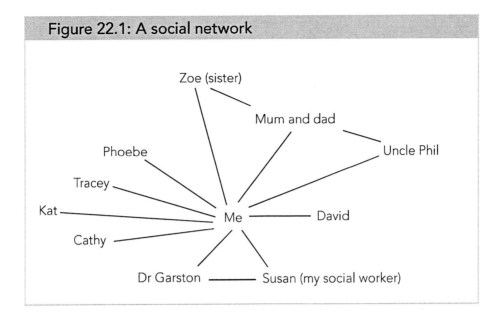

Practical support

It is probably true that everyone needs more than one type of supporter. One simple way to consider different types of supporters is that some will be good at communicating while others will be good with practical things. At different times in our lives we need different types of support. A client may be fortunate enough to have many friends and relatives who are happy to listen but they do not have anyone to turn to for help with the blocked sink!

Case study: Listening or practical?

When you visit Helena you find she is unusually tearful. As always, you listen to her over a cup of coffee. As you listen, you have a distinct feeling that she is not telling you the thing that is troubling her most. She is only talking about things you already know about and none of what she says seems to explain her low mood. She shows you her mood chart, which matches your view that she is moderately depressed. As you get up to leave she tells you that last week she hurt her back dragging her bed from one side of the room to the other.

You ask why and she tells you it was because the leak had started again and this time the drips were making the bedding wet and now she needs several buckets.

Consider

- Why do you think Helena did not mention her bad back earlier?
- Could the poor state of Helena's roof be her number one stressor at this time and be a big contribution to her low mood?
- Think about people you know. Do they have listening supporters or practical supporters?

National support groups

In addition to providing information and organising local groups, national organisations also act to lobby government on behalf of those with bipolar and hope to influence policy decisions through representing service users' views. They also help to raise public awareness about the disorder. Many such organisations also undertake and fund research. These same organisations benefit greatly from bipolar people who work efficiently during their periods of wellness. Is it possible that your client is passionate about making the world a better place and has skills these organisations need – perhaps with fundraising or research projects?

Organisations and support groups

Depression Alliance
Hearing Voices Network
Manic Depressive Fellowship
Rethink Local Carers Support Groups

Bipolar Disorder: A guide for mental health professionals, carers and those who live with it
© Pavilion Publishing (Brighton) Ltd 2012

Useful websites

Aware at www.aware.ie
Bipolar Scotland at www.bipolarscotland.org.uk
Depression Alliance at www.depressionalliance.org
Hearing Voices at http://www.hearing-voices.org/groups.html
MDF The Bipolar Organisation at www.mdf.org.uk
Sane at www.sane.org.uk
Shine at www.shineonline.ie

References

Ajayi S, Bowyer T, Hicks A, Larsen J, Mailey P, Sayers R & Smith R (2009) *Rethink Recovery Narratives Project Report 2009*. London: Rethink.

Green E (2010) Walking works wonders. *Pendulum* **26** (1) Spring 2010.

Murray B & Fortinberry A (2004) *Creating Optimism: A proven 7-step programme for overcoming depression*. New York: McGraw-Hill.

Wilson R (Director) (2006) *The Secret Life of the Manic Depressive*. BBC: IWC Media. (A two-part television documentary directed by Ross Wilson and featuring British actor and comedian Stephen Fry. It explores the effects of living with bipolar disorder, based on the experiences of Fry, other celebrities and members of the public with, or affected by, the disorder)

Further reading

Creating Optimism at www.creatingoptimism.com

See Me Scotland at www.seemescotland.org.uk

Chapter 23

Medication: the user's choice

Key points

- The role of medication is not just one of blind compliance.

- Professionals need to accept their client's individual perspectives and work in partnership.

- Self-monitoring for effectiveness and side effects is an important aspect of medicine management.

- Self-adjustment of medication is possible.

There are many different opinions regarding the effectiveness and value of medication in sustaining recovery. It is a personal consideration. The medical establishment will point to the dangers of relapse if the client stops complying with their medication regime. On the other hand, many clients will point out the relative inefficiency of much of the medication and its unpleasant side effects. However, as in many other aspects of life, it is wise to take into account a range of views and reach a compromise which suits an individual's circumstances and needs. Fink and Kraynak (2005) suggest that the options for a client are:

- accept professional help, medication and therapy and gain control of the disorder, and hence your life

- give trust to fate and risk losing your job, family, money and life.

These options could be considered to be simplistic as there are many variations and compromises between the two extremes which will work effectively for many people. It is natural to want to remain independent and resist medical intervention (or 'fly solo' as Fink and Kraynak put it), and often this is a necessary stage to go through on the way to making a decision that some sort of compromise is required.

A partnership approach

The goal, then, is a partnership approach to medication which is agreed by all concerned, with the client firmly in the driving seat. Working towards a 'self-managed' medication regime can be very liberating for the client, who traditionally will have been told exactly what to do and 'managed' by the medical establishment. Thankfully those days are long gone, though there are still pockets of outdated and paternalistic practice.

Question

What can a nurse do to give a client greater responsibility for their medication regime?

A first step is for clients to accept that medication is sometimes needed for their moods to stay within a range that is acceptable to them and those they are closest to.

Clients need to have an understanding of the purpose of each medication. Some clients will take several medications for years without ever questioning the types of medication. Some take an antipsychotic, a mood stabiliser and an antidepressant every day without paying attention to which is which or why such a cocktail might be necessary.

It is reasonable for clients to ask questions such as 'Am I taking this antipsychotic to lower my energy levels, or is it to help eliminate the overoptimism that has got me into trouble in the past?' It is also reasonable to try to find the answers to such questions, and knowing how medications are intended to work helps with effective self-monitoring.

Self-monitoring

The bipolar person can monitor their responses to medication. Both the effectiveness of the medication and the side effects can be recorded and charted. There are several rating scales that can be used, such as the Liverpool University Neuroleptic Side Effect Rating Scale (LUNSERS)

(Day *et al*, 1995). This is primarily for those using antipsychotic medication and cites a long list of possible side effects such as:

- rash
- drowsiness
- headaches
- poor concentration
- nausea
- weight gain
- reduced sex drive
- blurred vision
- shakiness
- bowel problems.

These are then rated according to how much they are experienced (not at all – very much) and degree of distress they cause (scaled from 1–10). Clients can draw up their own lists of the side effects they experience and find disturbing, and monitor the frequency and severity of them.

Self-adjustment

This refers to an agreed protocol whereby the client can adjust the dosages of their medication within certain parameters agreed mutually with the medical team. This allows the client to adjust their medication without seeking an appointment, giving them a larger degree of control over their treatment.

Lifestyle choices

There are many different side effects to psychiatric medication, as already explored. Occasionally these side effects are so severe that it becomes a real dilemma for the person. Weight gain is a common side effect and a very personal issue which can drive people to stop taking their medication. In circumstances such as these the nurse should help the person to explore, with their doctor, the possibility of alternative medications that produce fewer side effects. Side effects such as drowsiness can sometimes be overcome by altering the time the medication is taken. Other tactics which might help to alleviate the side effects are:

- moderately reducing the dose

- taking another medication to counteract the side effects

- drinking more water

- exercising more.

The dangers of feeling better

When a person begins to feel well they may start to question their need for medication. This is a danger point and stopping medication has caused many people to relapse. Maintenance of treatment needs to be discussed and attempts to see what life is like off medication need to be carefully planned and supported. There is an argument that psychiatric professionals can be too reluctant to take people off medication once they are being well maintained, but this is born of seeing many relapses when medication has been stopped.

Consideration point

- Should every patient have a carefully controlled drug-free holiday every few years if they request it?

Users' views: a wide range of opinions

The following case studies offer a selection of views on medication by people who have experience of bipolar.

Case study: The right to vary your dose

Terry has been taking an atypical antipsychotic every evening for five years. He has come to notice that when he takes it on Sunday–Thursday he wakes up with only the slightest headache and after a cup of tea he feels fully fit to drive the three miles to work. On Friday and Saturday nights he was taking the same dose but finding that he was waking up with a severe headache that would linger until mid-morning. Initially he thought this was due to drinking alcohol at the weekend, but after not drinking any alcohol for six months he has continued to record these headaches in his mood diary.

His wife has supported his decision to take half the normal dose on Friday and Saturday and this has solved the headache problem completely. They do not understand why this is true but to them it does not matter as eliminating the headaches has, in his wife's eyes, stabilised Terry's mood.

Consider

■ Is this something you would feel comfortable discussing with Terry's consultant?

■ Why might you not feel comfortable discussing this with Terry's consultant?

Case study: The desire to take less

James has been taking lithium for 22 years. He has had some relapses while taking his medication as prescribed and on one occasion he chose not to take his medication at all. He now accepts that medication is necessary but is concerned about long-term side effects.

Three months ago he decided to reduce his lithium to two tablets at night rather than the prescribed three tablets. A routine blood test showed he was below the 'therapeutic limit' and his psychiatrist asked to see him immediately.

James, who is as well as you have ever seen him, tells you that he attended with his girlfriend and the psychiatrist agreed with them that there were no obvious signs of mania or depression. However, James is furious because the psychiatrist is insisting he takes the full dose and did not respond to their concerns about side effects.

Consider

- How do you feel about either supporting the psychiatrist's view or accepting that after 22 years James may have gained a good understanding of his moods and the medications he feels he can tolerate?

Case study: A desire to keep taking the same medication

Jeanette tells you that two years ago she took an antidepressant from November to February, but within weeks of stopping it the depression returned until mid-summer. Last winter she took the same antidepressant 'to get through the dark months'. Yet her doctor insisted she try without in the spring and she had another bad depressive period.

With the clocks going back next weekend Jeanette wants your support in gaining a prescription that will allow her to have this particular antidepressant, which she says she 'gets on with' for a full six months. She thinks that because she does not leave the house or talk to the doctor during her worst depressions, her doctor does not appreciate how bad things have been for her during these last two years.

Consider

- Do you feel Jeanette's request is reasonable?
- Why might her doctor be reluctant to prescribe the same medication every winter?

Bipolar Disorder: A guide for mental health professionals, carers and those who live with it
© Pavilion Publishing (Brighton) Ltd 2012

Answer to question

What can a nurse do to give a patient greater responsibility for their medication regime?

- *Meet with the patient on a regular basis not just when things are going wrong.*
- *Form a good relationship and don't profess to be the expert.*
- *Get the patient to self monitor both side effects and effectiveness of the medication.*
- *Agree with the client and the team a protocol for the patient to self-adjust some aspects of their medication regime.*
- *Ensure the patient is invited to all meetings.*
- *Work together on lifestyle issues as well as medication.*
- *Remember that talk of reducing medication is usually healthier than talk of stopping a medication. Reducing medications by 'titrating-down' in tiny steps is usually far safer than sudden decreases and this is an option that patients who are dissatisfied with their medication should be reminded about. It is almost always appropriate to ask a patient if they have discussed small reductions in medication with the prescribing doctor.*

References

Day J, Wood G, Dewey M & Bentall R (1995) A self rating scale for measuring neuroleptic side-effects. *British Journal of Psychiatry* **166** 650–653

Fink C & Kraynak J (2005) *Bipolar Disorder For Dummies*. New Jersey: Wiley Publishing. (See Chapter 15 'Battling the Urge to Fly Solo'. This is an intelligent discussion of the issues regarding medication and the pros and cons of non compliance.)

Further reading

Bentall R (2009) *Doctoring the Mind*. London: Penguin Books.

Blackburn P (2011) Antipsychotic medicine and mental health. *Mental Health Today* July/August 25–27.

Lehmann P (1998) *Coming off Psychiatric Drugs*. Berlin: Peter Lehmann Publishing.

Manic Depressive Fellowship (2005) *Inside Out: A Guide to Self-Management of Manic Depression*. London: MDF – The Bipolar Organization. (See pages 15–16)

MIND (2007) *Coping with Coming off Psychiatric Drugs Guide*. London: Mind Publications.

Read J (2009) *Psychiatric Drugs: Key issues and service user perspectives*. Basingstoke: Palgrave Macmillan.

Wells A (2003) My right to choose. *Open Mind* **123** p13.

Chapter 24

Managing stress

Key points

- Stress is a major factor in influencing mood.
- Recovery involves learning to deal with stress and anxiety.
- There are a range of helpful coping mechanisms that can be tried.

What is stress?

Everyone has their own definition of stress. This can make it difficult to know where to start, even when clients are clearly experiencing a great deal of stress. It is good to start by clarifying the difference between pressure and stress.

'Stress is at the wrong end of a continuum that includes pressure–strain–stress.' (Mowbray, 2009)

'Stress is the adverse reaction people have to excessive pressure…' (Health and Safety Executive, 2008)

The word 'adverse' makes it clear there is no such thing as 'good stress'. Good stress, sometimes called 'eustress', is a myth (Bernstein, 2010). When managers fail to realise the difference between pressure and stress, employees start to experience stress-related illnesses.

Figure 24.1 shows the relationship between pressure and stress. As pressure increases so does performance, but eventually a point is reached where the pressure causes too much stress and performance drops off.

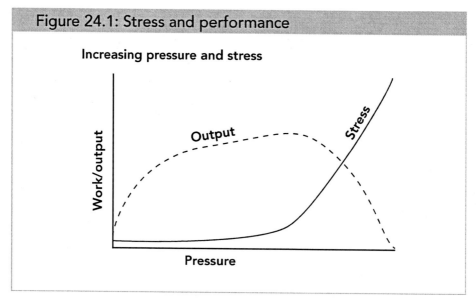

Figure 24.1: Stress and performance

Increasing pressure and stress

Work/output

Output

Stress

Pressure

It is often said that we do not feel stress but rather we feel the effects of stress. Each person will have a unique experience of stress so it is important to bear in mind that a client will experience stress in a different way to their supporter.

What is happening inside us?

Stress comes from the overactivation of the sympathetic branch of our central nervous system, which is responsible for the 'flight or fight' reaction. Stress initially increases the body's use of energy and also creates negative feelings and thoughts. This extra energy output and negativity generates the feeling of anxiety. Anxiety is the mood most closely associated with danger and as such it usually feels unpleasant. This unpleasantness gives us a desire to feel less anxious and so avoid further stress.

How stress influences mood

Stress can cause us to become more active, anxious or depressed. Stress always makes us less calm. The most common effect stress has on mood (by far) is increased anxiety. It is natural for people to be anxious from time to time. Anxiety is alertness and a feeling that we want to change our situation. However, prolonged anxiety takes its toll on the body.

Figure 24.2: Mood Map

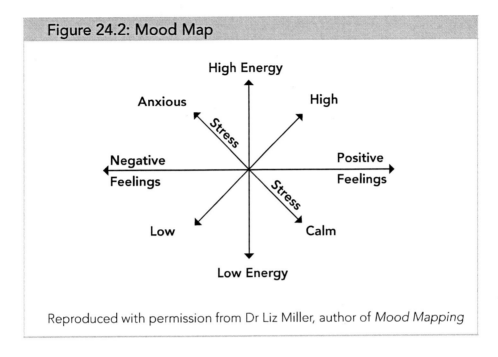

Reproduced with permission from Dr Liz Miller, author of *Mood Mapping*

With bipolar disorder, anxiety (perhaps described as worry or fear) can become disproportionate to the stressor(s) causing it. Anxiety then starts to interfere with everyday life and stress needs to be reduced to avoid illness.

Table 24.1: Warning signs of excess anxiety

Physical	Psychological	Behavioural/social
Dry mouth	Anxiety/worry	More/less sleep
Trembling, sweating	Anger	Indecision
Nausea, tiredness	Poor concentration	Making mistakes
Muscle tension	Fearfulness	Eating more or
Aches and pains	Confused thinking	Eating less
Headaches	Indecision	Argumentative
Indigestion	Negative thinking	Irrational
Palpitations	Gloomy thoughts	
Weight gain or loss		
Muscle twitches		

> ## Reflection exercise: Warning signs
>
> Some warning signs can be observed but the bipolar person may have to discuss the more hidden ones. In the table above there are some signs that are neither visible nor are likely to be talked about, even if asked about. An example is loss of sex drive. This may be a common effect of stress yet few people experiencing anxiety will mention it, but they may readily tell you about having a dry mouth, confused thinking or a lack of sleep.
>
> ■ Rearrange the signs in the three columns in Table 24.1 into one list. Put the signs you would most expect to see and hear about at the top list and those that are less obvious or less likely to be reported towards the bottom of the list.
> ■ Does anxiety affect you personally in ways not listed above?

Overcoming anxiety

It is good to start by understanding how the body responds to stress. On perceiving danger more adrenaline is produced, causing the heart to beat faster and the breathing to become shallower and faster. The mouth starts to dry and the skin pales as blood is diverted to the muscles needed for activity (flight or fight). Sweating increases and dizziness can occur due to a sudden change in blood oxygen levels. If all of the above happens in an extreme and sudden way it can be extremely unsettling, leading to a panic attack, which can feel like a heart attack. People may describe this as the worst experience imaginable.

For most people long-term anxiety is the bigger threat to physical and mental health. When everything mentioned above is occurring many times a day or is going on to some extent almost every minute of every day, the mind and body begin to suffer. Any number of the warning signs listed in the Table 24.1 may be happening.

When we consider anxiety as a mood we can actively do something to change our mood such as choosing a different way of thinking or behaving. People in control of their moods do this all the time, possibly unconsciously or consciously, using a well rehearsed technique (such as the relaxation techniques discussed later in the chapter). People with poor control of their moods either do not possess or fail to remember techniques they need when they are most anxious. Those who are unable to 'calm down' may have few other options as illustrated in the following examples.

Case study: When calm is not an option

'Things had gone terribly wrong and I was beginning to panic. The boss shouted at me to calm down and my heart started to beat so hard and fast that I was sure I could hear it. I was sweating like a pig and couldn't think what to do next. The boss told me to relax, which was the last thing I wanted to hear. I rushed out of the room knocking chairs over, ran down the corridor and out of the building. Half an hour later I was calm and apologised to everyone.'

Consider

■ Looking at the Mood Map in Figure 24.2, which mood did this person switch to when their anxiety became too extreme and they were unable to 'calm down'?

'The pressure had been building up for days. They were asking me to do more than was humanly possible. I wanted out of there but thought I would lose everything if I ever said, 'No'. I thought my anxiety was obvious to everyone but somehow they could not see I was at breaking point. Then it happened. I didn't say, 'No', in fact I didn't say anything. I just sat on the floor, covered my face and cried. I cried and cried with everyone looking on. Suddenly I didn't care what they thought. I no longer cared about anything.'

Consider

■ Looking at the Mood Map in Figure 24.2, which mood did this person switch to when their anxiety became too extreme and they were unable to become calmer about their situation?

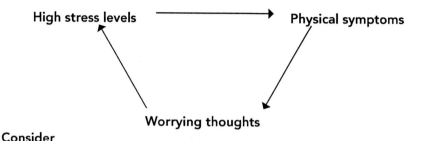

Figure 24.3: Stress trap

The mind's response: how thoughts increase anxiety

Misinterpretation of physical feelings makes matters worse and can set up a vicious cycle.

High stress levels   →   Physical symptoms

Worrying thoughts

Consider

■ Could you imagine that sometimes this process might work in reverse?

Anxiety and negative thinking

It is hard to say when anxiety is creating negative thoughts or when negative thoughts are creating anxiety. Anxiety is characterised by negative feelings and negative thinking. If we were feeling and thinking positively we would not be anxious.

Negative thinking is not always a bad thing. Without it we would be unable to see danger and would soon start to have accidents. Inappropriate and extreme on-going negative thinking is always problematic and can lead to the following traits:

■ jumping to conclusions...   'It will be awful.'

■ catastrophising...   'It will be the end of the world if I fail.'

■ self-doubt and self-criticism...   'I won't be able to cope.'

■ negative expectations...   'It will all go wrong.'

The language people use informs us of negative thinking and often the frequency of negative language informs us about how extreme and entrenched the negativity is likely to be.

Helping clients to exchange negative thinking for positive thinking helps them to move away from the extremes of anxiety and depression (see Chapter 26: Healthy thinking).

Avoiding stress

All stressors can be considered as avoidable or unavoidable. Stressors that could be described as avoidable include: reliance on alcohol and drugs, taking on too much, driving for too long without taking a break etc. Unavoidable stressors might include: a relative or close friend dying, an unavoidable accident, redundancy, Christmas and extreme cold weather etc. Be aware that people see stressors in different ways; what may be easily avoided for one person may not be the case for someone else.

For those experiencing anxiety, many everyday activities can become stressful.

Case study: Avoidance

Fiona has again been offered the chance to attend a self-management course for her bipolar disorder and although she has told you she wants to attend, she has now said that she will wait until next time. By patiently asking about all her reasons for not going, she tells you that she cannot travel by train due to panic attacks that she sometimes has when on crowded trains.

Consider

■ What might be the next steps for Fiona in 'getting her life back on track'?

Some stressors are best avoided while others need to be faced so that the stressor does not reinforce its power over us.

At times we all need to face our fears to overcome them. It is often possible to build resilience by allowing ourselves to be stressed. Even in the most stressful situations it is normal for anxiety to peak and fade. However, we need to take care if advising clients to face their fears and return to situations they have found unbearable in the past. You need to be sure that your client has appropriate coping techniques before they face their fears.

Case study: Nothing to fear but fear itself?

Conventional wisdom is that if we face our fears anxiety will begin to subside, which for some people can be good advice. This was not good advice for John who was told that he should not run away from his work colleagues when they taunted him. The next time this happened John stood his ground but his anxiety got the better of him and he lost his temper, drawing the attention of a manager who suspended him from work. Later, he explained to a friend this was almost exactly what happened last time he faced up to bullies and that was why he would walk away.

Consider

- What sort of help could John be given first if he wanted to control his flight or fight responses?

In order to help clients it is important to remember that their fears are based on past experiences and the power of these fears may be hard for others to imagine. Even with this in mind it is good to share the idea that when it is possible to tolerate stress it can be better to endure a stressful situation to see if the anxiety dissipates. This is very likely to be true if the stressor is the fear of the unknown.

Coping with stress

As we face up to stressful situations we need ways of coping. Everyone has a whole range of coping mechanisms already available to them, yet few of us will have been taught which coping strategies to use in which situations. Increasingly clients will be learning about ways of dealing with stress. However, when very anxious we have a tendency to use coping strategies that we learnt when we were much younger. Many of these built-in ways of coping give quick short-term relief rather than helping to build real resistance to stressors.

Case study: Bill

Bill says his biggest stressor comes from memories of his divorce, how his solicitor lied, and how he became homeless and spent six months on a psychiatric ward. He says these memories come back every time he is alone and it is quiet. He avoids this stressor by being with people or keeping the TV or radio on from early morning until late at night. When the memories come back he tells you that he copes by drinking all the alcohol in his flat. This used to get him into a lot of trouble. Now he says, 'I only keep a couple of bottles in now, then I have to go out to buy more and the walk to the off-licence seems to help at lot.'

Consider

■ Do you feel that Bill has reached a good compromise?
■ What alternative coping strategies might you suggest to Bill in case 'the bottle lets him down'?

Some ways of coping with stress

Welcome help	Nothing more, nothing less. Just accept it.
Talking	Talking with friends and family. Sharing problems and worries usually reduces stress. The support of good friends can be very helpful even when they just listen.
Sleep	Doing whatever is necessary to ensure a good night's sleep. It helps the body and mind to recuperate.
Exercise	Walking, walking the dog or volunteering to walk the neighbour's dog.
Gentle exercise such as yoga and tai chi	Aerobic exercise including swimming and dancing.

Exercising as part of a group	Exercise helps you to feel physically better and often more mentally alert. It uses up adrenalin and produces endorphins (natural painkillers) reducing anxiety, creating calmer feelings and helping you to sleep.
Animals	This could be stroking a pet, walking the dog or helping out at stables.
Slowing down	Try to take one thing at a time, walk slower, talk slower and avoid being rushed by others.
Relaxation and meditation	Many people find these very useful, when they find techniques that work for them. Some simple techniques are given later in this chapter. Suggest to clients that they explore local contacts to take this further. Aromatherapy and yoga are among the many techniques that can be tried.
Mindfulness	Being able to eliminate worries about things in the past that we cannot change and future events that may never happen reduces anxiety. (See websites in the reading list.)
Taking breaks	This can be as simple as remembering to have tea breaks and lunch breaks away from where you are most of the day. Taking time away from work or the home on holiday or with friends/family can be restorative making it easier to cope when returning. For some a 'change is as good as a rest' with time away relieving stress.
Time out	This is about making time for ourselves. It is important after recovery as a maintenance mechanism. This may include hobbies that take you away from your routine.

Writing	This may be writing lists and plans or just writing down your feelings in order to express them, which can be therapeutic in that you have discharged them rather than let them build up.
Planning	Planning and being sure what it is you would like to achieve is important. When anxious we can try to do too much and when we fail to complete our plans, become more anxious or become depressed. Consider how you might do less or work slower without upsetting those around you. Prioritise the things you have to do and remember that you can't do everything. Find out more about effective delegation.
Eating well and eating regularly	For some this is about sticking to a diet they believe in to help with stress, whereas for others it is about allowing themselves treats to get through stressful times. (See Chapter 27 – Food and mood)
Music	Listening to music can be a tremendous source of help, as can listening to a favourite programme on the radio.
Pampering	A long soak in a warm bath can be very relaxing. Some people find bubble bath and candles enhance this experience.
Assertiveness	This is an important aspect of recovery. (See Chapter 25 – Assertiveness)

And some things to have less of?

Drugs	Minimise your use of alcohol and caffeine. As a stimulant coffee is likely to make an anxious person more anxious. Do not cope by smoking more than normal – it is only a temporary relief.
Change	Big changes are a common cause of stress, as are too many small changes. Avoid changing too many things at once.
Ambition	It is important to have ambition although taking on too much and being too ambitious can itself be stressful. Be realistic in what you take on. When most anxious allow time not trying/pushing so hard.
Work	What is it about work that stresses you? What can you do to tackle specific issues? Can you adjust work so that it does not rule you? If financially possible it may be worth reducing hours, otherwise slow down and delegate more. Talk to your manager about alternative ways of working.
Stressful situations	Identify difficult situations in order to plan and rehearse what you might do or say to cope. Consider whether such situations be avoided completely.
Rumination	Do not dwell on the past – you cannot change it. Focus on things you can do something about.

Relaxation techniques

Slowing down the body using relaxation techniques can have a calming effect. Relaxation is a skill that can be learned. Initially it can help to practice at the same time each day. Regular use will give you mastery and allow you to do it where and when you need to, even in anxious situations so that you stay calm and in control.

One form of relaxation is called progressive muscle relaxation and works on the body's muscles from head to toe (or vice versa) by tensing and then relaxing muscles. Typically the muscles that are tensed and then relaxed are grouped as feet, legs, buttocks and abdomen, shoulders and neck, arms and fists, and the muscles of the head and face. An important part of this technique is noting the feeling of relaxation in these muscles as they relax, before moving on to the next part of the body.

Many relaxation CDs are available commercially. Some are set to calm music, many also ask the listener to visualise a pleasant environment such as a warm beach. You can use or adapt the following simple exercise. Once you are familiar with it you will be able to do it without having to re-read the instructions.

Relaxation exercise

Preparation

Choose a quiet room; a warm and comfortable place where you will not be disturbed. Dim the lights and put on some pleasant, soft instrumental music. Lie down or sit back in an armchair. Make yourself comfortable, and close your eyes and concentrate on your breathing. Breathe slowly and calmly. Concentrate on each breath as it goes out and as you slowly breathe back in. Count in, two, three and then out, two, three and say the word 'calm' each time you breathe out.

This exercise will go through the muscle groups in turn asking you to tense the muscles and hold that tension and feel it, then relax the tension and feel the tension flow out of the muscles. All the time you will breathe slowly and calmly, breathing in when you tense the muscles and out as you relax them.

Hands

Clench your fists tightly and feel the tightness and tension in your hand and forearm. Release the tension and feel it flow out along your fingers. Notice the difference between the tension and relaxation and feel any slight tingling in your fingers as the tension goes.

Arms

Bring your fists up to your shoulders and squeeze them tight to your body, hold this and feel the tension in your biceps, then relax.

Legs

Straighten your legs out tight in front of you, pointing your toes towards your head, feel the tension in your knees, toes and legs, hold and then relax.

Buttocks

Squeeze your buttocks together tightly, hold and relax.

Abdomen

Tense your tummy muscles and squash them tightly, hold and relax.

Shoulders

Shrug your shoulders up towards your ears and squash them inwards, hold and then relax.

Neck

Press your head as far back as it will go and feel the tightness in your neck. Hold, then relax.

Face

Frown as hard as you can, screw up your eyes, scrunch up your brow and purse your lips, hold and feel the tension all over your face, then relax.

Relaxation as part of a lifestyle

You may well find that the people you help to manage stress already know many relaxation techniques but are not using them regularly. When in a high mood, relaxation exercises can seem boring and when depressed it can be too much effort even to do breathing exercises.

'In my experience teaching the techniques is about one per cent of the challenge faced by the carer – the other 99% is working out how to persuade the bipolar person that the exercises are worth doing and continuing with.' Stress adviser

Consider

■ How could you make relaxation techniques more interesting so that clients practise between visits?

Meditation

Meditation exercise one

This simple exercise will take about 15 minutes and helps you to relax and clear your mind if you are beginning to worry too much. Use a room in which you will not get disturbed and sit comfortably; relax, lie back and close your eyes. Spend a few minutes getting comfortable. Breathe quietly and gently, in through the nose and out through the mouth. Let your attention focus on the breathing. Slow it down and relax.

- Begin to count your breaths from 1 to 10.
- 1 is the whole cycle of inhalation and exhalation.
- 2 is the next complete cycle.
- When you get to 10, start again and repeat.
- If you are distracted or lose count, start again.
- Do this for about 10 minutes.
- Next slowly focus on your body.
- Be aware of its weight.
- Open your eyes.
- Stretch and come back to full alertness.

Meditation exercise two

Lie down in a quiet darkened room and breathe slowly and calmly. Imagine you are lying on a soft warm beach. Imagine the sound of the waves lapping on the shore, a gentle breeze rustling some palm tree leaves, the warmth of the sun on your face, the feel of the sand on your skin and between your toes. Feel your body becoming heavier and heavier with each breath. As you breathe out, feel yourself sinking a little way into the warm sand.

Meditation exercise three

Examine one item and try and notice all of its minute details. Try to block out all other distractions and focus on the object. This exercise helps to distract you from worrying thoughts.

Breathing exercises

For people with bipolar disorder, being able to regain the ability to control breathing is considered to be particularly important (Straughan, 2009).

Stress brings with it certain physical responses; the heart rate increases, we sweat, breathing becomes more rapid and muscles tense up. These physical feelings add to the sense of panic and anxiety. It is possible to reverse this and slow down the heart rate to relax. This is achieved by slowing and deepening our breathing.

Focusing on your breathing

Breathe in and out slowly counting in 1, 2, 3 out 1, 2, 3 and so on. Concentrate on each breath and notice the air flowing in and the tension flowing out. Just concentrating on breathing and trying to cut out all other sensations is very relaxing.

Breathing and holding

It is easy to introduce pauses in our breathing. Breathe in and hold the breath for five seconds, then breathe out and hold breath for another five seconds. Continue to do this and your breathing will be slower and deeper.

Abdominal breathing

The idea is to breathe more deeply by breathing from the abdomen rather than the chest. Filling the lungs with more air will make you breathe more deeply and slow down your breathing. Breathe through your nose, slowly and deeply.

Place a hand on your chest and the other hand on your abdomen and breathe such that the hand on your abdomen rises higher than the one on your chest.

Fill your lungs to capacity and hold the breath for 6–7 seconds then slowly breathe out through the mouth for 6–7 seconds. Squeeze your abdomen muscles to help expel all the air. It is by expelling all the air from the lungs that we achieve the deepest breathing. Do this for about five minutes.

A simpler regime

Breathe in for three seconds, hold it for three seconds and then breathe out for five seconds. This is useful if you are in a public place as it can be done discreetly without anyone else noticing.

References

Bernstein A (2010) *The Myth of Stress*. London: Piatkus Books.

Health and Safety Executive (2008) *Working Together to Reduce Stress* [online]. Available at: http://www.hse.gov.uk/pubns/indg424.pdf (accessed November 2011).

Miller L (2009) *Mood Mapping: Plot your way to emotional health and happiness*. London: Rodale.

Mowbray D (2009) The prevention of stress at work. *Stress News* **21** (4).

Straughan H (2009) *In-Sight: A holistic approach to recovery training for people with bipolar disorder or depression*. Brighton: Pavilion.

Further reading

Cooper C, Cooper R & Eaker L (1988) *Living with Stress*. Harmondsworth: Penguin.

Ingham C (1993) *Panic Attacks*. London: Thorsons.

Jeffers S (1987) *Feel the Fear and Do it Anyway*. London: Vermilion.

Powell T & Enright J (1990) *Anxiety and Stress Management*. Oxford: Routledge. (This is comprehensive, well written and backed up with some typical case studies. It is also essentially a very practical book)

Useful websites

Australian National University at http://counselling.anu.edu.au/brochure/10-best-ever-anxiety-management-techniques

Be Mindful at http://www.bemindful.co.uk

Mind http://www.mind.org.uk/help/medical_and_alternative_care/mind_guide_to_relaxation

Mindfulness at http://www.mindfulness.com

Chapter 25

Assertiveness

Key points

- Learning to become more assertive can aid recovery.
- Being assertive improves self-esteem.
- Assertiveness skills need to be practised.

Assertiveness can be a great help in aiding recovery as being assertive improves a person's confidence and self-esteem. The more someone behaves in an unassertive way, the more they fail to get what they want, and the more other people take advantage, the worse they feel about themselves. The result can be that the person comes to see themself as being weak and this can cause their self-esteem and confidence to drop. A lot of energy can be wasted in trying to please everyone else. If you are assertive in your communications, people tend to respect your wishes and needs.

Being assertive is a way of behaving and communicating which avoids ambiguity and clearly states one's wishes. It is an honest communication which takes into account the views of others and avoids being aggressive or passive.

Being assertive will enable someone to:

- say no to unreasonable requests
- ask for what they want
- openly express they feelings
- express their views
- reclaim their self-esteem
- be happier.

> ## Case study: Why might bipolar people be less assertive than they need to be?
>
> Gillian had been one of the brighter girls at her school. When in an energetic mood, she would not only have her hand up first, but would shout out answers and want to give a rather too full explanation to questions put by teachers. Several teachers saw this as 'a bit too aggressive' and said other pupils 'were hardly getting a look in'. Some pupils felt the same way.
>
> Increasingly, Gillian was told to 'shut up' and to only speak when spoken to. This was exactly what she had been doing during her low energy phases. Teachers and friends found the low energy Gillian easier to get on with and gradually Gillian's communication style became very passive, with any assertiveness being seen as out of character.
>
> **Consider**
>
> There are many ways people can learn to be unassertive.
>
> ■ Can you think of an example where someone may gradually become more aggressive?

How to be assertive

First, it is necessary to recognise unassertive ways of communicating and behaving and to stop doing them. Next, is learning new assertiveness skills and putting them into practice.

Being unassertive means that people cannot defend their rights and they find it difficult to:

■ refuse requests

■ make requests

■ negotiate with others

■ return something to a shop

■ complain about bad service

Bipolar Disorder: A guide for mental health professionals, carers and those who live with it
© Pavilion Publishing (Brighton) Ltd 2012

- express anger or dissatisfaction
- stand up for themselves.

This unassertiveness manifests itself as passive behaviour in which people do not express their true feelings, rather they are overapologetic and allow others to get their own way. They skirt around the issue and even find it hard to talk clearly, possibly stuttering and mumbling and adopting a submissive, slouched posture. Common phrases used by those who are unassertive are *'I'm sorry to bother you, but....'* and *'I, err, wonder if you err, might.....'*. It is easy to refuse requests that lack conviction.

The ability to be assertive depends on our mood

Anxiety generates the flight or fight response. Flight, the feeling of wanting to escape danger, will generate passive responses. Fight, the feeling of wanting to challenge threats, will generate aggressive responses. For this reason assertiveness is closely linked to the ability to understand stressors and minimise anxieties (Lindenfield, 2001.

Whether we are seen as aggressive or passive is largely determined by our mood. When depressed we rarely challenge anyone or anything and so are seen as passive. When we are overactive we have the energy to challenge everyone and everything and this behaviour is often seen as aggressive.

It is easiest to be assertive when we are feeling positive and we are not too energetic. In other words we may be most assertive when we can remain fairly calm.

Assertive behaviours and tactics

- Eye contact should be firm but not staring.
- Do not fidget.
- Use a firm and steady voice.
- Stand tall and confident, don't slouch.
- Listen actively.

- Negotiate and be fair. Be prepared to listen to the opinions of others, discuss options and look for a win-win outcome. Assertiveness is not about someone getting their own way over and above everybody else, it is about finding an acceptable solution for both parties. You may have to adjust your request a little, without giving too much away.

- Anticipate when someone is likely to make an unreasonable demand on you or when assertiveness is most important.

- Be clear and concise. Spend some time in finding the right language and words you want to use. Be precise and specific about what it is you want. Keep to the point and do not beat around the bush.

- Rehearse what you will say and how you will say it. Practise saying it until you sound confident.

- Avoid or minimise excuses as these weaken your stance. If an explanation is necessary, keep it short.

- Stick to your decision. Use the broken record technique if necessary. 'What I was saying was...', 'I am still sure the best solution is...'

- Say 'I'. Make it personal... 'I think', 'I feel', 'I want'.

- Accept valid criticism. There is no point in denying it. Accepting will usually disarm an aggressive accuser and it is an opportunity to think about what you might want to change.

- Explore criticism. When a criticism does not make sense, feel able to ask for evidence or clarification.

Three stage response

Assertive responses can be seen as a three-stage process.

1. Express your feelings eg. 'I feel ...'

2. Identify what you disagree with/do not like, describe specific behaviours eg. 'when you ...'

3. State clearly what you need eg. 'I need you to ...'

Developing assertiveness will take time and practice, so trying to approach situations being faced as opportunities to try out these techniques may be beneficial.

Case study: Becoming assertive requires re-training and practice

Between bipolar episodes, Robert worked in a laboratory. He was regarded as a good worker because of his attention to detail and his willingness to focus on whatever work he was given. Robert found one of his co-workers, Maria, to be aggressive towards him and he was aware of his own passive behaviour whenever she was working in the same area. Several times after he had laid out the glassware he needed for the day, Maria simply helped herself to his beakers, flasks and funnels rather than walking to the far end of the building to get her own. The day after going on an assertiveness course Robert saw Maria taking something he needed and decided to assertively ask for it back. For a moment Maria was shocked then said that she did not take it. Although Robert was thinking, 'Be assertive', an argument soon developed. Their manager called them into his office and said he did not care who started it, the incident would be recorded in their files. The manager said, 'Robert, it is not like you to cause a fuss. Are you taking all your medication?'

Consider

- How do you think Robert felt immediately after this incident?
- Do you think that confronting the bully, with unpractised assertiveness skills, worked out well for Robert in the longer term?

When providing assertiveness training we may need to make suggestions about appropriate times and people to try out new skills. It takes time to learn balance and avoid jumping from passive to aggressive.

References

Lindenfield G (2001) *Assert Yourself: Simple steps to getting what you want* (3rd edition). London: Thorsons.

Further reading

Powell T (2009) *The Mental Health Handbook: A cognitive behavioural approach* (3rd edition). Milton Keynes: Speechmark Publishing.

Websites

Assertiveness Skills: The Art of Saying No at www.assertiveness.org.uk

Mind at http://www.mind.org.uk/help/treatments/how_to_assert_yourself

Chapter 26

Healthy thinking

Key points

■ Depression and anxiety distort how someone thinks.

■ Learning to think more positively can help to overcome low self-esteem.

■ Simple cognitive behavioural techniques are useful in combating the negative thoughts that often accompany depression and anxiety.

Mood depends on energy levels and on how we feel, while being able to moderate our mood depends on being able to think in the right way. We can describe 'thinking in the right way' as healthy thinking. To be able to think healthily we need to be in a reasonably healthy state physically and emotionally, which makes this a good time to remember that a holistic approach is needed in managing stress and maintaining good health.

What is healthy thinking?

Healthy thinking can involve any or all of the following:

■ being able to take on new ideas

■ thinking logically

■ being able to reason

■ seeing more than one side to an argument

■ being able to move on when an argument is futile

■ the ability to plan ahead

■ having plenty of positive thoughts, yet not too many

■ being able to rationalise negative thoughts.

Unhealthy thinking

Unhealthy thinking could simply be said to be a lack of, or imbalance in, any of the above. Often unhealthy thinking is described as various habitual traits or thinking distortions that hinder healthy thinking. The following list is adapted from McKay *et al* (1981). People with bipolar disorder can have a few or even nearly all of these with the severity of each relating to their moods or their circumstances.

Table 26.1: Thinking distortions

Being right	Being wrong is unimaginable and one will do anything to prove one is right, even when everyone seems to be disagreeing.
Believing in universal rules	Frequent use of 'must', 'should' and 'ought' indicate rules learnt early in life. This can increase anxiety as people feel they need to conform to these rigid 'rules'.
Blaming others	Others are responsible for one's problems. 'It's your fault, don't blame me.'
Blaming self	Believing one is responsible for everything that goes wrong and is totally responsible for one's own problems including any mood disorder.
Catastrophising 1	Referring to small setbacks in life as disasters eg. spilling a drink and saying, 'What a disaster!'
Catastrophising 2	Expecting a real disaster to strike at any moment.
Changing others	Believing one can change anyone's mind to fit in with your plans.
Comparing	Comparing oneself to others too often/too much.
Control fallacy	Believing one is responsible for just about everything.
Emotional reasoning	Believing what one feels is fact. 'I feel stupid therefore I am stupid.'
Filtering	Magnifying negative details while filtering out positives.
Overgeneralisation	Coming to a general conclusion based on a single piece of evidence/incident.
Perfectionism	Needing to be perfect and if not perfect then this is failure.

Personalisation	Thinking one is at the centre of everything that is going on.
Pessimism	Something bad happens once then expecting it to happen again and again.
Polarised	Seeing everything as good/bad, right/wrong, only black or white with no middle ground.
Reward fallacy	Making many sacrifices/being prepared to be bullied in the belief that there will be a reward sometime in the future. Possibly then feeling bad when there is no reward.
Victim fallacy	Believing one is helpless – simply a victim in every way.

More about thinking distortions

Poor self-opinion

When we compare ourselves with people we consider to be admired and successful we can form a low self-opinion. Depression exaggerates the distortion with everyone seeming to be more successful, attractive and capable than us and we can then denigrate all our efforts. In mania a person feels they are admired and successful and that others are barely worthy of their time.

Self-criticism

All bad events are due to our own shortcomings and ineptitude. This becomes a vicious spiral where low self-opinion leads us to expect and demand perfection from ourselves. Our unrealistic expectations set up a spiral of defeat. We blame ourselves for the non-attainment of unachievable goals and so believe that we are useless. In mania a high opinion of the self and our abilities renders us more likely to be critical of others who cannot see or share our visions.

Negative interpretations

Everything is interpreted in a negative way. A person only sees weaknesses and ignores any positives or strengths. In mania only the positive is seen and we are sure that all our schemes will flourish and nothing can get in the way.

Negative expectations

A belief that a person's current problems will last forever – failure is expected. The present is hopeless and the future is futile. There is no point in trying to do anything because you will fail. In mania you will succeed – there is no doubt.

Overwhelming responsibility

The feeling that you can't possibly cope and the things that you can normally cope with become enormous mountains. Physical anxiety is experienced when you try to do anything. The world is on your shoulders. In mania nothing is too much – there is nothing you cannot do or turn your hand to. You may feel no responsibility for others and just want to pursue your goals unhindered.

All or nothing

You generalise and have sweeping, all embracing thoughts such as 'I'm hopeless'. There is no middle ground. This is extreme black and white thinking where ideas such as 'Everything is useless'. In mania, 'I'm totally brilliant' can become fixed in the mind.

Catastrophising

This is caused by exaggeration, where all is doomed. Small difficulties become disasters; everything will go wrong. You overestimate failure and underestimate your ability to cope. In mania, the opposite is the case, nothing can possibly go wrong. All is wonderful.

Bipolar Disorder: A guide for mental health professionals, carers and those who live with it
© Pavilion Publishing (Brighton) Ltd 2012

Personalising

You take responsibility, blaming yourself for anything and everything. Things that have little to do with you or do not normally bother you are focused on; they are your fault and you interpret innocuous comments as put downs. In mania it can seem that it is all down to you but it is all brilliant.

Jumping to conclusions

These are negative conclusions whatever the facts, and despite the facts you predict gloom; you believe you will make a mess of it. In mania the conclusion is bound to be positive, you will succeed where others have failed.

Note: In the above nine examples, 'in mania' refers to the optimistic mania rather than mania involving high levels of anxiety.

Cognitive therapy

Cognitive therapies help with recognition of thinking styles, positive and negative thoughts and regaining healthy thinking.

Cognitive behaviour therapy (CBT) for depression

This is a way of combating 'errors' of thinking and the evidence suggests that it is helpful in preventing a relapse (Davidson & Blackburn, 1990). The bulk of today's CBT derives from the work of Beck who developed it in relation to depression and anxiety (Beck *et al*, 1979). There have been numerous books outlining its use. A key principle in CBT is helping people to realise that our interpretation of what is happening often (perhaps usually) has a greater impact on mood than the events themselves.

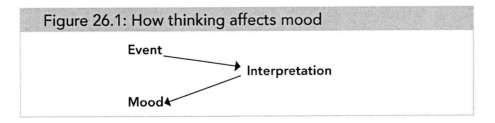

Figure 26.1: How thinking affects mood

Cognitive behaviour therapy hinges on the fact that errors in thinking are caused by and perpetuate negative feelings. Such feelings cause us to jump to wrong conclusions which seem to confirm our misery. For example, you are walking down the street and you see a friend who completely ignores you. Your negative thinking causes you to believe he has turned against you and rejected you and your opinion that you are not worth bothering about is enhanced: 'nobody likes me, I'm worthless'. Later, you see him and he apologises, explaining that he was preoccupied and didn't even see you.

The cognitive therapist works with the depressed or anxious person to test the validity of their thoughts by applying reason and logic. The client hopefully becomes aware of the link between the negative feelings and the unreasonable negative thoughts, and hence mood. Negative thoughts are often errors of judgement, caused by the negative feelings, but which rapidly become self-fulfilling prophecies. In the depths of depression this can become a vicious spiral into which you sink deeper and deeper.

The crux of cognitive therapy is:

- recognise distorted thoughts
- replace thoughts with more realistic thinking.

Clients are asked to think about and write down negative thoughts and identify the thinking distortions they are using. They are asked to challenge them and to write down alternative explanations.

Questions

CBT depends on clients having a level of healthy thinking such that they can take on new ideas and challenge false ideas.

1. Why might CBT be less effective if used for patients while experiencing severe depression?
2. Give reasons why CBT might be more effective/less effective if used by clients at home who are hypomanic?

In extreme depression it is very difficult to believe in anything other than a doomed outlook on the future, total futility and that you are completely worthless. These negative thoughts mainly arise because of the depression and have no basis in truth. Beliefs such as these lock you into a depressive world view. These negative thoughts have to be challenged and replaced with more realistic and more positive views. Re-emergence of negative thoughts can be a key early warning sign.

In bipolar disorder there is also the possibility of the re-emergence of overoptimistic thoughts and as is the case with depression, these need to be recognised, challenged and replaced by more realistic views. Such overoptimistic thoughts can be challenged in the same way by considering the possible consequences and trying to formulate more realistic views.

Reflection exercise: Thought distortion

I'm not good enough	It's all because of me
I have nothing useful to say	I can't live without her
Everybody loves me	I am worthless, totally useless
Nothing can go wrong	Nothing can hold me back
Nobody likes me	This will be the best thing ever
There is no point in trying	They are so much better than me
I should be the prime minister	I'll never cope, it's all too much

- Read the statements and identify the types of distortion.
- Write down more realistic interpretations of what these people may be facing.

Thinking distortion in mania

An additional thinking distortion seen in mania is grandiose thinking. This certainly exists as clients often seem to have ambitions that far exceed their capabilities. There is a significant risk of damaging recovery here, as a feature of a grandiose idea is that the client does not see it as grandiose. They may well appreciate that it is 'grand', but in their elevated state it will seem perfectly realistic and well within their capabilities. If in mild hypomania, they may even be progressing nicely with their plan, thus reinforcing their view that it is do-able.

Describing their idea as grandiose may:

- bring them to their senses

- simply be shrugged off as others have probably already told them to be more realistic
- accidentally spur them on, with an enhanced view that their work is worthwhile, challenging, amazing and exactly what the whole world is waiting for.

If the third option happens this could increase the hypomania and possibly increase the likelihood of a manic episode. Although, in a few cases, being told 'you are being grandiose' has spurred bipolar people onto greater achievements than anyone thought possible (Copeland, 1997).

Delusions

Occasionally, distorted thinking reaches delusional proportions in both mania and depression.

Mania example
Mind reading and starting to believe one instinctively knows (with no evidence/explanation) what others are feeling and why they do what they do.

Depression example
Hypochondriacal ideas – believing that small pains indicate severe illnesses even though there is no evidence.

Consider

- What other examples of delusion beliefs can you identify for mania and for depression?
- How would you apply cognitive therapy to such beliefs?

Practice

It is a good idea to keep a diary to record negative thoughts and substituting more realistic explanations. It is important also to try to examine the consequences of the distorted thought and come up with a positive action.

Depression example

Distorted thought: I'll never be able to succeed
Negative action: I don't try, so no chance of success
Rational thought: There is a good chance of success
Rational action: I give it a go and it works

Mania example

Distorted thought: This project can't fail
Negative action: I go ahead and it fails
Rational thought: This project could fail
Rational action: Plan; discuss with partner; we succeed

Defence mechanisms

Defence mechanisms can be unconscious (or sometimes conscious) methods of coping with stress. Using these 'tricks' to avoid confronting problems can be an aspect of unhealthy thinking. It is a form of avoidance. The recognition of defence mechanisms enables us to consider how we are using them and whether we could tackle the problem in a healthier way than avoiding it. Defence mechanisms can include the following.

Suppression
Putting feelings or impulses out of mind. Example: *Not thinking about a loss.*

Denial
The reality is so painful that its existence is denied. Example: *The belief that a loved one has not died or the alcoholic who believes they are a social drinker.*

Displacement
Anger directed at an unconnected person or object. Example: *You have a bad day at work so you argue with your teenage child.*

Intellectualisation
Ignoring the emotional content of a situation and thinking about it in a cold, factual way. Example: *Paramedics frequently do this.*

Projection

Putting the blame on to someone else. Example: *An aggressor accusing his victim of being aggressive.*

Rationalisation

Finding an acceptable explanation for something you feel is unacceptable. Example: *I'll quit smoking after the exams.*

Regression

Reverting to less mature behaviour. Example: *Becoming aggressive when things do not go our way.*

Repression

Keeping painful or guilty thoughts out of mind in the unconscious. Example: *Having no memory for a traumatic event.*

Reaction-formation

Doing the opposite of what you feel or think. Example: *A driver who uses a mobile phone yet campaigns for harsher driving penalties.*

Sublimation

Diverting your aggression onto something more acceptable. Example: *Taking up boxing instead of fighting at football games.*

Consideration points

- Think about how much these defence mechanisms can protect us from feeling bad about ourselves and how often they can lead to later problems.
- Look at the thinking distortions listed in Table 26.1. Note which ones appear to be associated with depression and which are associated with mania.
- Now see if you can describe the exact opposite and say whether you would expect this in the opposite mood.
- You may find that the list of 'Some more thinking distortions' will help with considering opposites.

Bipolar Disorder: A guide for mental health professionals, carers and those who live with it
© Pavilion Publishing (Brighton) Ltd 2012

Answer to questions

1. **Why might CBT be less effective if used for patients while experiencing severe depression?**

In the depths of a depression the person has no motivation to engage with therapy and has little energy for anything. The client is thus both unwilling and incapable of engaging with CBT, which demands a certain level of thinking ability, which is absent in a deep depression.

Even when they are getting better and coming out of the depression, it may just not be right for that client. Many depressed people do not respond to CBT and other remedies must be sought.

When a client's depression is due to poor diet it will continue to be difficult to think positively until the diet is improved. For example, low levels of many vitamins lead to depression that is only reversible when vitamin levels are corrected.

After a CBT session some clients will talk about 'not getting on with' the therapist. This contrasts with patients who make exceptionally rapid recoveries when working with a therapist and telling friends 'I can tell this therapist is really listening to me'. This may or may not reflect on the therapist's skills as the quality of this connection is likely to be mainly influenced by personality

2. **Give reasons why CBT might be more effective/less effective if used by clients at home who are hypomanic?**

The hypomanic client can be capable of taking to new ideas with huge enthusiasm and with an insight into the need to take control of their moods, they may quickly start to use new ideas to improve their health. Conversely, the therapist may have great difficulty as a hypomanic client may have such a short attention span, with so much else on their mind and so much to say in response to each idea that progress can be frustratingly slow.

References

Beck A, Rush A, Shaw B & Emery G (1979) *Cognitive Therapy of Depression: A treatment manual*. New York: Guilford Press.

Copeland ME (1997) *Wellness Recovery Action Plan*. Dummerston: Peach Publishers.

Davidson K & Blackburn I (1990) *Cognitive Therapy for Depression and Anxiety* (2nd edition). Oxford: Blackwell Science.

McKay M, Davis M & Fanning P (1981) *Thoughts and Feelings*. California: New Harbinger.

Further reading

Beck A & Greenberg R (1974) *Coping with Depression*. New York: Institute for Rational Living. (Cognitive therapy is attributed largely to Beck and this is one of the original articles).

Blackburn I & Davidson K (1990) *Cognitive Therapy for Depression and Anxiety* (2nd edition). Oxford: Blackwell Science. (See Chapter 2 for an overview of the cognitive therapy model and an examination of the claims of its efficacy)

Powell T (2009) *The Mental Health Handbook: A cognitive behavioural approach* (3rd edition). Milton Keynes: Speechmark Publishing.

Chapter 27

Food and mood

Key points

- Mood influences what we eat.
- Food has as a large impact on mood.
- An awareness of what affects us as individuals is important for recovery.

Mood affecting diet

Why do we eat?

A common answer for why we eat is that it is all to do with nutrition. This is largely true, but on the other hand, most decisions about food are made according to the way we feel. What we eat, when we eat, who we eat with, how quickly we eat and so on are all determined by our feelings, which are directly linked to our mood. We eat when we feel hungry, when we feel like a quick bite, when we feel like something crunchy or sweet. Some will choose foods based on nutritional properties, but even these choices are based on feelings to a degree.

Reflection exercise: Food feelings

Discuss and list your feelings about food. List the factors which determine when you eat, what you eat and how much you eat.

What factors affect our choice?

In a country where food is readily available and relatively cheap it is not necessary to spend long consciously thinking about what to eat. These days we often have no contact with the raw ingredients used in many of our meals. Busy lifestyles mean that supermarkets, fast food outlets, ready meals and snacks from vending machines can separate us from ingredients. Feelings and choices about food are also influenced greatly by packaging and advertising.

Some reasons why people choose particular foods

People choose foods for a variety of reasons. It could be that it is: clean, organic, fresh, colourful, tasty, spicy, hot, cold, smooth, juicy, substantial, warming, crunchy, brittle, bitter, sour, high in protein, high in fibre, low in fat, to calm the stomach, to avoid constipation, it contains vitamins or minerals, it is cheap, expensive, exotic, recommended by a friend, advertised on TV, nostalgic, slimming, calming, sweet and so on.

Consideration points

Read the above list and imagine which ideas a bipolar person would be able to relate to:

■ when in a depressed state
■ when in a high state.

For some there may be a steady continuation from not having the energy or interest to eat anything when totally depressed through to eating anything and not caring what those foods might be when manic. It is probably rarely this simple. The only certainty is that food preferences will vary according to mood. Sometimes food choices may be influenced in unexpected ways by paranoid thoughts that might reach extremes during a manic episode. Sometimes an occasional comfort food or a favourite meal such as fish and chips will be eaten frequently and so cut down healthy variations in day-to-day diet.

Diet affecting mood

Different views

- Some people accept that certain foods affect their mood and on some occasions take this into account when making food choices.

- A lot of people give little thought to how their moods are being influenced by food. For these people the idea of studying food and mood can seem unnecessary because they do not feel affected.

- Other people's moods are extremely and rapidly affected. These people need to make careful selections every time they eat. Consider children (and their parents!) who are hyperactive after eating certain food colourings.

Some ways in which food may affect mood

Direct chemical effects: These include the immediate effects of stimulants such as caffeine and the depressant alcohol.

Appearance: Just looking at food can raise or lower the mood depending on memories associated with that type of food. For example, a bland, basic meal may bring memories of hospital. Similarly, an appealing plate of food can cheer us up.

Aroma: The smell of fresh foods or cooking is likely to be good for most people's mood, but sometimes a food smell can remind us of unpleasant times when that smell was in the air, such as the distinctive smell of school meals. Many people who have been manic report a heightened sense of smell during an episode. This could lead to a more intense recall of feelings associated with certain smells.

Taste: An enjoyable meal or tasty snack can improve mood, although it can be difficult to prove the link with taste as our enjoyment depends on so many other factors, such as who you are with and where you are at the time. People often turn to comfort foods to improve their mood.

Feeling of fullness: Eating the right amount is good for mood. When moderately depressed or hypomanic, under-eating or overeating are likely to be more common. The resulting discomfort can make the mood swing worse.

Indigestion: Not a good thing to get when already feeling low.

Excess eating: In hypomania people tend to lose weight or simply remain thin, however, medications that reduce mania tend to cause great hunger with the possibility of rapid weight gain. Some antidepressants are also associated with weight gain.

Weight gain: Many bipolar people on medication tend to be overweight (or at least consider themself to be overweight). Often they are only slightly overweight but the psychological effects can be great if prior to diagnosis and medication they had always been lean and athletic. The rapid change (possibly in less than a month) of their self-perception from fit to extremely unfit can be devastating and can be part of the low following on from a major high.

Poor nutrition: When mood instability continues for many months or years, health problems from poor nutrition are likely. These could be physical health problems ranging from minor ailments to diabetes. Poor nutrition can also lead to further mental health problems and may well exacerbate the mood disorder.

Reflection exercise

In understanding mood swings and helping bipolar people it is important to recognise that short-term and long-term effects both need to be taken into account.

Read through the above list again and discuss which effects might be short-term or long-term.

Types of food that affect mood

Each type of food has the potential to affect mood and people will be affected in different ways. The result is that we are unlikely to meet two people with an identical set of food/mood reactions. To understand a client's food and mood reactions it is important to spend time with them, considering some of the typical effects of food components that are well known for altering mood.

The most talked about mood-altering food components tend to be alcohol, caffeine, chocolate, artificial food colourings and sugars.

Table 27.1: Reactions to food		
Food type	Typical and less typical reactions	Timing
Alcohol	The taste and social aspects of drinking can initially make the mood more positive and increase our confidence, which most people find a pleasurable experience. Ultimately though, after several drinks the alcohol acts as a depressant. Long-term alcohol dependence is strongly linked with depression.	Depressant effect can begin after only a few drinks.
Caffeine (typical)	Increases energy, but may cause a lower mood overall as any initial boost wears off. Some claim the small caffeine content in chocolate is enough to keep them awake.	Raises mood almost instantly – craving for more caffeine may be after just a couple of hours. Probably only relevant if eating late in the evening.
Caffeine (less typical)	For those with ADHD tendencies, caffeine is frequently said to have the reverse effect, calming the mood.	Many people with ADHD claim caffeine acts like Ritalin, making them less active.

Food type	Typical and less typical reactions	Timing
Chocolate	Calms and gives a secure feeling. Improves mood. Can temporarily alleviate depression. For some it helps to sooth anxiety and hence bring mood down into normal range.	Often instantaneous, as mood can be linked to the taste of chocolate as well as to its unique chemical constitution.
	Weight gain, damaged teeth – concern about self-image.	Months – it is of course rare that one food type will be responsible for such effects.
Sugars	Can cause rapid changes in energy. 'Sugar-sensitive' individuals have stronger cravings for sugar and refined carbohydrate. (DesMaisons, 1999)	Simple sugars are quickly digested. For those affected the cycle is just a few hours.
Artificial colours	Extreme reactions are: lots of energy, racing thoughts, a need to do something/anything, a desperate feeling that things are not right. (Hanssen, 1984)	In some children the reaction can be very rapid. In adults the reaction is likely to be a few hours after consuming the highly coloured food.

Some of the food and mood choices discussed in self-help groups

Complex carbohydrates and fibre

This idea is related to the possibility that excessive sugar is bad. Sugar is digested very quickly and causes blood glucose and insulin levels to fluctuate. Complex carbohydrates (essentially sugars in a form that can only be digested slowly) allow glucose to be released steadily into the blood throughout the day. When mood is significantly affected by glucose levels, reducing the intake of simple sugars and increasing the intake of complex carbohydrate is likely to stabilise the mood throughout the day. In turn this can lead to a more stable mood in the longer term. A major advantage of this approach to diet is that it is approved of by almost every nutritionist in the world as a means to improving physical health. This improvement to general health will almost certainly help with mental health in the longer term.

Essential fatty acids

Fats are especially important for young people while their brain develops and they continue to be important for the ongoing maintenance of the adult brain. Fat is transported as soluble fatty acids in the blood. The brain needs very specific fatty acids that cannot be manufactured by the body and makes us reliant on our diet to supply them. If these fatty acids are not in our diet we can develop emotional sensitivity, undue anxiety and disturbed sleep–wake cycles (Yehuda, 2003). The fatty acids most needed by the brain are often referred to as omega-3. There is strong evidence that low levels of omega-3 lead to mood swings (Watts, 2008).

A well-balanced diet will probably supply sufficient omega-3 fatty acids. However, in recent decades diets in many countries (including the UK) have changed to include more fat, most of which is devoid of omega-3. Sources of omega-3 include oily sea fish, walnuts, linseed and watercress. Many bipolar people report an improvement in mood stability by taking omega-3 supplements. An American Psychiatric Association review of evidence on the benefits of omega-3 for mental health recommended that those with 'psychotic disorders' take 1g per day (Freeman *et al*, 2006).

Habits and social considerations

There are few things we do as habitually as choosing what to eat. When we decide to make changes to our diet in order to lose weight or eat more healthily, once we start to lose weight, feel better or sleep better we often find ourselves giving in to old habits. Relapse can also be due to social pressure from those we live and eat with, the places where we eat or because our culture reinforces certain ideas about food through advertising and the placement of goods in supermarkets.

To overcome cultural influences bipolar people may appreciate help, such as:

■ reassurance that the diet that they have chosen is keeping them well and is not in any way abnormal

■ simple tips such as making a shopping list rather than buying on impulse

■ discussing diet with other people in the household; it is likely that others will have not thought about the food and mood experience in the way that the bipolar individual has

■ if alcohol is a problem then having alcoholic drinks in the house may be too much of a temptation

■ for a habitual coffee drinker who wants to stay off caffeine the smell of coffee can be very difficult to resist; others in a household should be aware of this

■ introduce the person to others who have made similar lifestyle choices.

Consideration points

■ How realistic is it to persuade other members of a household to adjust their diet, including when and where they eat and drink?

■ What possible strategies are there for staying off caffeine after the initial addiction has been broken?

Dieting to lose weight

Body weight and body image influence how we feel about ourselves and our mood. If weight is not lost or gained during a diet it is likely to depress a person's mood, which could be a significant risk if they already have a low mood. Frequent dieting to lose weight and then putting weight back on ('yo-yo dieting') is also likely to contribute to mood swings. More permanent changes to diet that give gradual weight loss and steadier weight are likely to help decrease mood swing risks (DesMaisons, 1999).

It is what you believe!

As mentioned previously, when it comes to food and mood what we *believe* counts for a great deal, and often more than what is scientifically proven. If a bipolar person says that consuming a particular food or avoiding a food keeps their mood steady, then there is almost certainly some truth in it. They know how they feel and probably have their own explanation as to why this choice is effective. Noticing these choices and listening to any explanations will be useful. It could be that you can help to ensure the person gets the foods they need.

References

DesMaisons K (1999) *Potatoes not Prozac*. London: Simon & Schuster.

Freeman MP, Hibbeln JR, Wisner KL, Davies JM, Mischoulon D, Peet M, Keck PE, Marangell LB, Richardson AJ, Lake J & Stoll AL (2006) Omega-3 fatty Acids: evidence basis for treatment and future research in psychiatry. *Journal of Clinical Psychiatry* **67** (12) 1954–1967.

Hanssen M & Marsden J (1904) *E for Additives: The complete 'e' number guide*. Wellingborough: Thorsons Publishers.

Watts M (2008) *Nutrition and Mental Health: A handbook*. Brighton: Pavilion.

Yehuda S (2003) Omega-6/omega-3 ratio and brain-related functions. *World Review of Nutrition and Diet* **92** 37–56.

Further reading

Geary A (2001) *The Food and Mood Handbook*. London: Thorsons.

Glenfield M (1999) *Natural Alternatives to Dieting*. London: Kyle Books.

Holford P (1997) *The Optimum Nutrition Bible*. London: Piatkus.

Useful websites

ADD and ADHD Treatments at http://www.add-adhd-treatments.com/Caffeine.html

Black Dog Institute at http://www.blackdoginstitute.org.au/public/bipolardisorder/bipolardisorderexplained/maniahypomaniadefined.cfm

Chapter 28

Lifestyle choices

Key points

- Some of the stressors which can cause relapse are avoidable.
- Many stressors can be modified by lifestyle changes.
- Getting a good balance between activity and rest is an important factor in alleviating stress.

People with ongoing mood problems can have lifestyles that fail to avoid or cope with stressors that other people deal with or see as avoidable.

Consideration points

Consider whether the following stressors are avoidable or unavoidable.

- A parent with a serious illness
- Facing the possibility of redundancy
- Working late or taking on too much work
- The car keeps breaking down
- Spending all night on the computer
- Agreeing to look after your friend's dog for a month
- Having mounting debts

Reflection exercise: Stressors

Would all of the above be stressors for you?

- Consider which of the above are unavoidable and which are avoidable.
- Think of another six unavoidable stressors and another six avoidable stressors.
- Compare your answers to other people's and explore the reasons for your differences.

When our mental health is good most stressors seem avoidable and we make reasonable efforts to avoid those which cause the most problems. For example, if spending all evening on the computer is causing problems, a person with good mental health will think of ways to change their computer usage. For continuing recovery and improvements to well-being it is useful to review areas of life that might seem unconnected with the disorder such as diet, sleep, work, pastimes, finances and relationships. (Diet and relationships are examined in their own chapters). In this chapter the focus is largely upon activity and rest and getting this balance right. Managing these aspects helps people to stay well and recognise how, if left unmanaged, they could contribute to relapse.

Activity

Many bipolar people lead busy lives and are well aware of doing too much while recognising their lack of assertiveness and poor delegation skills. Rather than simply confirming the need for better time management skills they may need help in re-examining their activity levels and creating more realistic plans. Career, home maintenance, car ownership, gardening, children, parents, pets, hobbies etc. can take up all a person's time. Sometimes people need to drop some responsibilities or tasks in order to allow themselves more 'me' time or just time to rest. If people feel that their lives are too full and that they never have time to relax, they need to think about what exactly it is that they do in order to look at where they might cut down. It might help to chart this over a week and write down all that is done each day in a notebook. Checking at the end of the week can reveal what can be cut out or delegated to somebody else. This simple exercise might be quite revealing as we often do much more than we think and there is often much that we do not really need to do.

Another aspect of activity is to ensure that we have time to do those things which we treasure. This can be many different things such as family time or socialising with friends and others, the need to pursue a long-held hobby or sport, for some it is a blend of all of these and more. The answer is often not to overdo it and to learn to sacrifice that which is held in low esteem for that which gives more satisfaction. Chores will still need to be done but can be put aside in favour of a night out or a favourite walk. It may be that we need better time management. A good start is to have a timetable. It could be a written one or, for example, simply ensuring every Tuesday night is free for socialising and Fridays are free for the running club.

It is of course important to keep time for maintaining relationships with friends who are a source of support but it may be worth reappraising these relationships and taking stock of those which are helpful and those which are disrupting mood. The former being encouraged and the latter gradually lost.

A hobby may not necessarily be relaxing and might unwittingly be stressful in a way you do not recognise. Remember that it is important to have time to do nothing, just sitting watching television, reading a book or the papers, or taking a long soak in the bath. It is good to have time for recuperation, doing little physically and mentally can 'recharge your batteries'.

The importance of exercise

It is easy to slip into a 'lazy cycle' where the less we do, the less we feel like doing. This can then cause us to feel worse and do even less, and so on, until we fall into a lethargy trap. Increasing exercise can help us feel less tired as well as less guilty about resting. When exercise becomes part of an established routine it helps with general health and mood stability. Exercise also releases endorphins, which are the body's natural relaxants, and gives a feeling of well-being.

It's not what you do but how you do it!

Data on the comparative effects of recreation and housework suggest that quality of time, and not mere energy expenditure, must be taken into account in attempts to explain the psychological benefits of physical activity (Stephens, 1988).

It seems that even the most moderate exercise can be very beneficial when compared with no exercise at all. Many people say that exercise as simple as walking to a local shop helps enormously with steadying the mood. Beyond this, a lifestyle that includes more vigorous walking, cycling, running or swimming for about 30 minutes every day is likely to be useful both physically and mentally. It can also help with meeting people regularly, increase time in the fresh air/daylight and help to control body weight.

Rest and sleep

Lack of sleep is characteristic of hypomania. Those who have experienced mania talk about a complete breakdown of sleep patterns leading up to episodes. Sleeping too much (or too little) can bring on lethargy and low moods. Understanding and achieving appropriate rest and sleep is essential if we are to improve mood stability. The following advice is often helpful.

Having a regular and adequate sleep pattern is crucial. Bipolar people often believe that they thrive by staying up late or being up early. This is usually not helpful. There may be times when individuals are especially creative and focused during the night, but usually this is draining and not a good long-term plan. If we are up very early or going to bed very late, we need to be aware of whether this is helping or hindering our wellness. Being out of synch with society can help us to be creative and achieve more but it can take a toll in the longer term and needs to be monitored. Some action is usually needed if there is a continuing drift towards ever earlier waking or later bedtimes.

■ A routine of getting up at the same time everyday and going to bed at the same time every night with only minor alterations for nights out and the odd lazy weekend sleep-in helps most people.

■ Daytime naps are best avoided because they can lead to less sleep at night. However, when we are so tired that we cannot keep our eyes open, a daytime nap can be the best and safest option. An alarm set so as not to sleep for too long can be useful.

■ Try to make the hour before bed a relaxing one by starting to wind down. Perhaps by watching TV or reading. This usually helps take the mind off worrying thoughts which might keep us awake.

■ Relaxation CDs or music often help with sleep.

- A warm bath can be relaxing.

- Drinking stimulants such as tea, coffee and cola before bedtime can keep you awake. Similarly, do not have a big meal before going to bed as this will often make it harder to sleep. If particular foods keep you awake, avoid eating these in the evening.

- Avoid smoking before going to bed as this also acts as a stimulant.

- Exercise can be a stimulant. If this is the case for an individual they could do their vigorous exercising earlier in the day.

- Most medications for bipolar disorder cause a lowering of energy after each dose. This can come on in minutes or after an hour or so. Being aware of how medication affects sleep is important. Often medications prescribed to be taken in the morning and which cause some drowsiness can be taken in the evening. As with all medication issues it is essential to talk to the doctor or psychiatrist before making any change. It is important to remember that medications which help with sleep are only a short-term solution and can be addictive.

- It is worth trying herbal teas such as camomile or valerian as many people find these helpful.

- Using relaxation techniques will also help with sleep, as will breathing exercises. Linking these to imagined, peaceful scenarios can help to eliminate worrying thoughts.

- Be aware that trying too hard to sleep can keep you awake. If you are unable to sleep just try laying with your eyes closed as this calm and rest can be valuable. If unable to settle, some people benefit from staying up until they feel sleepy.

Case studies: Links between exercise and sleep

In trying to help people control activity levels it is important to be aware that mania consists of a combination of high physical activity and high mental activity. Using a lot of energy does not make people manic. In fact having a lot of 'pent up energy' is far more likely to lead to a range of mood problems.

Consider the following examples for people who have bipolar diagnoses.

Steve is a professional football player. An injury means it will be three months before he can play again. He tells you his sleep is rapidly deteriorating.

Julie cycles five miles to work six days a week and swims on Sundays. With recent family troubles she tells you: 'I cannot switch my brain off. I just lie awake worrying.'

Ahmed describes himself as an academic and is proud of his PhD and research post. He believes his sleep problems are entirely due to excitement, saying 'I hardly go outside because I am on the phone with colleagues 24/7. The final submission of my work is next week. It has to be word perfect. This is a fantastic opportunity for me. It has to be right.'

- Which of these bipolar people is likely to benefit from more exercise, and what types of exercise might you want to discuss with them?
- For whom do you think extra exercise would be of little benefit and which options for improving sleep would you most want to discuss with them?

Diet

Diet is covered in detail in Chapter 27: Food and mood but it is important to mention it here in relation to overall lifestyle. Depression can lead to overeating as well as a loss of appetite as people turn to food for comfort in much the same way as some people turn to alcohol. The resultant increase in body weight and size due to overeating will serve only to depress the individual further and give them a weight problem to add to their burdens. The path to recovery is a combination of healthy eating, exercise and medication control, as medication can also have an adverse affect upon weight and subsequent body image.

Employment

Most people cannot afford to give up work and so it can be a major area of stress. The transition back to work and the support of an employer is often very important in recovery. Apart from the money, work also provides security, to a degree, and this fact in itself can make life less stressful. For those lucky enough to enjoy their jobs, work also provides a great deal of satisfaction and self-esteem.

Part of the health professional's role can be to help the bipolar person to negotiate with their employer.

- The transition back to work needs to be carefully managed so as not to put the person under too much strain too soon. This can be achieved by negotiating clear boundaries about roles and in planning a gradual reintroduction to work such as working up from one day a week to a full week. Under the Disability Discrimination Act (2005) employers must make reasonable adjustments in accordance with the employee's needs.

- Involving the employer in a relapse prevention plan.

- It might be necessary to negotiate time off for support meetings and therapy. Health professionals can help with this especially when employers lack understanding.

- It may be possible to negotiate an alternative role or position within the company which is less stressful.

- It is also useful to discuss and plan what to tell work colleagues.

To disclose or not to disclose

Whether to disclose a diagnosis to an employer – given the history of stigma surrounding mental illness – is a difficult decision. On the plus side, it can be a relief not to have to keep it a secret and it may open doors to support and help that you did not know existed. The negative side is that a person could become regarded as a risk to the company and become marginalised. Future promotion prospects may be lost and colleagues could shun you.

Consider

- What can be done to avoid a negative scenario?
- What can be done if the negative scenario becomes a reality?

It might also be possible to consider changing jobs or working part-time. A change is as good as a rest, especially if a job causes too much stress and is not enjoyable. Going part-time may be much less stressful than working full-time. However both of these are major changes and should not be tackled too soon after an acute episode.

Voluntary work

If unemployed, it is important to have things to do and ideally have meaningful daytime activities. An empty day is an invitation for boredom and depression to creep in. It might be worth considering the possibility of voluntary work in such areas as community, social or conservation work. This can be a great source of social contact and give self-esteem a boost. It will also provide a routine. Voluntary work can vary from the informal to the formal whereby a commitment is made to undertake regular hours and this can also help in the transition to paid employment. Exploring the possibility of further education is also useful as this can provide structure and increase social networks.

Drugs and alcohol

Drugs and alcohol are frequently used as coping mechanisms by many, including those with mood swings. For some they act as a temporary relief but for many people the gradual build up of reliance leads to dependency and further problems. There is also the risk of adverse interactions with drugs taken on prescription.

If dependency occurs a local support group can be very useful in offering support to reduce drug reliance and explore other means of coping. If abstinence does not seem like an option, drug-free days may be a way to limit intake. The number of drug-free days may be gradually increased. Substituting the alcohol or drug for another pleasure can be effective. It is sometimes better to gradually cut down and succeed than try to give up completely and fail. It helps to avoid other drug users as well as situations and places that lead to drug use. It is important to use the support that is available, be prepared to admit to having an alcohol or drug problem and seek professional help.

Case study: A drink problem

Jeff used to run the village shop. Since the shop closed he has been spending more time at the only place where villagers regularly meet – the pub. Jeff is well aware that his medication is less effective when he drinks alcohol and his drinking often causes him to relapse into depressive states. He has tried drinking soft drinks and non-alcoholic beer, but tells you that the guys at the pub do not understand and that he would rather drink the same as they do.

Consider

■ How could you help Jeff explore alternative lifestyle choices?

Finances

If a person is unemployed or on a very low income it can be useful for them to be referred to a social worker for a financial assessment to check out that they are receiving their full benefit entitlement.

If a person has debts they can be referred for debt counselling and helped to work on a plan to eliminate the debts. Once debt free, the person should be advised to stop using credit cards or get strict limits set on them which cannot be exceeded.

If excessive spending has been a problem in the past then having someone the person trusts to look after bank cards may avoid generating new debts.

References

Department of Health (2005) *Disability Discrimination Act 2005*. London: HMSO. Available at http://www.legislation.gov.uk/ukpga/2005/13/contents

Stephens T (1988) Physical activity and mental health in the United States and Canada: evidence from four population surveys. *Preventive Medicine* **17** (1) 35–47

Further reading

Fink C & Kraynak J (2005) *Bipolar Disorder for Dummies*. Indiana: Wiley Publishing. (See Chapter 13: Restructuring your life.)

MDF (2008) *Manic Depression/Bipolar affective disorder*. London: MDF The Bipolar Organisation.

MDF (1995) *Inside Out: A guide to self-management of manic depression*. London: MDF The Bipolar Organisation.

Raglin JS (1990) Exercise and mental health: beneficial and detrimental effects. *Sports Medicine* **9** (6) 323–329.

Straughan HJ (2009) *In-Sight: A holistic approach to recovery training for people with bipolar disorder or depression*. Brighton: Pavilion Publishing.

Chapter 29

Dealing with stigma

Key points

- Many people still consider those who have mental health problems to be dangerous or helpless.

- Stigma is arguably the largest barrier to real social inclusion and thus recovery from mental illness.

- A large part of the health professional's role is helping to combat such stigma.

Mental illness continues to be portrayed negatively in the media, although in recent years this has improved with some hopeful and more positive storylines in TV soaps and films. Bipolar disorder, in particular, has been fortunate in recent years to have had celebrities admitting to having the diagnosis or simply saying they are 'a bit bipolar'. This has helped to normalise the disorder so that fewer people are shocked when they hear that a friend or colleague has the diagnosis. Unfortunately, stigma remains firmly embedded and may take a long time to overcome. Much of the prejudice that still exists ignores the nature or extent of the mental health problem and is unfortunately largely maintained by media reporting (Rethink, 2009).

Case study: Prejudice

Yes, they did attack me physically! While my mental health had been good my neighbours accepted me, even though I was the only foreigner in the block. It was when things went wrong and I had to own up to having a diagnosis that the trouble started. All of a sudden they did not want me there. It was recorded as racial violence, but I do not think that was right. They were OK with the colour of my skin until they found out about me seeing a psychiatrist.

> **Consider**
>
> ■ This incident happened a few years ago. Do you think this is likely to happen today?

For people with bipolar disorder stigma is often something they are very aware of but struggle to explain how and where it is happening. This may in part be because prejudice is often covert and subtle.

Box 29.1 Stigma: the facts

Many research reports have identified the impact of stigma on those with mental health problems. These findings show that:

■ 87% of those with mental health problems have been affected by stigma

■ those with mental health problems have a lower rate of employment than any other 'disabled group'

■ less than 40% of employers would employ a person with a history of mental health problems

■ a third of those with mental health problems report having been dismissed or forced to resign from their job because of discrimination

■ 70% are put off applying for jobs

■ 20% of the public think that those with a history of mental illness should not hold public office

■ 36% of the public think that those with mental health problems will be violent

■ one in eight people say they would not want to live next door to someone with mental health problems

■ 60% of the public describe someone with mental health problems as needing to be kept in a psychiatric hospital

■ a third of the public believe that those with mental health problems should not have the same rights to a job as everyone else

■ people with the most severe mental health problems die on average 10 years younger.

Other key areas of concern include problems with insurance, travel visas, predominantly negative media coverage and social exclusion.

(Sources: NMHDU, 2009; Time for Change, 2008; TNS UK/DH, 2008)

Stigma in the medical profession

'Once psychiatric diagnosis or medication history was known, their medical complaints were not taken as seriously.' (Wahl, 1999)

Consider

■ Why do you think this happened?

Case study: Work

Phil tells you: *'I didn't tell my employer about my bipolar diagnosis. Fortunately, I have not had any episodes since starting this job two years ago. What is bothering me is that it takes so long to get from work, 15 miles away, to attend my cognitive behaviour therapy so I have to take half a day off every other week. Although I am using my holidays for these medical appointments my boss wants me to explain why I do not take holidays in a block like others in our department do. I am terrified of people at work finding out that I have a mental illness as I know their views are backward to say the least.'*

Consider

■ Do you feel Phil's fears of his disorder being found out are valid?
■ Do you think there are many workplaces where it is impossible to take time off for medical reasons without having to reveal that the appointments are linked to mental health?
■ What fears might be associated with working with people with 'backward views' of mental health?

Shame is the other half of stigma

As we have grown up in a society that is intolerant of mental illness we are likely to feel shame as well as stigma when we experience it. It can be difficult for us to appreciate that it is not our fault as social attitudes – and even our own attitudes – make it difficult to reject the idea. In short, wherever there is stigma, there is an element of shame.

Case study: Appendicitis?

I was 140 miles from home when I was admitted to a psychiatric unit. A few days later my parents came to visit me and stayed in a hotel overnight. They needed to ask the neighbour to look after the dog and explained their sudden need to visit me by saying, 'Penny has been rushed to hospital with appendicitis.' Two weeks later they visited me again and continued to do so for the rest of that year. I have always wondered what the neighbours must have thought about the appendicitis that strangely went on and on. Perhaps they did not dare to ask as it was so obviously a cover up.

Consider

If Penny's parents were regularly lying about her health:

- How might this be beneficial to Penny?
- Suggest some ways in which such lies might lead to greater troubles in the future.

A lot of stigma comes from stereotypical thinking about what a person with bipolar may be like. Recent attempts by TV soaps to accurately portray bipolar disorder will have helped as viewers may now be able to more easily recognise symptoms. However, soaps may also hinder progress as the short scenes depicting the disorder are necessarily simplified and often extreme, with the periods of stability being far shorter than experienced by the majority with the disorder.

People endure the disorder itself plus the attitude of people they come into contact with. '*Some young people and their families have described the experience of stigma as being equal to and sometimes worse than having a mental health problem.*' (Young Minds, 2010)

Another form of stigma occurs between the person enduring the disorder and their well-meaning family/friends/colleagues who know some details of their disorder. They now run the risk that every time they cry, or get angry, it is dismissed as being a part of their mental illness. All the person's feelings are seen to be generated by the mental illness and none are seen to be relevant or valid.

Bipolar Disorder: A guide for mental health professionals, carers and those who live with it
© Pavilion Publishing (Brighton) Ltd 2012

Case study: Unpaid chambermaid

Helena has three children who used to help around the house. During several long depressions the children had to do everything, including preparing their mother's meals. Eventual diagnosis with bipolar disorder and appropriate treatment has allowed Helena to recover well and become capable of everything that needs to be done around the house. As Helena gradually took back duties from the children, the children took to doing less and less and now do nothing at all towards running the house.

As Helena is collecting dirty dishes from her son's bedroom then moving on to pick up clothes left on the floors of her daughters' bedrooms she increasingly feels that the children are using the house as a hotel with her as an unpaid chambermaid. She calls the children together and explains how she feels, and in tears, asks if they could do a few chores. The oldest turns to the others and says: 'It's OK, Mum is just having one of her mood things, she probably needs more medication. Let's stay out of the way.'

Consider

Imagine yourself in Helena's position.

■ Is it reasonable to ask for help?
■ What would be your advice to Helena?

What to do about stigma

The context of stigma is described by Thornicroft (2006). People are largely ignorant of the facts of bipolar disorder and many believe what they read in newspapers or what their friends tell them. These beliefs or attitudes become a prejudice and when this prejudice is translated into behaviour it becomes discrimination. The effects of this discrimination are described in Box 29.1 Stigma: the facts. Positive strategies towards overcoming stigma include:

■ viewing the experience of mental illness as a positive asset in the mental health professions ie. actively recruiting those with experience of mental health problems

- becoming active in the local mental health voluntary sector

- declaring a diagnosis; research suggests that direct social contact with people with mental health problems is by far the best way of changing public attitudes and overcoming stigma and discrimination

- working towards changes in employment legislation to allow more flexible working.

Question

How might mental health professionals work towards these goals?

Answer to question

How might mental health professionals work towards these goals?

In order to answer this question and find some fresh ideas it can be useful to arrange a few meetings with mental health nurses and practitioners and engage with local mental health voluntary groups to get their ideas and find out what they are doing. There are many good national campaigns that are slowly making a difference, but try to think about what is going on in your own locality.

Two very useful ideas are mental health practitioners going into schools to run mental health awareness and 'how to look after your mind' workshops. The other is engaging with local groups to run mental health film nights or music and comedy nights that have an entertainment value to pull people in, and an educational value as they double up as mental health awareness events with information about how to look after yourself and how to access services.

References

National Mental health Development Unit (2009) *Factfile 6: Stigma and discrimination in mental health*. London: NMHDU.

Rethink (2009) Rethink challenges tabloid over 'Schizo' headlines. *Your Voice* Summer 5.

Thornicroft G (2006) Challenging discrimination against people with mental health problems. In: C Jackson & K Hill (Eds) *Mental Health Today: A handbook*. Brighton: Pavilion.

Time for Change (2008) *Stigma Shout: Service user and carer experiences of stigma and discrimination*. London: Time for Change.

TNS UK for the Care Services Improvement Partnership/DH (2008) *Attitudes to Mental Illness 2008: Research report*. London: DH. Available at: http://www.dh.gov.uk/en/Publicationsandstatistics/Publications/PublicationsStatistics/DH_084478 (accessed August 2011).

Wahl O (1999) *Telling is Risky Business: Mental Health Consumers Confront Stigma*. New Jersey: Rutgers University Press.

Young Minds (2010) *See Beyond Our Labels: Young Minds briefing on young people's views about mental health*. London: Young Minds.

Further reading

NHS Information Centre (2011) *Attitudes to Mental Illness 2011: Survey report*. Available at: http://www.ic.nhs.uk/pubs/attitudestomi11 (accessed September 2011).

Useful websites

Active Minds at www.activeminds.org

National Alliance on Mental Illness at www.nami.org/stigma

Mental Health Commission at http://www.mentalhealthcommission.ca/English/Pages/OpeningMinds.aspx

Mental Health Matters at www.mentalhealthmatters.com

Scottish Recovery Network at www.scottishrecovery.net

See Me Scotland at www.seemescotland.org

Chapter 30

Advance statements

Key points

- Advance statements are an important recovery tool.
- Health professionals need to both advocate their use and heed their content.
- Advance directives are legally binding.

What is an advance statement?

During a period of well-being anyone can create an advance statement to express what they would like to happen should they become unwell. For it to be valid the person must have capacity when creating the statement, as defined in the Mental Capacity Act (2005). The advance statement describes preferred care and support should the person become unwell and lack capacity.

An advance statement can consist of both *advance preferences* and *advance directives*. Advance preferences relate to what the individual would like to happen and advance directives relate to what they do not wish to happen – only the latter have legal status.

> ### Question 1
>
> What do you consider might be the advantages of such statements?

The two components of advance statements

1) Advance preferences

An advance preference is an expression of wishes about future support and care. There are no restrictions on what can be said in a preference. This part of the statement is not legally binding and can be expressed in any format. Often it is simply a verbal agreement. This can be between the individual and anyone who knows them. It can be recorded in any format – even an email can count as an advance preference. Advance preferences do not need to be signed or witnessed. However, preferences are most likely to be effective, and wishes adhered to, when written clearly, signed and distributed to everyone concerned.

Health professionals are duty bound, although not legally bound, to meet the individual's wishes providing that any treatments they request are likely to be in their best interests. Health professionals need to take wishes into account even if a patient is sectioned.

Preferences:

- outline what a person would like to happen
- are informal
- have no legal standing
- are agreed with others.

2) Advance directives

An advance directive means an advance *refusal*. This can be the refusal of a particular treatment but it can be the refusal of almost anything else eg. 'I do not want my uncle to visit me in hospital. Do not allow him on the ward.' Directives should not contain refusals of basic care or ask a doctor to act unlawfully as these options are not valid.

An advance statement can contain many advance directives, with each one being *legally binding* on medical staff. Even for patients subject to compulsory powers (ie. who have been sectioned), staff need to consider directives carefully and be able to explain any choices they make that go against the patient's wishes.

Directives:

- state what a person is refusing

- are formal

- are legally binding

- can be negotiated with the team

- are clear about the circumstances when they are to be used.

Question 2

Why might an advance statement be of particular interest to someone who experiences extreme mood swings?

Common issues

Issues that are frequently raised when discussing advance statements are medication and electro-convulsive therapy (ECT). Medications such as typical antipsychotics (eg. haloperidol) are targets for refusals, especially after severe side effects have been experienced in the past. Such requests are very reasonable considering that the newer medications are said to have fewer severe side effects. It is not possible to refuse all medications.

ECT refusals come from people who have experienced ECT and believe it has caused memory loss, from people who find the thought of being sedated and given electric shocks too unpleasant, or from people who disagree with it. Conversely, some people who believe ECT has previously helped them have preferences stating that it is OK to use ECT as soon as it seems necessary.

A third issue – often seen as a major one – is whether or not to refuse admittance to a specific psychiatric ward. A person can refuse to be admitted to a particular ward but they cannot refuse to be taken to a place of safety, or all wards and hospitals.

Case study: Graham

Graham has a bipolar diagnosis and has had bad experiences on psychiatric wards in the past. He has a legally valid advance statement and copies of it are with all the health health professionals he comes into contact with. It states that he must never be admitted to the local psychiatric ward. It includes an agreement that no matter how ill he becomes he will be able to stay with his parents. Five years after the creation of this advance statement he enters an extreme manic phase. It is clear to the community mental health nurse that his parents are struggling to cope.

Questions

3. What are the options for the health professionals, considering that they must both give the best care but also not break the law by disregarding what appears to be a valid legal document?
4. Why might a person's refusal to go to their nearest psychiatric ward be a bad idea?

What else goes into an advance statement?

For most people with a bipolar diagnosis there are likely to be more dos than don'ts in their advance statements. That is, more preferences and perhaps fewer directives.

People sometimes need help with giving examples of everyday activities that need to be taken care of in the event of illness. These are things that are important but often overlooked. This is because people with bipolar disorder are often well for a lot of the time and are likely to be leading busy lives, doing many things. Many of these things are likely to fall to someone else when a crisis occurs.

The following is a list of the type of ideas/questions that clients will be considering.

- Who will look after pets and plants?

- Who should be told/not told if hospitalisation becomes necessary? (Parents, children, siblings, aunt/uncle, friends, neighbours)

- What should happen about financial matters such as any regular bills not paid by direct debit?

- Should the message on the answering machine be updated?

- Who do you want to visit/not visit you?

- Therapies that helped? eg. 'John and Sue – please encourage me to walk more.'

In many ways, there is no end to the possibilities and everyone's list will be unique. Some people will be greatly reassured by just writing down the most important things and feeling sure that they will be taken care of. Others will want a longer list and may find this reassuring even if it is never completed.

Important guidelines for staff and carers

Discussing with clients any examples of things that could be in an advance statement is unwise. This can too easily be seen as directing the person to say certain things and however well meaning your efforts, this could invalidate the statement. All ideas and exactly how these are worded must initially come from the client.

The staff/carer role is to explain what an advance statement is and where to get support with further understanding and creating of an advance statement. When anyone shows you a completed statement you can help by reading it carefully and asking any questions necessary for clarification. Doing this while the patient has capacity is useful, and some might say essential.

Some benefits from creating an advance statement

- It gives a greater feeling of control for the person experiencing mental health difficulties.

- It can reduce anxiety and concerns about what may happen during a crisis.

- It is a way of improving understanding and communicating hopes and fears.

- It may prevent a crisis as issues are thought through and possibilities for early intervention become apparent.

What can supporters do to help with the creation of an advance statement?

- You can encourage a person to think about starting one.

- Give enough information so that the person can make their own choices.

- Encourage independence in filling it out.

- Give contact numbers for advocates.

- Read what the person has written, understand it and ask questions to clarify.

- Help to clarify who will be keeping copies and how it may be updated.

- If asked, assist with distribution of the statement and let other health professionals know about the statement.

What must supporters not do when helping with the creation of an advance statement?

- Never force anyone to create an advanced statement.

- Never tell someone what to put in it. It has to be what the individual would like, not what you think is best.

- Do not be present while the advance statement is being written.

Bipolar Disorder: A guide for mental health professionals, carers and those who live with it
© Pavilion Publishing (Brighton) Ltd 2012

Question 5

What are some of the dangers with nurses on psychiatric wards helping patients to complete advance statements before discharge?

Is this ever the right thing to do?

Pro-formas

It can be useful for clients to have a proforma with spaces to write or type in the following:

- names, addresses, phone numbers for:
    - themselves
    - people who have agreed to help
    - people and places who/where copies the statement will be stored
    - the witnesses to the statement
- any/all of the preferences they are stating
- any/all of the directives they are making
- space for signatures and dates.

Good proformas will come with an example for a statement of intent, which is essential if the advance statement is to be legally binding (Shaw & Smith, 2011).

Having two witness signatures can add 'weight' to the advance statement if there is any dispute should the client lose capacity.

Answers to questions

1. **What do you consider might be the advantages of such statements?**

Beyond the obvious advantage of giving supporters and the health professionals clearer information, advance statements can provide increased confidence and less anxiety for clients who know that their wishes are likely to be followed.

2. **Why might an advance statement be of particular interest to someone who experiences extreme mood swings?**

Bipolar is an episodic disorder which means that many (not all) clients will unfortunately become unwell again through changes in mood. All clients who have periods of stability have the opportunity to create an advance statement. This can be done in the hope of never having to use it, just as anyone can create a statement for any eventuality they are concerned about.

3. **What are the options for the health professionals considering that they must give the best care but also not break the law by disregarding what appears to be a valid legal document?**

It will be useful to know if Graham's advance statement has been updated since it was created five years ago. It has been argued that statements that are not reviewed every few years may be obsolete.

Clients with old advance statements may be advised to review these, but only if they have capacity and no one is coercing them to make specific changes.

- *The health of Graham's parents should be taken into account. If their health is far worse than when the statement was created then their ability to care for Graham may be questioned.*
- *His parents' wishes will also need to be taken into account as they have been specifically named in the statement.*
- *Is Graham so manic that he needs to be sectioned for reasons of safety?*

Note: Overall there may be no clear cut answer and this is why advance statements sometimes need to be discussed by health professionals before making a decision.

Bipolar Disorder: A guide for mental health professionals, carers and those who live with it
© Pavilion Publishing (Brighton) Ltd 2012

4. **Why might refusing to go to your nearest psychiatric ward be a bad idea?**

■ *As the statement is believed to be legally binding possibilities of transport to an alternative ward (in a different town or county) will need to be investigated. This can take time, delay admission and might have detrimental consequences.*

■ *Health professionals must always act in the patient's best interests and provide basic care. If this is considered to mean admission to the local psychiatric ward their directive may carry little weight.*

■ *Remember that if a person is sectioned their directive will simply be treated as a preference, so stating a preferred psychiatric ward could be at least as effective as refusing one in the case of sectioning.*

Note: When making this type of directive clients need to think through the alternatives eg. can they name a similar ward with similar journey time from their home or perhaps a ward close to their parents' home?

Are directives that at first glance do not look like the ideal solution more likely to be followed when they are seen as having been clearly thought through?

5. **What are some of the dangers with nurses on psychiatric wards helping patients to complete advance statements before discharge?**

■ *An advance statement is about an individual's own ideas so you should not be assisting anyone with creating theirs other than in ways described above, such as saying where to find out more about the subject.*

■ *A psychiatric ward is never a good setting for creating an advance statement because later on there are likely to be doubts about the capacity of a patient, even if you and other staff believe they are recovering well. Such doubts will almost certainly invalidate any directives in the statement.*

Is this ever the right thing to do?
■ *There is a short answer: no, it is never a good idea!*

References

Shaw R & Smith RA (2011) *Advance Training Workbook*. Nottingham: The Rushcliffe Mental Health Support Group.

Further reading

Atkinson J (2007) *Advance Directives in Mental Health: Theory, practice and ethics*. London: Jessica Kingsley Publishers.

Atkinson J (2011) Advance directives. In: P Parker (Ed) *Mental Health Ethics: The human context*. London: Routledge.

Straughan J (2009) *Insight: A holistic approach to recovery training for people with bipolar disorder or depression*. Brighton: Pavilion.

Chapter 31

Family, friends and carers

Key points

- Bipolar disorder can put an enormous strain on relationships.
- Family members, friends and carers can play a huge supporting role.
- Family members and carers have their own needs in relation to caring.

This chapter emphasises the role of the carer in developing empathy for the person with bipolar disorder and the opening up of healthy communication channels between the carer and cared for. The chapter also looks at what the particular needs of families and carers are in relation to living with a person with bipolar.

Case study: A partner's support

Richard knew I had a bipolar diagnosis before we married. He did not anticipate any difficulties as I had been well for a long time. I came off all medications when expecting our child and my moods became erratic. I was aware that I was not being logical, as one minute I would be as calm as anything and then I would be screaming at him for something he hadn't done that I thought he should have done.

Richard never stopped being supportive, even when I told him to leave and he moved back to his father's place for a week.

He was present for the birth but then had to endure the deepest depression I had ever had. This was followed by a new antidepressant and a mania that caused chaos. When I came down, I thought how amazing it was that Richard was still with me. Just one of many crazy things I did was to phone his boss at 2am to say that Richard hated him, hated the job and was quitting! Richard told me later that the next day was his 'most interesting' ever at work!

What I did not know at the time was that Richard had spent that week at his father's reading a pile of library books about bipolar disorder, so in many ways nothing I did shocked him.

Strong, loving, supportive and mutually respectful relationships are vital in helping a person with bipolar disorder to stabilise their moods. Good friends can encourage a person back to social interaction following the depths of a depression and can suppress and modify the overzealous plans and ambitions of hypomania. Depression can leave loved ones feeling helpless and desperate while manic episodes can cause frustration and extreme exhaustion. Friends and family who accept the disorder are less likely to be critical of the person who behaves erratically due to the disorder. They will learn to reject behaviour without rejecting the person. Friends can help by being supportively critical and being prepared to risk upset rather than see hypomania escalating. Strong friendships are those which remain after the fun elements of a high are gone and can persevere after rejection through depression. Those with bipolar need such people around them.

Case study: Difficulties and frustrations of a carer

My son is about to move out for the second time. He came back to live with me 10 years ago after some big changes in our lives. First, he told me and my husband that he was gay. It was no big surprise or big deal for me. His father struggled with the idea and I think this contributed to the next change. My son started using street drugs and one night we were phoned from a psychiatric ward to say he was there and we were asked if we would visit in the morning.

This was a whole new world for us. We started visiting every day. Then his father and I separated. It was not only because of the strain of mental illness in the family but this was the last straw for our relationship that had been shaky for a long time.

It was a full year before diagnosis and discharge and that was when my son came back home having had his own flat prior to the hospital admission. It has taken a full 10 years to just begin to get to grips with what bipolar is, what it means, and what a mother's choices are in supporting her son. I do not see myself as a carer as such. He looks after himself as much as any son does, except when he is poorly and the health professionals are caring for him then. I have certainly been his supporter and greatest 'fan'. I can see he has so much potential now he is back on his feet and going back out into the world.

Relationships

People who can identify others they fully trust and can rely on in any circumstance are fortunate. Friendships like these reduce anxiety and provide stability. Those with a bipolar diagnosis sometimes cannot identify anyone they fully trust as all their relationships have been affected in some way by the disorder.

When a person is depressed it can seem that they have few friends. While manic it may seem that they know everyone in the world and everyone knows them. When a person is well and in a steady mood, creating a relationship wheel (see Reflection exercise below) to map close relationships can help to put things into perspective, especially if recent episodes have caused changes in levels of trust.

Reflection exercise: Relationships wheel

- Write your name in the middle of a piece of paper. Draw lines like bicycle wheel spokes from the circle and at the end of the lines write the names of all the people or groups with whom you interact. Include family, close and distant friends, work colleagues, health professionals, voluntary groups etc.
- Draw a circle around those who give you the most support. Think about any other people who are reliable and trustworthy who might be a good source of support.
- How can you develop these relationships?

Cultivate supportive relationships

Having a range of supportive relationships to turn to can be very reassuring for an individual, and increasing the number of supportive relationships will ease the pressure on those closest to the person if there is a crisis.

Rebuilding relationships

Both mania and depression can damage relationships. When moods are out of order a person can be unaware that they are upsetting people. They may be so wrapped up in their own troubles that they miss the obvious signs. Those who know the bipolar person best can tell them who has been upset during such episodes.

When people have been upset some thought is needed as to how much explanation is necessary. If something strange was said at a supermarket or a petrol station, then it is probably best to forget the event and move on as the person may never need to meet those particular people again. If close family members have been offended then apologies are needed, together with an explanation as to what is going to be different in the future. Friends or work colleagues who have been upset may also be hoping for an explanation, but not in too much detail. A balance is needed on who needs explanations/apologies and how detailed the explanations need to be.

Sometimes it has to be accepted that there is little chance of repairing some relationships. It is common to have to move on after episodes, accepting that those who cannot cope with the disorder may well not have been such true friends after all.

Maintaining good relationships within the family

- Remember that most bipolar people are well most of the time. Bipolar disorder is episodic. Sometimes it may not seem that way as one episode may blend into the next. It is an important point as between episodes a bipolar person will hopefully be able to appreciate not being 'the patient'. With a steadier mood it is reasonable for them to be fulfilling any role such as parent, 'bread-winner', home-maker, decorator, gardener, family taxi service etc.

- Open communication is essential for a long-term trusting relationship. Arguments and big scenes are almost always unhelpful. Try to allow mistakes without criticism to nurture a relaxed atmosphere. Being more relaxed allows issues to be discussed without fear of being criticised.

- High levels of 'expressed emotion' including a critical atmosphere, being overprotective, having a blame culture, sarcasm, being intolerant and not listening to each other will hinder recovery. Try to remain 'low key' and avoid heated emotional exchanges or being critical. It is important to avoid an atmosphere of surveillance and bombardment with advice. This can feel like being treated as a child and lectured at. It may be appropriate to play the incident down and shrug it off as a learning experience.

- Learning about triggers, warning signs and coping strategies that apply to loved ones is essential for family members who hope to help avoid future episodes. These are also important for helping to build resilience between episodes. Once aware of warning signs, a common mistake is to see anything that is unexpected as a warning sign.

Case study: worries from the past

Harry had depression all winter and he was barely able to smile. His wife, Jean, was relieved when the spring came and he started gardening again as this greatly improved his mood.

Suddenly during a comedy programme that he had never even smiled at in the past, he burst out laughing. Jean, without thinking, asked if he was alright. Harry apologised, saying he found that one bit especially amusing. Jean apologised to him, saying that she was worried about the mania returning. An argument ensued, with Harry saying he felt overprotected and he just wanted to get on with his life.

Consider

- How can Jean learn to distinguish between happiness and hypomania?
- What tactics can she employ so she does not overreact?

The role of family, friends and carers

It is important to discuss the need to act and seek medical advice at times of impending relapse. For an individual, it can be useful to agree on the actions to take and emphasise their own needs frankly. An agreed plan increases the supporter's confidence to act as agreed in a crisis.

- Family members should learn about bipolar disorder. Reading and attending training workshops should not be left just to the bipolar person – share responsibility for finding out more. The more a family understand about the disorder the more they will be able to understand behaviour in the context of the disorder, and the less readily they will be to make personal criticisms.
- Have open and frank discussions about what is helpful and what is unhelpful. Allow partners to express the same.
- Avoid overprotection, being judgemental and a blame culture; it is necessary to accept the disorder for what it is rather than trying to deal with it without understanding.
- When someone is expressing their feelings make a point of actively listening to them, this will foster a sense of democracy and openness that is healthy for family life.
- Focusing on positive feelings rather than negative ones and noticing successes rather than failures is usually very helpful.
- It may be necessary to set clear limits in order to discuss and identify unacceptable behaviours.
- Strain in relationships can also be alleviated by ensuring that both the person and the support still do things that give them pleasure eg. meals out, cinema trips, outings etc.

Unhelpful relationships

Some of our relationships are not healthy and it can be helpful to eradicate those that do not help us.

> ## Reflection exercise: Relationships wheel – unhelpful relationships
>
> - On the wheel you have drawn showing all the people you interact with, take a fresh colour and draw a circle around those you feel are not helpful.
> - Think about and discuss options for discontinuing some of the least helpful relationships.

How family and friends can help

In depression

It is hard for family members not to feel rejected if a person rebuffs all attempts to help them. It is important to avoid becoming irritated with a depressed person because of their lack of effort and apparent indifference. The depressed person will often neglect their basic needs and this can give rise to frustration and anxiety on the part of the carer.

Patience is the biggest virtue a carer can have and, while worried, they must do all they can to preserve the depressed person's physical well-being by encouraging them to drink, have a balanced diet and look after their personal hygiene. When depressed, a person can feel indifferent about having an unkempt appearance and reduced hygiene standards. It can even feel right as it matches their mood.

Having a routine and fitting in with the family is often helpful for recovery. However, encouraging routine may be difficult for the family when it seems this could make the depression worse and when suicide risks seem very real.

Where suicide appears to be becoming a possibility, professional help must be sought.

Warning signs for suicide

- Changes in normal behaviour patterns
- Withdrawal
- Self-neglect
- Expression of suicidal ideas
- Verbalisations and expressions of intent
- Making preparations eg. writing a will and giving possessions away
- Talking about a plan and a method
- The writing of suicide notes

In mania

Warning signs and responses

It is essential for the family to be aware of the typical warning signs of hypomania. It is equally important to know which warning signs the person has exhibited before. If what a family member considers to be key warning signs do not match their relative's view of their warning signs then it is important that they talk and gain a better understanding of each other's views.

Families need to appreciate that happiness and mania are not necessarily related. Watching for increasing happiness as a warning sign is not at all helpful. Overexcitement and a need to be at the centre of attention are usually clear warning signs where the spouse or carer can try to limit exposure to stimuli/exciting situations. Unfortunately, a relative is likely to be seen as a killjoy who is interfering unnecessarily in their enjoyment of life. A fine balance is needed, and this takes time to learn.

If the frequency and severity of warning signs for mania start to increase the person affected needs to be urged to seek professional help. At first a relative may not want to tell them this for fear of a backlash, however, if they wait too long they may be less likely to take any notice.

Practicalities

Help with the practicalities of life will allow the hypomanic person to be calmer, which in turn will help them to rest, sleep and feel they have time to eat a more balanced diet. As with depression, family can remind their relative that personal hygiene is associated with a steady mood.

Medication compliance is important and there will almost certainly be times when the bipolar relative will want to stop, such as when they are feeling better or wanting to regain lost feelings. Be prepared to listen and discuss such ideas and especially ask about side effects. Help the person to negotiate issues with medication with the professional team.

Finances

People in hypomania have spent exessive amounts of money by using credit cards and have put their family in debt for years. If a loved one has a history of spending sprees a relative will need a plan for keeping finances in control leading up to and during any episodes. When they are well, many bipolar people who have made bad financial errors will voluntarily cut up their credit cards. Less drastically, partners are often trusted to look after a credit card other than when it is needed for agreed essential purchases. Again, balance is essential as too much or inappropriate control will lead to tension.

Routine

A haphazard lifestyle with no regular times for bed, breakfast etc. are typical as mania develops, whereas developing a routine is typical of a person in recovery. Take opportunities to encourage routine and think carefully before suggesting anything that might disrupt established routines.

Reflection exercise: Consequences

Sharon has the opportunity to drive 100 miles to her sister's 40th birthday party that is advertised as being from 9pm until very late!

She thinks of two options:

1. Suggest that her bipolar husband drives them there. She will not drink alcohol so she can drive home and he can drink whatever he wants and then take his medication when he gets home.
2. Apologise, saying that her last late night party was great but these days it is too many miles to be driving at night.

- What might be the consequences of option 1?
- Can you think of any other options?

It is important not to take the disorder too personally. In manic states the person can make very hurtful comments and can be aggressive and critical. In depression they can be rejecting and irritable. It is important to remember that it is the disorder that drives these behaviours and words, and not the person.

When to seek help

Despite having had an episode and being stable and feeling in control of the disorder, people can have relapses. It is important that family carers remain practical and alert for early warning signs of impending relapse. Self-neglect, not eating or drinking, and some uncharacteristic behaviour need to be taken as warning signs and the need for a state of heightened awareness. The continuation of these behaviours indicates the need to seek a review by a health professional. Identifying a possible episode early on can prevent it or reduce its impact.

Looking after children

When a parent is unwell with bipolar disorder it can be frightening and confusing for children. It is important that children understand the disorder and are given appropriate information. It can be very disturbing to witness a parent's uncharacteristic behaviour without knowing why it is happening. A child's behaviour may become problematic and the carer needs to remain sensitive to their needs. An adult should explain to the child that the behaviour is part of the disorder and this is why their parent is behaving differently.

Keeping the child's normal routine will help to preserve a sense of normality during the confusion, as will the other relatives' calmness. Older children who are aware of the difficulties facing the carer need to be asked to help. They may be helped to contact groups for teenage carers where they may talk with their peers and gain support from them.

Consideration point

Stigma may be an issue in relation to children accessing support groups Why might this be so?

(See Chapter 29: Dealing with stigma for more information.)

It can be difficult for parents to talk about the effect bipolar disorder has on their children (see case study below).

Case study: Do my children need to know?

How do you explain to a 10 year old and a 12 year old that you temporarily lost touch with reality? Is there any way to begin to explain where delusions about needing to act on God's every word, the apocalypse, a new holocaust, and being chosen to join the space programme all came from? There wasn't! And there still isn't!

My children have grown up now and it turns out they didn't need to know. All they needed to know was that I was going to get better and everything would be as it was before; before they had to suddenly grow up and find out their world was going to be a whole lot more challenging than it was for their school friends and their cousins.

The children visited the psychiatric ward with their mother most days through the summer. The ward was not a great environment for young children so we were lucky to have a month of good weather and the visits were moved to the hospital lawn, with ball games in the sunshine. I cannot help but cry when I look back to those times and some of the music from that period still triggers some difficult memories.

Looking after yourself

An exhausted supporter will lead to the collapse of both the supporter and the supported. It is important that the supporter can recharge their batteries and have necessary breaks from caring. Having close friends and other family members to confide in will be useful as will more formal support mechanisms such as bipolar support groups. Take the time to find accessible and trusted professional contacts. Some carers will receive the regular support of a community mental health nurse who will develop an understanding of their needs.

Reflection exercise: Support from a community mental health nurse

Many bipolar relatives believe that it is difficult to access a health professional for their own support needs.

With nearly 600,000 people with a bipolar diagnosis in the UK, how realistic is it that someone in each family affected will receive the regular support of a community mental health nurse?

Discuss this with a community mental health nurse to ascertain how important they see this aspect of their role to be and how they try to achieve this.

Although NHS resources are limited it may be worthwhile finding out if support from a community mental health nurse is available in the area. Find out about crisis teams that can be accessed during working hours and out of hours, as just knowing that such teams are there can be helpful. Carers can be referred to a social worker to have their own needs assessed and to identify any help they may be entitled to.

Summary of what is helpful

- Learn as much about the disorder as possible
- Be a partner in the disorder
- Look for early warning signs
- Offer hope and encouragement
- Keep communication channels open
- Avoid being overemotional
- Help to identify and practise coping strategies
- Help with action planning
- Develop a shared relapse and management plan
- Help with coping strategies
- Don't take it personally – remember it is the disorder
- Join a support group
- Encourage medication compliance

Bipolar Disorder: A guide for mental health professionals, carers and those who live with it
© Pavilion Publishing (Brighton) Ltd 2012

- Help with practical matters
- Keep to a daily routine
- Maintain the fun elements of family life
- Be patient

Further reading

MDF The Bipolar Organisation (2008) *Manic Depression: Bipolar disorder information for family and friends*. London: MDF.

Useful websites

Bipolar Significant Others at www.bpso.org

Carers at www.carersuk.org

Young Carers at www.youngcarers.org.uk

Section 4
Related conditions
and conclusions

Chapter 32

Related conditions

Key points

- Bipolar disorder shares similar symptoms with other mental health disorders and there is often much overlap between diagnostic categories.

- There is much individual variation in presentation and symptomology.

- Seasonal affective disorder, post-natal depression and puerperal psychosis are particularly closely related conditions.

Overlapping diagnoses

Many mental health disorders overlap in terms of causes, symptoms, treatment and recovery. It can be useful to view this in a visual form as a diagram with overlapping circles to show that most people with one diagnosis will have elements and symptoms of other diagnoses (see Figure 32.1).

Bipolar people often point to a single traumatic event as the start of their troubles and so consider their disorder to be similar to post-traumatic stress disorder (PTSD). Many health professionals, however, would probably argue that there are many distinctions between PTSD and a traumatic trigger event leading to bipolar disorder.

Consideration points

- What important lessons can you take from these differing points of view?
- What do these differing perspectives tell you and how can this inform your practice?

Many bipolar people will talk about anxiety, stating that it is the worst part of their mental distress. The overlap with depression is clear as many people diagnosed with clinical depression have symptoms of bipolar II. Some people with a bipolar II diagnosis believe their diagnosis to be wrong as all their troubles stem from the depressive side of the disorder.

Figure 32.1: An infinite number of possibilities

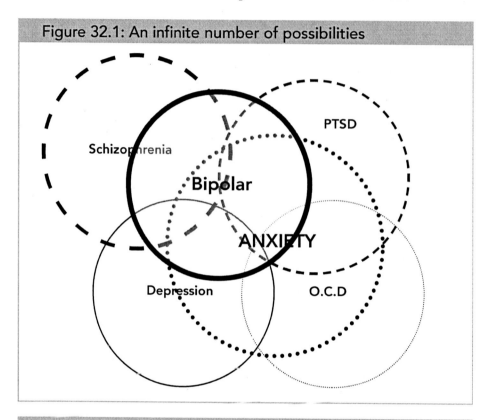

Reflection exercise: Diagnostic circles

Many disorders have similar and hence, overlapping symptoms as Figure 32.1 shows. This exercise was used in a workshop with participants creating their own view of how symptoms and diagnoses overlap. All the images that were produced varied as they depend on individual knowledge and experience of each diagnosis. A health professional's view of the pattern might well vary from that of the client.

■ Try creating your own diagram to show how symptoms and diagnosis overlap for a range of disorders you might consider to be related to bipolar disorder.

In Figure 32.1, there is a small overlap between OCD and bipolar. Bipolar people who are anxious may display behaviours that mimic obsessive and/or compulsive behaviours. Ruminating on negative thinking is a common trait in depression eg. 'I can't do it', 'It is no good' and 'I am hopeless'.

Reflection exercise: Differential diagnosis!

It was previously hinted that it can be very difficult to pigeon hole any group of symptoms into one diagnostic category. Two more examples are below.

Schizophrenia

'... bipolar spectrum disorder ... the person is susceptible to ups and downs – but might include people ... diagnosed as having bipolar disorder, severe depression and schizophrenia.' (Craddock, 2007).

Craddock goes on to say that bipolar and schizophrenia could be more closely related than previously thought, which would explain why some people are given one diagnosis, which is later changed to another (Craddock, 2009).

Schizoaffective disorder

This is as the name suggests – a disorder that is somewhere between bipolar disorder and schizophrenia.

Consider

- Are these merely points of view or are they evidence that we should be questioning the value of diagnosis?
- Should we reject the labels and just regard illnesses and disorders as individual presentations of a group of symptoms of a psychotic nature?
- Do we just fit individuals into the diagnoses or do we alter the diagnosis to the fit individual?
- If we cannot fit every presentation into a diagnosis, do we need to add more diagnoses to the list?
- How else might we view this dilemma?
- Once diagnosed, do people change their behaviour to fit the label, or the behaviour that is expected of them? Does the label become a self-fulfilling prophecy?

Case study: Diagnosable?

When Alan was a teenager his doctor thought he had seasonal affective disorder and after a third winter of low mood, she prescribed him an antidepressant. This seemed to help. However, in the spring Alan started to lose touch with reality. His doctor wrote, 'possible BP II' in his notes.

On becoming captain of the university rugby team, Alan felt almost obliged to drink excessively with his mates. One night after drinking a lot of alcohol, he took an illegal drug, had hallucinations and found himself wandering around town feeling extremely paranoid. When someone put a hand on his shoulder in the dark he instinctively lashed out, knocking the person to the ground. He had hit a policeman, which landed Alan in court and later in front of a psychiatrist, who having listened about the hallucinations and paranoia, without knowing about the illegal drug, wrote 'possible schizophrenia'.

Consider

- Do you think Alan would benefit from:
  - more psychiatric help
  - a diagnosis
  - prescription medication to control his moods?
- Can you think of other forms of help that might be better for Alan?

Seasonal affective disorder (SAD)

Seasonal affective disorder affects mood according to the season of the year, with people typically feeling depressed during the winter months. For many people it is a serious illness that prevents them from carrying out their normal level of functioning. The Seasonal Affective Disorder Association (SADA) estimates that it affects around 7% of the UK population (SADA, 2011). People with a milder form are said to have the 'winter blues'.

Symptoms reflect those of depression and include:

- loss of motivation
- lethargy

- depression

- anxiety

- low self-esteem

- apathy

- withdrawal and social isolation

- aches and infections

- poor sleep

- overeating and weight gain

- irritability.

For some people these symptoms fade as spring progresses but for others there is a sudden improvement in mood and symptoms as light levels increase, and this can be accompanied by a short period of hypomania.

The causes of SAD are uncertain but it seems to be triggered by the shorter days and lower light levels in the winter months, though what makes someone vulnerable to it is still open to debate. Seasonal affective disorder is rare close to the equator where high light intensity persists throughout the year.

Biochemistry

It is likely that serotonin and melatonin play a part in episodes of SAD as darkness seems to lower levels of serotonin. Shorter days in the winter may reduce serotonin production, leading to the possibility of negative feelings and a low mood. Each evening the dimming light increases our levels of melatonin, a hormone that normally helps us to sleep. It is possible that darker days cause higher melatonin levels, which in turn lower energy levels. If this is the case it would explain why SAD tends to start as the days become shorter. For some people the negative feelings and lower energy can lead to depression.

Consider

- Do you feel that discussions like this one on biochemistry are useful for clients? Or is it better to keep things simple and help people to focus on a balanced diet and getting outdoors whenever they can?

Another theory suggests that SAD is due to circadian rhythm imbalance due to lifestyles that no longer revolve around natural daylight. We often work and live in artificial light, stay up late, and in so doing upset our natural rhythm, resulting in SAD symptoms.

Treatment through the use of light therapy has been beneficial to many. SADA suggests that a success rate of 85% can be achieved when exposed to four hours of very bright light daily, though usual doses are 30 minutes to two hours, with 30 minutes being sufficient for most people. Ordinary household lighting is not of sufficient intensity and special light boxes are used. Treatment is normally daily from autumn through to spring. This is time-consuming and evidence suggests that this is a factor which puts some people off.

Antidepressants are used but the older tricyclic antidepressants tend to induce lethargy and so should be avoided. Newer SSRI antidepressants can be used in conjunction with light therapy. However, it should be noted that antidepressants will only alleviate the symptoms and not tackle the cause. Other useful treatment options are to sit near windows as much as possible, spend time outside each day and access supportive counselling and relaxation therapy.

Case study: My SAD

I cannot remember a time when I did not have a lower mood in the winter than the summer. I believed this to be normal and paid little attention to my sleeping more and doing less in the winter. I certainly would not have thought of it as a disorder.

My promotion from programmer to systems analyst one summer was good for my career, but I never could have imagined the consequences. I moved to a desk where there was no direct line from me to any window. Two people in my new department were on long-term sick and I was covering for them by working 6am to 6pm under fluorescent lights. Early in December I quite suddenly found that I couldn't cope and I was prescribed an antidepressant.

Occupational health were great, and although the company never accepted responsibility, by the new year our work area had been assigned for storage only and we were moved to the top floor. I have not had time off since, but in my own mind the damage was done that winter as the mild depressions I had prior to that turned into a worse mix of anxiety and depression that sets in every autumn when the clocks go back. I am studying CBT and fully appreciate that a lot of the problem is due to faulty thinking.

Post-natal depression

Mothers who feel irritable and sad for a few weeks after giving birth are said to be experiencing the 'baby blues'. More extreme depression, typically starting from 3–6 weeks after birth, is known as post-natal depression or post-partum depression. This affects 10–15% of mothers. It is suggested that the depression may arise because of:

- stress and anxieties about motherhood and caring for the baby, as it is more prevalent in those with poor social support mechanisms

- hormonal imbalance

- genetic predisposition.

A combination of these factors will increase risks but incidence is higher among those who have had previous mental health problems. As with other forms of depression/anxiety, common features are irritability, poor sleep, poor appetite, lethargy and feelings of guilt. These may persist for up to a year with some risk of neglect of the child.

For breastfeeding women who have a new episode of mild or moderate depression during the post-natal period, the following are recommended: self-help strategies, exercise, counselling and CBT. If symptoms are more severe then antidepressants may be useful (NICE, 2007).

Puerperal psychosis

In about 1 in 1,000 births psychosis occurs in the first few weeks after giving birth. It can present in many different ways and the baby may be at considerable risk of neglect and harm. Alongside delusional thoughts there are often hallucinations and other thought disorders. When there is a loss of contact with reality a hospital admission may be the safest option. Specialist mother and baby units exist but they are by no means universal. The presentation can be either unipolar or bipolar. In manic presentations there is overactivity and disinhibition, while in depressive presentations the symptoms are severe.

It is essential to know if the mother is breastfeeding before beginning antipsychotic medication, antidepressants or mood stabilisers. ECT may be considered in severe cases that do not respond to drug treatment.

Post-partum psychosis: Out of the blue

The fourth day after the birth of my first baby was the start of my meltdown. I had no history of mental health issues. Confusion, extreme anxiousness and terror mounted and I hadn't slept for four days. It happened suddenly and severely, within hours. I was manic and couldn't walk, talk or think. I held my phone but couldn't work out how to call for help. Over two weeks I had delusions and scribbled notes frantically. My mind was spiralling yet I had moments of clarity. My thoughts raced so fast that I developed a stutter. I felt like a baby re-learning how to eat, walk and talk. It was exhausting. I couldn't read or watch TV and was terrified by people moving or speaking too fast; I couldn't process thoughts quickly enough to understand. I was learning how to care for my baby at the same time as trying to survive myself. I was scared I'd be separated from my baby. I wanted information but nothing was explained to me as they thought I was crazy. Severe depression developed. I was numb and rarely left the house. It took a year to bond with my baby and I was suicidal for three months. After two years I made a full recovery but chose not to have any more children.

Bipolar disorder in pregnancy

When considering pregnancy, potential parents should carefully discuss medication options with their medical advisers. There are certain medications that should not be routinely used in pregnancy but are commonly part of bipolar treatment. These include valproate, carbamazepine, lamotrigine and lithium. Risks include cardiac defects in the foetus. Similarly, these drugs are not recommended if a woman is considering breastfeeding and antipsychotics are more likely to be used.

Lithium should be gradually reduced and swapped for the lowest possible dose of an antipsychotic. If it is necessary to continue lithium, extreme care is needed. Taking lithium during pregnancy is potentially very risky for the baby's health. All staff involved with the pregnancy need to understand the risks in order to ensure the greatest possible protection of the baby from lithium.

It is essential that the babies of mothers who were on psychotropic medication during pregnancy are carefully monitored for possible adverse drug effects.

Clients wishing to conceive should be aware that antipsychotics may also reduce the chances of conception. If an antipsychotic is necessary during pregnancy, more frequent reviews of the dose should be considered in order to minimise effects on the foetus.

(NICE, 2006)

Case study: Being pregnant and on medication

My first husband was violent and used to beat me. By the end of the divorce I had taken no end of medications and had a bipolar II diagnosis. By the time I married again and we felt confident that we could raise a child, I was 39 years old.

My GP and my psychiatrist emphasised that there were going to be exceptional risks with the pregnancy and I would need to work with them to minimise the medication. I cut back my hours at work and stopped smoking and using alcohol. My moods changed from moderate lows of about a week to much quicker and more confusing fluctuations.

My pregnancy is halfway (I have 20 weeks to go) and today is a rare good day. I have had nights without sleep, thrown up, turned to drink and smoked a few cigarettes – I have been struggling. I am ashamed of the way I have behaved, although I have at least been totally honest with the health professionals and they believe the worst may be over now. My husband continues to be supportive. I am looking forward to getting back on the full dose of mood stabiliser once our baby is born.

> ### ADHD
>
> Attention deficit hyperactivity disorder (ADHD) also has some similar traits to bipolar disorder. An early and correct diagnosis is of great importance. (See Chapter 33: Bipolar children.)

References

Craddock N (2007) Unlocking the future of bipolar treatment. *Pendulum* Spring 2007 **23** (1) p7.

Craddock N (2009) Old thinking about bipolar must go, says MDF expert. *Pendulum* Summer 2009 **25** (2) p4.

NICE (2006) *Clinical Guideline 38. Bipolar disorder. The management of bipolar disorder in adults, children and adolescents, in primary and secondary care.* London: NICE.

NICE (2007) *Antenatal and postnatal mental health; clinical management and service guidance. NICE Clinical guideline 45.* London: NICE.

SADA (2011) SADA.org.uk [online]. Available at: www.sada.org.uk (accessed September 2011).

Useful websites

Information on season affective disorder at Mind at www.mind.org.uk/help/diagnoses_and_conditions/seasonal_affective_disorder

National Childbirth Trust at www.nct.org.uk/home

Post-natal depression and puerperal psychosis at www.puerperalpsychosis.org.uk

Royal College of Psychiatrists at www.rcpsych.ac.uk

Seasonal Affective Disorder at www.sad.org.uk

Chapter 33

Bipolar children

Key points

- The average age of diagnosis was 39 years old but it has recently dropped to 19 years old.

- Younger people with the disorder and their family carers have specific needs that need to be addressed.

For a parent, accepting that your child has bipolar disorder is not easy. It is natural to be reluctant about giving a child what might turn out to be a damaging psychiatric label, and yet there is a dilemma here. If a parent refuses to get a diagnosis they may be cutting their child off from help and treatment.

Question 1
What reasons might there be for the recent increase in younger people becoming diagnosed with bipolar disorder?

Reflection exercise: The parent's dilemma
Write a list of the pros and cons of accepting a diagnosis.

Young people with bipolar disorder

There is no simple explanation for when bipolar disorder may develop. It is worth bearing in mind that no one is born with a diagnosis of bipolar disorder. It is reasonable to ask: 'How early in life can a person be judged to be experiencing mood disorders?'

Diagnosis can only be made based on behaviours. It is difficult to recognise a mood disorder in a very young child as rapid shifts in mood (without much provocation) are normal for most children. It is normal for children to laugh, cry, sulk, have tantrums and so on, and then gradually grow out of these behaviours to become an apparently more stable adult.

In the mid 1990s very few young people were diagnosed with bipolar disorder in the UK. The increase since then has been dramatic. There is a large discrepancy between diagnosis in young people in the USA and UK. In the UK very few children (under 16) have been diagnosed with bipolar disorder, although the numbers displaying symptoms associated with extreme moods is probably not very different between the two countries.

Diagnostic difficulties

It can be difficult to arrive at a diagnosis in younger children as depressions and highs might not be as obvious or clear cut, or as long or as deep as in adults.

Behaviour that is regarded as being normal in adolescence, such as being 'moody', may be dismissed as being clinically insignificant. How do you tell a stroppy, emotionally labile, normal teenager from one who has bipolar disorder?

As with adults, it is when such symptoms persist over time and begin to interfere with the normal activities of life that we need to be alert and seek help. However, arriving at a consensus as to what is normal for adolescence can be equally difficult!

Adolescence is a time of testing things out, trying to find ourselves and making sense of the world. Normal adolescents get depressed, experience anxiety, can be obsessive, act impulsively and compulsively, have sleep difficulties, get stressed and may experiment with drugs.

Similarly, hyperactivity is not necessarily manic behaviour, while ADHD may be indicative of underlying bipolar disorder.

It can also be difficult to uncover unhealthy family dynamics that may be driving behaviour. For example, where abuse is part of the picture the abuser and abused can be equally unlikely to share the whole truth.

Mood instability in children is frequently diagnosed as ADHD. Many children diagnosed with ADHD are later diagnosed with bipolar disorder.

Attention deficit hyperactivity disorder (ADHD)

It is important to be able to distinguish between ADHD and bipolar disorder as the treatments are different. Treatments for ADHD are likely to overstimulate the bipolar child and mood stabilizers do not offer much help to those with ADHD. In both disorders there is an increase in activity levels, increased talking, poor impulse control and a low tolerance to frustration, resulting in behavioural problems.

Two differences a nurse or parent can look for:

1. In a bipolar presentation there is likely to be some evidence of 'cycling' or episodes as contrasted with ADHD in which the behaviour is more consistent over time.
2. Children with ADHD usually have persistent low self-confidence despite their outgoing behaviour. This contrasts with the variable bipolar traits of occasionally being 'grandiose' or overconfident of abilities and status.

Both disorders will present with sleeping difficulties and it is also possible that the child has both, or neither!

What may help

- Be hopeful of recovery and share that sense of hope for the future with a child.

- Ensure that specialist help is obtained in determining if a diagnosis is actually needed.

- Don't blame the child! Don't place the family's problems on the child. Often children present with behavioural difficulties due to stresses caused by family dynamics. If parents are arguing, undergoing separation, drinking heavily, being violent etc. then the child will react in ways that may inadvertently bring them into contact with services. Parents need to be honest and admit their own problems. They must avoid blaming the child and giving them a problem not of their own making. When this is possible family therapy is likely to be useful.

- Engage the child in the debate, assessment and treatment. Use mood charts and consider all aspects of life such as home, school, friends etc.

- Ensure the child is made aware of the facts and has a chance to give informed consent and be part of the process.

- Allow the child separate appointments if they want them.

- A parent should not take the disorder personally or blame themselves for poor parenting.

- Blame the disorder and not the child.

- Keep calm. Foster a family environment with low expressed emotion. Don't develop a blame culture and offer support not criticism.

- Be open about the use of medication. Debate it openly with the child.

- Keep the school informed and access school-based support systems. Teachers can only adapt if they are aware of the child's needs. Help to educate the teachers about your child and the diagnosis.

- Discuss therapy with your child as speaking with a counsellor may help the child to understand the diagnosis and learn to manage it in the future.

- Lifestyle changes. Pay attention to sleep, diet, exercise, socialising and hobbies.

Working with very young people who have bipolar disorder has at least one big advantage in that poor lifestyle choices are unlikely to be 'fixed in stone'. The biggest disadvantage may be that a lack of life experience may make it more difficult to explain why changes are needed for recovery and to build resilience.

As with adults, we need to look for triggers. Remember that bipolar disorder is made up of episodes – we need to remember to look for what is triggering the episodes. If there are no obvious triggers, such as bullying/abuse, parents separating, changing school, then it is worth enquiring about diet, eating and drinking behaviours.

Consideration point

- What dietary factors might you need to take into consideration for children displaying mood swings?

Bipolar Disorder: A guide for mental health professionals, carers and those who live with it
© Pavilion Publishing (Brighton) Ltd 2012

Hope

Hope is difficult to define yet it is arguably the most important factor in determining whether the child starts to recover or gets worse. If the child believes they have a disorder that can be treated, their mindset is likely to be positive and hopeful. If the parents behave as if the child is beyond help and the situation is hopeless, then the child's mindset will be negative.

A lack of hope can cause the bipolar person, no matter what their age, to swing between the lows of depression and uncontrollable highs. A child without hope may start to alternate between longing for death to escape their 'prison' to trying for even greater highs as these may be the only way to forget the hopelessness they are feeling.

Recovery workshops facilitated by 'survivors' tend to stress and demonstrate hope.

Case study: A daughter's view

My mother works hard at resisting the urges to wrap me up in cotton wool and protect me from myself. She loves me when I am high and even when I have been in bed for a week and won't shower.

It doesn't matter which version of myself is in front of her, she treats me the same and will not give any attention to my more disruptive bipolar traits. She watches, but doesn't interfere. She has my back, but lets me sort it out for myself. She doesn't let me get away with anything, just because I have bipolar – and I do try to use that excuse regularly!

Case study: What is the most important thing your mother does for you?

The most important thing she does for me is to refuse to pander to my every whim or change in mood. She listens, but doesn't offer opinions or advice unless I ask. She just lets me vent (and probably smokes 10 cigarettes once I'm gone!). That's an amazing ability I think, to truly listen to someone but not speak and offer your own thoughts/advice. I know I can't do it.

Case study: A mother's view

It seems normal for the mother to bear the brunt of everything. The child with bipolar can take frustrations and anger out on the one person they feel safe with. When you have consistently tried your best and bipolar has worn you down it is hard when people suggest the child's problems are the result of bad parenting. Finding the right medication has been pretty much trial and error. Growing bodies add an extra problem. Medications and dosages are changed and then changed again. Am I overprotective? Yes, I probably am. But you don't see my child on the streets and getting into trouble because of her poor impulse control and believing everyone she meets is her best friend.

Case study: A father's view (USA)

My son was diagnosed with bipolar three years ago when he was nine years old. He is already on his fourth medication. It is the medication that worries me more than anything at the moment. He seems so fragile and the medication can be so powerful. I have to admit that I am way out of my depth and all I can do is talk to the doctor as much as I can to let him know what is going on at home. I know I have done some good in getting the dosage corrected, but I have little confidence that the latest cocktail of medication is going to be the last. I am frightened by the whole thing and pray that research is going to change things so he can have a better future.

Case study: A parent considers the value of diagnosis and medication (USA)

My child was first diagnosed with ADHD. This seemed like a step forward as the overactivity could be controlled by Stratera. At age 11, bipolar was added to the diagnosis. It seemed to me that the ADHD medication caused moody and aggressive behaviour, as each dose wore off. The school could not handle the extremes and we have been encouraged and supported with home teaching. Each medication for the disorder modifies behaviour but we still have disruption here every day. So far for bipolar we have had Risperdal, piperazine, Wellbutrin, Abilify and Depakote. The only good thing to have come out of the bipolar diagnosis is that it has sorted out some insurance issues and our child now gets weekly counselling, which is where we are pinning all our hope for understanding and regaining some normality in our house.

Question 2

How do you feel about young children (see examples above) being given a bipolar diagnosis?

Answers to questions

1. **What reasons might there be for the recent increase in younger people becoming diagnosed with bipolar disorder?**

- *A change in diagnostic criteria in the USA may have influenced some psychiatrists in other countries.*
- *There is also much greater recognition of mental illness in general, increasing possibilities that links between behavioural problems and mental illness will be made.*
- *Medication is increasingly being used for young people seen to experience ADHD, anxiety and depression. Strong reactions to these often results in the early identification of bipolar disorder.*
- *Greater public knowledge of bipolar disorder makes it likely for some parents and children to be looking for symptoms that in the past would have been seen as typical childhood/teenage behaviour. For example, frequent tantrums, truancy, damaging property and getting into trouble with the law may lead to parents taking the child to their GP or to a psychiatrist to discuss the possibility of bipolar disorder.*

2. **How do you feel about young children being given a bipolar diagnosis?**

This question is very much about how you feel. Your feelings may depend on the extent to which you see recovery as being likely, versus how much you believe bipolar disorder can continue to be a 'life sentence'.

Bipolar Disorder: A guide for mental health professionals, carers and those who live with it
© Pavilion Publishing (Brighton) Ltd 2012

327

Further reading

Aiken C (2010) Family *Experiences of Bipolar Disorder: The ups, the downs and the bits in between*. London: Jessica Kingsley Publishers.

Johnston J (2005) *To Walk on Eggshells*. Helensburgh: The Cairn Publishers.

Johnston S (2004) *The Naked Birdwatcher*. Helensburgh: The Cairn Publishers.

MDF (2008) *Bipolar Disorder in Children and Young People*. London: MDF.

NICE (2006) *Clinical Guideline 38. Bipolar Disorder: The management of bipolar disorder in adults, children and adolescents, in primary and secondary care*. London: National Institute for Health and Clinical Excellence.

Chapter 34

Achieving balance

Key points

- Achieving a degree of stability helps people to stay well.
- The key to stability lies in balancing different aspects of our lives.

It is possible to think of episodes of mania and depression as periods of imbalance with the relative wellness between episodes as periods of stability. Mood swings can be pictured as rapid changes in the balance between high and low moods.

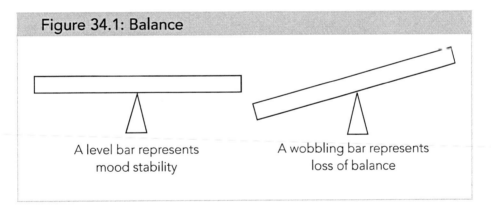

Figure 34.1: Balance

A level bar represents mood stability

A wobbling bar represents loss of balance

In Figure 34.1, the two bars depict a stable mood and an unstable mood. Imagine the bar as a spirit level with the goal being to make corrections as soon as mood tips in either direction.

Figure 34.2 shows changes in mood as represented on a graph. The goal here would be to smooth out the peaks and troughs to create stability.

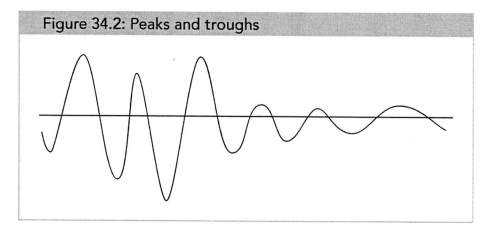

Figure 34.2: Peaks and troughs

The concept of balance can also be applied to the extremes that are characteristic of bipolar disorder, such as extremes in thinking, physical activity, socialising etc.

Table 34.1: Examples of extremes in mood

	Extreme in depression	Extreme in mania
Thinking example:	I can't do anything at all	I can do absolutely everything
Physical activity example:	Staying in bed for 24 hours	Redecorating all night
Socialising extreme:	Not even wanting to see family	Moving from party to party

Reflection exercise: Extremes

Identify other areas of life where people with bipolar may go to extremes.

Not all extremes should be described as a loss of balance as for a bipolar person there is a likelihood of extremes being related to mood swings.

Looking at Figure 34.1, how quickly the balance is lost, the extent of the loss and whether a quick return to stability is possible will depend on everything from personality to robust coping strategies.

Case study: A healthy obsession?

Brothers, Simon and Jamie, were keen tennis players prior to Simon's bipolar episodes. Jamie decided to take up tennis again and asked Simon to train with him. They both took the training very seriously. Jamie found all the exercise helped him to be calmer at work and sleep better. Prior to their first doubles tournament Simon said he would have to pull out as he could feel himself becoming increasingly manic. Later, Simon explained that he had been having extra tennis coaching every day and watching Wimbledon videos during the night.

Consider

■ How might you be able to help Simon to maintain his balance?

Balancing any one aspect of our lives can be difficult. If a colleague is on sick leave it may be reasonable to do extra work, and for a while our work-life balance will be upset. There are many aspects of our life that may need balancing, such as work, family, leisure, etc.

Exercises such as the Circle of life in Figure 34.3 can help with understanding how our lives are balanced and can give clues as to where we may need to focus our energies to improve overall balance. The exercise simply involves drawing a large circle and dividing it into segments to represent aspects of a person's life.

Figure 34.3: Circle of life

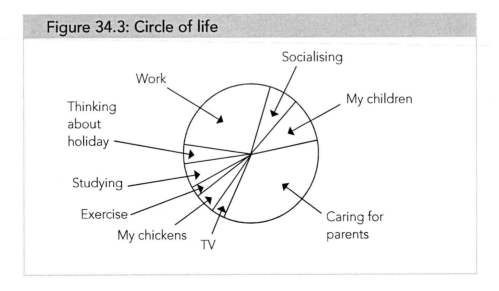

In Figure 34.3 the segment labelled 'caring for parents' seems particularly large. If this represents a moment in time this may be fine, whereas if this is going to be the picture for many years to come there may need to be efforts made to alter the balance between the segments/aspects of the person's life.

Reflection exercise: Circle of life

Draw a circle of life for your current lifestyle. Can you identify areas where you would like to make changes?

When there is something terribly wrong with our lives we can latch onto a single idea that we hope will put everything right. The tendency to do this is probably even greater for bipolar people. The distress caused by episodes can lead to desperation and desperation can lead to too much hope being placed in one solution. Health professionals can also make this mistake.

Case study: Chemical imbalance?

A social worker told me: 'You simply have a chemical imbalance. All you need to do is to take the medication and wait for the balance to be corrected.' I liked the idea that someone else was thinking about balance, but he was wrong – my problems were not just about chemicals. I needed to balance my diet, exercise, talking, sleeping and a whole lot more.

When medications like modern antipsychotics rapidly improve a person's well-being it is easy to start thinking that medication is the key to resolving mood disorders. A better view is that medication is just one aspect of achieving balance. Ultimately, the people who stay well for the longest are likely to be those who develop the capability to balance the many other aspects of their lives. Another important balance is that between having too few interests and having too many – the latter being common in mania. Balance needs special consideration in the period immediately after episodes as there can be a danger of imbalance as clients attempt to quickly put right everything that went wrong while they were unwell.

Carer's balance

A useful idea for the health professional supporting the carer could be to ask them to draw their own circle of life. This exercise may reveal imbalance in the carer's life.

Consider

- If the carer thinks that the segments relating to caring are too large, how might you be able to help them make changes?
- What role might local support groups play?

Further reading

MDF The Bipolar Organisation (2007) *A Balancing Act*. London: MDF The Bipolar Organisation. Available at: http://www.mdfwales.org.uk/?o=238659 (accessed October 2011).

Smith R (2006) *Achieving Balance*. Available at: http://www.bipolarrecovery.org/articles/balance-si07.htm (accessed October 2011).

Straughan J (2009) *Insight: A holistic approach to recovery training for people with bipolar disorder or depression*. Brighton: Pavilion Publishing.

Chapter 35

Creativity

Key points

- The link between bipolar and creativity is often referred to in texts on bipolar disorder.

- There can be no doubt that some bipolar people are very creative and creativity is not limited to people with bipolar disorder, but whether they are any more creative than the general population remains to be proven.

- A good deal of literature deals with bipolar disorder and gives an insight into varying experiences of the disorder.

Lists of well known people who have experienced extremes of mood and been both creative and successful can be inspirational and give hope.

Person	Profession	Ways their changeable moods have been described
Buzz Aldrin	Astronaut, pilot of first craft to land on the moon	'Aldrin suffered from bipolar disorder, resulting in bouts of depression. His books *Magnificent Desolation* and *Return to Earth* all provide accounts of his struggles with depression and alcoholism during the years after retirement. He reiterated that the cause was not being prepared for the fame that followed landing on the moon.' (http://www.famousbipolarpeople.com/ buzz-aldrin.html)
Bill Oddie	Presenter, writer, comic actor, musician, and naturalist	In a magazine interview, Oddie explained how after many years of depressive episodes he was diagnosed with manic depression at 67.

Person	Profession	Ways their changeable moods have been described
Frank Bruno	Boxer and mental health activist	Frank Bruno talks openly about his diagnosis of bipolar disorder. The headline 'Bonkers Bruno' has since been used as an example of how mental health should not be portrayed in the media.
Nicola Pagett	Actress	Nicola Pagett recorded her experiences of manic depression in her book *Diamonds Behind My Eyes*.
Paul Gascoigne	England international football player	Paul Gascoigne hit the headlines when he cried on the pitch during the 1990 World Cup. His progress with a bipolar diagnosis has been reported many times in the papers.
Spike Milligan	Author, comic actor, poet	Spike Milligan wrote a great deal about his experience of 'shell shock' and later living with manic depression.
Stephen Fry	Author, game show host, comic actor	Revealed his diagnosis to two million viewers through presenting of the television documentary *The Secret Life of the Manic Depressive*

Speculation

The reporting of celebrities said to have bipolar disorder has increased dramatically in recent years. Much of this is speculation as there is rarely access to medical records or interviews with the named celebrities. It seems a celebrity only needs to mention the word 'bipolar' or be seen to act erratically for a myth to be created.

There are many lists of creative bipolar people on the internet. These lists often include people who have no official diagnosis, people who deny having the diagnosis and historical figures whose mood swings were noted at the time. Many lived before the terms 'bipolar disorder' and 'manic depression' were used.

Some of the many creative historical people said to have experienced extremes of mood include:

Winston Churchill – prime minister, author, artist
TS Eliot – author
Isaac Newton – scientist
Alfred, Lord Tennyson – poet
Vincent van Gogh – artist
Mark Twain – author

The lists are impressive but do they really help us to connect bipolar with creativity?

The trend towards more celebrities being said to have bipolar disorder may have a downside. It gives the message that it is OK to have a disorder. Some people are interpreting this in a way that suggests bipolar disorder is not a serious disability or life-threatening. Perhaps a way to put the advantages of having bipolar disorder in proportion is to look at the achievements of people who have other disorders and this can turn out to be just as impressive.

Consideration points

- It is often said that people who have extremes of mood are particularly creative. Why might this be?
- Is it equally suggested that exposure to extremes of mood can severely limit our ability to be creative. How might this be?

Why would extremes of mood make people more creative? A great deal of poetry and painting comes from the extremes of anxiety and depression. The choice to create poetry or art could be because of the difficulty in finding ordinary words to describe such emotional anguish. These forms of expression also seem possible without recovery, for example Vincent van Gogh was creative while being hounded by negative feelings.

With extremes of mood, ideas can seem to flow at an overwhelming pace. This is well known in manic states while in depression the ideas can be more repetitive, yet still lead to creative works as the ideas can be markedly different from those of the bulk of the population. There is, however, no correlation between numbers of ideas and creativity. A person in mania may have (or feel they have had) a thousand original ideas yet create nothing at all. A calm person may have just one original idea and gradually develop this idea to create something. The danger is that people with extreme moods can create a great deal of poor quality work without appreciating that it is poor quality. Creating quality work usually requires periods of stability or at least some short periods of calmness in which to appreciate how others may be experiencing the work.

It is possible for a person in the grip of mania to create awe-inspiring works but this is an exception rather than the norm. Usually mania has to be controlled and harnessed to some degree for it to be creative. The ability to improve mood control is at the heart of recovery work.

Case study: The early morning thinker

George is a web designer who typically wakes at 3.30am. He knows this is a warning sign of hypomania. He knows that if he gets up at that time it will disturb the family and quickly escalate into mania. As he lays awake ideas flow through his mind. Most just come and go but among these are good ideas for his work. Over the years he has learnt to pick out just one useful idea and keep it in mind for when the alarm goes off at 6.30am. He incorporates this one new idea into his work, which he says is his 'edge' over his non-bipolar competitors. George describes this as a routine that works.

It has been reported that the creativity associated with bipolar disorder lessens with age. Claims that long-term medication lessens creativity are difficult to prove, although it would seem likely that excessive medication and side effects would make creativity less likely. Many bipolar people say that medications reduce their creativity. Certainly antipsychotics and mood stabilisers are likely to reduce a flow of ideas.

There are also many bipolar people who say they have become more creative since starting on certain medications. They tend to say it is due to increased focus and the ability to be calm enough to use the ideas gained while high. Lithium is often blamed for taking away creativity, yet even lithium is praised by those who have taken it and found it has helped them to see creative projects through.

Bipolar in the arts

Literature

Literature can offer insight into how others experience and cope with mental illness. The following are good examples.

72 Hour Hold by Bebe Moore Campbell
A Can of Madness: Memoir on bipolar disorder and manic depression by Jason Pegler
An Unquiet Mind: A memoir of moods and madness by Kay Redfield Jamison
Beloved Stranger by Clare Boylan
Finding Jericho by Dave Jeffrey
Hurry Down Sunshine: A father's story of love and madness by Michael Greenberg
Lies in Silence: Lessons about Bipolar and co-occuring disorders learned through advocating for appropriate treatment for my family by SJ Hart
Love in the Asylum: A novel by Lisa Carey
Notes from an Exhibition by Patrick Gale
Polar Bears by Mark Haddon
The Bird of Night by Susan Hill
Wide Sargasso Sea by Jean Rhys

Bipolar in film

Mr Jones (1993)
Pollock (2000)
Sylvia (2003)

Points to consider about the portrayal of mental health in the media

- How realistic are the events that depict mental illness in film?
- Are events sensationalised or exaggerated to make them more marketable?

- Are there links between the author's mental health and the story?
- Do the books and films perpetuate stereotypes?
- Do the stories and portrayals give us any extra insights?
- Do the books and films portray mental illness in a positive or negative way?
- Are they giving a hopeful or a pessimistic message?
- Could watching the film or reading the book be therapeutic?

Further reading

Gluck J (2009) *Bipolar Reflections: Light on water*. UK: Chipmunka Publications.

Zurn J (2009) *Memoirs of a Bipolar Soul*. UK: Chipmunka Publications.

Useful websites

Bipolar Lives http://www.bipolar-lives.com/movies-about-bipolar-disorder.html

Internet Movie Database www.imdb.com

Madness and Literature Network http://www.madnessandliterature.org/

New York University Literature, Arts & Medicine Database at http://litmed.med.nyu.edu/Main?action=new

Psychiatry in the Cinema http://priory.com/psych/psycinema.htm

Chapter 36

The future

Key points

■ Bipolar is a relatively new diagnosis and there is still much we need to learn about it.

■ There is growing appreciation that drugs alone are not a long-term solution.

■ Holistic approaches to care are still quite uncommon.

Today there is much more awareness and understanding about mental illness, and social attitudes are changing and becoming more positive and less stigmatising as indicated by recent surveys on public attitudes (DH, 2010). However, the strain on health services as a result of a growing population, limited resources and funding cuts are a challenge for the future, along with the stigma that still surrounds mental illness.

Coming out

The situation is helped by those with mental health issues such as bipolar disorder 'coming out' and going public. A significant factor in prolonging fears regarding mental illness is the fact that the public is rarely aware of people with mental health problems who are well and getting on with their lives, and these people are the great majority of those with mental health problems. Therefore it is helpful when people are prepared to admit to their disorder so that the public can see recovery in action and see successful people who have learnt to live with or overcome their mental health issues.

Society needs more people like Stephen Fry, Alistair Campbell, Ruby Wax and Alison Faulkner to come out and talk about their mental health issues.

We all need to make a commitment to continue to combat stigma in the future because this will improve the lives of people with mental health problems as much as advances in treatment.

Old and new viewpoints

The concept of bipolar disorder is new, having been first considered to be a diagnosis as recently as 1980. Swinging between two specific moods is very much a modern western idea. For most of human history variations in mood were believed to originate from the body (for example, the heart, gut, liver etc) rather than from the brain. In some parts of China, it is still believed that feelings such as agitation are caused by 'fire in the liver'. From a nutritionist's point of view there is a great deal of logic in this idea belief as moods depend on the processing of nutrients, much of which happens in the liver.

Rather than high and low moods, the ancient Greeks and Romans, and subsequently, Islamic and European physicians considered there to be four 'humours' until the 19th century. Mood mapping revives this as four moods – anxiety, activity/mania, reflection/depression, and calm, with, for example, the Greek mood of 'melon chole', (melancholic) matching the reflection/depression mood. As more experts adopt this 'new/old' approach, the need for bipolar diagnosis can seem unnecessary as people often fit the choleric/anxiety mood rather than the extreme sanguine/manic mood. The appropriate treatment is then that for anxiety rather than that for bipolar disorder.

A very different approach is that of 'bipolar in-order' put forward by Tom Wootton, where the bipolar person focuses more on how to live well and fit into society with the symptoms, rather than focusing on eliminating symptoms. This is not an anti-psychiatry view but one of clients working even more closely with their professional supporters. The need for new approaches is clear as recovery rates have continued to decrease with the increasing use of psychiatric medications (Whitaker, 2010).

Wider and better treatment

The future may hold the promise of medication that is more effective and has fewer side effects. The challenge for pharmaceutical researchers is that the brain has been found to be far better at adapting than was known when the first neuroleptic medications were introduced. The brain begins to adapt to any new chemical that is in the bloodstream and in doing so all drugs have some element of addiction. Doctors are becoming better at explaining this to patients with the need for a planned withdrawal programme becoming more widely recognised. Medications that can help in the short term while causing the minimum undesirable changes in brain structure are likely to aid recovery.

It is hopeful that there is an ever increasing acceptance of the hugely beneficial role that non-drug therapies play. The hope is that these are likely to become more accepted and more widely available. The role of exercise and an improved diet are two examples of key areas that may need a greater focus.

Support

The importance of the role of support is increasingly recognised and this provides greater hope for the future. The growth of bipolar support is largely due to the efforts of those who have bipolar themselves. The value of local support groups is immense and any action plan for the future of bipolar disorder must include increasing support for local initiatives. The national picture is important but when people need support they need it promptly and locally. Another hopeful sign is the growth of internet sites dedicated to giving support and spreading the word about bipolar disorder and mental illness. The growing abundance of bipolar internet chat forums and blogs is refreshing as people can connect with a huge range of fellow bipolar people and compare experiences, tips, coping mechanisms, recovery strategies and generally support each other.

There are also very good internet sites and forums for carers and younger people. There is a healthy openness and frankness about these forums. However, a word of caution must be expressed here because there are many 'inexpert experts' out there and some very professional-looking sites that merely broadcast the personal opinions of the site's author. Better support may be gained from forums that let everyone have their say. These allow people to form their own opinions and connect with those they find common ground with.

Funding

How the limited money available for therapies and recovery is used will continue to impact on how quickly improvements can be made. Mary Ellen Copeland, the creator of the Wellness Recovery Action Plan (WRAP), notes how the research that she started while an inpatient depended on a health professional securing a grant for her. This work led to WRAP, which is now available in many countries. WRAP led to many other recovery programmes such as MDF The Bipolar Organisation's self-management training programme. However, each of these recovery initiatives can only be rolled out when funding can be found. Places on recovery courses continue to be rare and courses by experts through experience even more rare.

Case study: Experts by experience

Trainers with a bipolar diagnosis can be said to be abundant in the UK. Unfortunately opportunities for such experts to work in mental health are limited.

Jerry's situation

I enjoyed being a trainer on the bipolar self-management programme. Unfortunately the £150 honorarium for delivering the three-day course just was not enough considering all the unpaid travel time, development and preparation days. Overnight stays away from my partner and young children put a strain on our marriage. I took a full-time job with a charity, but it did not last. The next job was in customer services but it just wasn't me. I had learned so much about mental health recovery and how to teach recovery, and that was what I wanted to do, but not for £50 a day. I set up my own business and it is tough. We still have no money for holidays or even trips out. We have become resourceful, such as being able to conserve my medication to save £60 on prescription charges this year. Yes, these are desperate times. I have the qualifications and I can do a good job. I just need to be recognised by the NHS.

Consider

■ How might this situation be altered and what opportunities can you see locally and within your practice to engage the services of user experts?

Personal futures

It is important for everyone, diagnosis or not, to have things to look forward to. After a crisis there is a need to review what the future may hold, whether you talk of this as aims, targets, goals or using other terms. There are many examples in literature and many of the people the authors have spent time with in preparing this book talk of how the diagnosis has changed their lives as they realised new possibilities.

Two recent Mind Champion of the Year awards were for people previously diagnosed with bipolar disorder – Liz Miller (medical doctor, researcher and author) in 2008 and Rachel Perkins (clinical psychologist and author) in 2010. Only a fraction of those diagnosed with bipolar will want to research, write about or talk about the disorder. Even so, everyone will need personal goals in relation to their future and what they want to achieve post-diagnosis.

Contributors to this book have included owners of established and start-up businesses, computer programmers, voluntary workers, psychiatrists, doctors, psychologists, full-time parents/home-makers, lecturers, authors, a chemist, a local government worker, an artist, researchers, a shop assistant, an architectural draftsman, a customer relations manager, an engineer, and a professional photographer. Almost any career is possible after a bipolar diagnosis, although the challenges of coping with medication side effects and stigma must never be underestimated.

There were also many contributors who have been struggling to come to terms with bipolar disorder and are in need of better information, support and generally more hope in their lives.

There is a need for people to identify what they want their futures to include, then have a plan and timetable for achieving a better life. Success here will give more hope and help to demonstrate to others that they can expect a successful life with bipolar or beyond bipolar.

References

Department of Health (2010) *Attitudes to Mental Illness 2010: Research report*. London: Office for National Statistics. Available at: http://www.ic.nhs.uk/webfiles/publications/mental%20 health/mental%20health%20act/Mental_illness_report.pdf (accessed September 2011)

Whitaker R (2010) *Anatomy of an Epidemic*. New York: Random House Publishing.